Test-Driven Development
with PHP 8

Build extensible, reliable, and maintainable enterprise-level
applications using TDD and BDD with PHP

Rainier Sarabia

BIRMINGHAM—MUMBAI

Test-Driven Development with PHP 8

Copyright © 2023 Packt Publishing

Group Product Manager: Pavan Ramchandani
Publishing Product Manager: Bhavya Rao
Senior Editor: Mark D'Souza
Senior Content Development Editor: Rakhi Patel
Technical Editor: Simran Udasi
Copy Editor: Safis Editing
Project Coordinator: Manthan Patel
Proofreader: Safis Editing
Indexer: Manju Arasan
Production Designer: Roshan Kawale
Marketing Coordinator: Anamika Singh

First published: January 2023
Production reference: 1161222

Published by Packt Publishing Ltd.
Livery Place
35 Livery Street
Birmingham
B3 2PB, UK.

ISBN 978-1-80323-075-7

www.packt.com

In the memory of my aunt Rose, who raised me, and to my family and friends. To Eva, for the unending encouragement. To my partner, Frezel Enriquez, for the love and support throughout my journey in life.

– Rainier Sarabia

Foreword

I have known and worked with Rainier Sarabia for more than 5 years. In this book, *Test-Driven Development with PHP 8*, Rainier takes you on a learning journey that started in the late 1990s, with not only PHP but test-driven development itself. For more than 20 years, PHP has continued to evolve to meet the needs of developers around the world. In parallel, test-driven development and agile principles have also evolved, culminating in this book combining all three to demonstrate how easily an application with frameworks, environments, and toolchains can be built rapidly, and more importantly, with rock-solid reliability.

In his presentations and examples, Rainier shows how easy it is not only to create consistently tested applications but to have consistent environments to run those tests in, no matter whether they are on your machine, a fellow developer's machine, a cloud-based CI, or in a test environment.

With *Test-Driven Development with PHP 8*, you'll learn the best practices for writing reliable, maintainable code with PHP's object-oriented architecture. After you complete Rainier's book, you'll understand how to take full advantage of test-driven development in PHP.

Beyond developing apps, you'll learn how to quickly and easily bootstrap applications in cloud services using containerized environments, giving transportability and consistency to your application.

Rainier encapsulates the knowledge gained through years as a world-class software engineer and passionate advocate. With his words, step-by-step instructions, screenshots, source code snippets, examples, and links to additional sources of information, you will learn how to continuously enhance your skills and applications.

Ben Hansen

Directory of Quality Assurance, PayGroup Ltd.

Contributors

About the author

Rainier Sarabia is a Software Engineering Manager, who currently works in Melbourne, Australia for Astute Payroll, a Deel company. He has worked on hundreds of complex software projects, including massive enterprise SaaS products while leading and training senior engineers from all over the world. His favorite programming languages are PHP, C#, Java, and Javascript which he uses for both professional and personal projects. He co-founded his first tech company back in 2014, with over 400,000 users. Outside of working hours, he is an amateur astronomer. He spends most of his time doing astrophotography focusing on deep-sky objects like nebulae and galaxies.

I want to thank the people who have been inspiring me and helping me in writing this book. I'd like to thank Eva Bellaire, Ilia Mogilevsky, and Ben Hansen for spending so much of their free time and weekends helping me with this book, I really appreciate it.

To the Packt team: Manthan Patel, Rakhi Patel, Mark D'Souza, Bhavya Rao, thank you so much for your patience and guidance, I've learned so much from you!

My mates from Exsentriks: Jan Albee Angeles, Joms Calma, Blink Easley, Randy Porcioncula, Vincent Rafols, William Dela Pena, and Richard Coles, thanks so much for the support and ideas I always love and enjoy our C#, PHP, Java, and Javascript discussions!

For the past 6 years, Astute Payroll, and PayGroup have been very supportive of me and my ideas! To Luke Zawadzki, thank you so much for all the help and guidance, mate! I'd also like to thank, Eloise Roberts, Sally Laycock, Mahin Sonia, Johnny Yu, Trang Dinh, Adi Setiono, Tadek Chavez, Marcus Webb, Shelley Mackie, Nicole Poulton, Adam Perks, Paul Radford, Rudy Compayan, Joyce Orevillo, Tao Ding, Tim Evetts, Julian Calaby, Mac Wilgucki, Tim Malone, Ginli Chew, Mitch Collins, Trish Scally, and Rick Measham. And I'd also like to thank Adam Parrish, Andrew Sekula, and Vik Radha for the great table tennis battles we had in MIM! Lastly, I also want to thank Erin Jan Gandia, Oleg Posternatsky, Matteo Bortolu, Dexter Naag, and Andre Bellaire for all the support.

About the reviewers

Ben Hansen has been a QA professional his entire IT career, starting as a purely manual tester, then learning and working up to automation testing, QA lead, and now QA director overseeing large international teams. Specializing in various CRM, accounting, and payroll applications, he has pioneered many testing techniques and technologies, reducing testing times from months to weeks for features in some applications while increasing quality.

Eva Bellaire is a CPA-qualified leader who has worked in multiple positions in accounting and project delivery with both agile and waterfall methods. Her experience includes management and oversight of projects for organizations in a diverse set of industries including mining and engineering, professional services, higher education, and financial services. She is experienced in enterprise transformation and technology enablement across finance, planning, payroll, HR, and analytics software. She has a passion for continuous learning as well as mentoring and people development.

Ilia Mogilevsky is a Ukrainian-born Jewish immigrant who is currently leaving in Melbourne, Australia, with his beautiful wife, two young inquisitive children, and his always playful golden retriever, Daisy. He is an industry-certified professional with over 20 years of full-time commercial experience as a code wrangler, technical lead, solutions architect, and engineering manager. Ilia has worked in various areas of software engineering, ranging from big digital agencies such as Next Digital, massive B2B and B2C companies such as Hanes Australasia (Bonds, Sheridan, Berlei, Champion), and small start-ups such as Combitel, where he helped develop a data-driven web-based application for IPTV streaming. As of 2022, he is currently employed at SmartBear as an engineering manager, working with the PactFlow team to help engineers all over the world build more robust testable software. In recent years, he turned his passion for technology with a wide breadth of software engineering knowledge, skills, and experiences to helping businesses achieve their critical goals by building successful technology-centric teams and continuously cultivating his growth mindset while helping and supporting his peers through mentoring, coaching, and best practices.

In his spare time, he loves to travel with his family and has become a keen landscape photographer.

Table of Contents

3

Setting Up Our Development Environment Using Docker Containers 39

4

Using Object-Oriented Programming in PHP   49

Part 2 – Implementing Test-Driven Development in a PHP Project

5

Unit Testing   79

6

Applying Behavior-Driven Development   127

7

Building Solution Code with BDD and TDD   147

8

Part 3 – Deployment Automation and Monitoring

9

10

11

Monitoring   293

Index   305

Other Books You May Enjoy   312

Preface

For the past few years, I've been helping friends and colleagues learn more about PHP and **Test-Driven Development (TDD)**. I realized that I found myself repeating some of the things I'm discussing with different people. I told myself, it would be great if I could just point my friends and colleagues to a collection of my notes so that I could help them with developing applications in PHP from the start of the project, up to deployment. Unfortunately, my notes only made sense to me.

In 2009, I was working as a C# developer and made friends with my colleagues who were fellow programming enthusiasts. Unfortunately, we haven't been in touch for a long time. 11 years later, in 2020 while in COVID lockdown, I got in touch with my long-lost friends, and we started chatting about programming. They told me that they were very keen on learning about TDD with PHP. We then did a screen-sharing tutorial session on a weekend, and I realized that I seriously needed to start writing something a bit more organized to help other people who are interested in learning about this topic.

I do self-training most of the time. I buy books, read them, and watch tutorials about things I want to learn myself. I then decided to write a book about TDD with PHP. Since I have learned a lot from the books published by Packt, I thought I should reach out to them.

Reading this book will help you start organizing your thoughts and the things you need to build for a project as a software developer. You will learn how to write and use automated tests to help improve the quality of the software you produce, and you will also learn how to use tools to automate the execution of your tests, as well as the deployment of your code onto remote servers. I'm aiming for the reader to understand the value of TDD as a process, and not just learn about writing automated tests. That's why I have covered topics from starting a project to deploying it on a public-facing server.

Who this book is for

If you're a professional PHP developer who's getting tired of working on applications that are not easily testable or maintainable, this book will help you be a better professional PHP developer. You will learn how to utilize **Test-Driven Development (TDD)** and **Behaviour-Driven Development (BDD)** to help you produce more structured and maintainable software.

What this book covers

Chapter 1, What is Test-Driven Development and Why Use it in PHP?, Goes through the definition of TDD, what problem it tries to solve, what are the benefits of PHP and what we developers will get from implementing it. This chapter will also make you understand the value of TDD in large projects and how it helps reduce regressions.

Chapter 2, Understanding and Organizing the Business Requirements of Our Project, explains how to interpret business requirements into an organized list. The list can be used to help developers prioritize and determine what features we need to build, and which features we need to build first.

Chapter 3, Setting Up Our Development Environment Using Docker Containers, is all about Docker containers for development. Using containers will help developers get more consistent application setups in different server environments.

Chapter 4, Using Object-Oriented Programming in PHP, goes through the **Object-Oriented Programming (OOP)** concept in PHP. Understanding OOP in PHP is crucial for implementing TDD, and BDD.

Chapter 5, Unit Testing, covers the basics of unit testing. The lessons learned in this chapter will be the foundations for the concepts that will be discussed in applying TDD and BDD in the following chapters.

Chapter 6, Applying Behavior-Driven Development, provides an introduction to the process of BDD. The BDD process will help software developers ensure that the expected behavior of a software product is achieved.

Chapter 7, Building Solution Code with BDD and TDD, demonstrates how to use BDD and TDD together. Implementing BDD and TDD together will help ensure that the expected behavior is delivered, and it will also help increase the reliability of the software being produced.

Chapter 8, Using TDD with SOLID Principles, involves following the SOLID principles in a project. This will help developers implement the SOLID principles while following TDD in a more realistic use scenario.

Chapter 9, Continuous Integration, details **Continous Integration (CI)** for test execution. CI is used to help merge reliable code to the master branch of a project by making sure that all automated tests pass first.

Chapter 10, Continuous Delivery, discusses using **Continuous Delivery (CD)** to automate the release process. Going further than CI, we will automate the deployment process of the product.

Chapter 11, Monitoring, unpacks how to use monitoring tools for deployed applications. Applications running in production will need to be maintained and having monitoring tools help developers to get on top of possible issues in production.

To get the most out of this book

The instructions in the book are Unix based. The development machine used as an example host machine in the book runs on MacOS 12.3 and should work on later versions as well. However, the Docker containers should also run on Windows and Linux machines.

Software/hardware covered in the book	Operating system requirements
Docker	macOS, Linux, or Windows
PHP 8.1	Linux
MySQL 8	Linux
PHPStorm	macOS, Linux, or Windows

If you are using the digital version of this book, we advise you to type the code yourself or access the code from the book's GitHub repository (a link is available in the next section). Doing so will help you avoid any potential errors related to the copying and pasting of code.

Download the example code files

You can download the example code files for this book from GitHub at `https://github.com/PacktPublishing/Test-Driven-Development-with-PHP-8`. If there's an update to the code, it will be updated in the GitHub repository.

We also have other code bundles from our rich catalog of books and videos available at `https://github.com/PacktPublishing/`. Check them out!

Download the color images

We also provide a PDF file that has color images of the screenshots and diagrams used in this book. You can download it here: `https://packt.link/BwjU3`.

Conventions used

There are a number of text conventions used throughout this book.

`Code in text`: Indicates code words in text, database table names, folder names, filenames, file extensions, pathnames, dummy URLs, user input, and Twitter handles. Here is an example: "The test class name needs to be suffixed with `Test`, and it extends the `PHPUnit\Framework\TestCase` class."

A block of code is set as follows:

```php
<?php

namespace App\Validator;

use App\Model\ToyCar;
use App\Model\ValidationModel;
```

```
interface ToyCarValidatorInterface
{
    public function validate(ToyCar $toyCar): ValidationModel;
```

Any command-line input or output is written as follows:

```
$ cd docker
$ docker-compose build && docker-compose up -d
```

Bold: Indicates a new term, an important word, or words that you see onscreen. For instance, words in menus or dialog boxes appear in **bold**. Here is an example: "Paste the script into the text area and click on the **Commit File** button."

> **Tips or important notes**
> Appear like this.

Get in touch

Feedback from our readers is always welcome.

General feedback: If you have questions about any aspect of this book, email us at customercare@packtpub.com and mention the book title in the subject of your message.

Errata: Although we have taken every care to ensure the accuracy of our content, mistakes do happen. If you have found a mistake in this book, we would be grateful if you would report this to us. Please visit www.packtpub.com/support/errata and fill in the form.

Piracy: If you come across any illegal copies of our works in any form on the internet, we would be grateful if you would provide us with the location address or website name. Please contact us at copyright@packt.com with a link to the material.

If you are interested in becoming an author: If there is a topic that you have expertise in and you are interested in either writing or contributing to a book, please visit authors.packtpub.com.

Share Your Thoughts

Once you've read *Test-Driven Development with PHP 8*, we'd love to hear your thoughts! Scan the QR code below to go straight to the Amazon review page for this book and share your feedback.

https://packt.link/r/1803230754

Your review is important to us and the tech community and will help us make sure we're delivering excellent quality content.

Download a free PDF copy of this book

Thanks for purchasing this book!

Do you like to read on the go but are unable to carry your print books everywhere?

Is your eBook purchase not compatible with the device of your choice?

Don't worry, now with every Packt book you get a DRM-free PDF version of that book at no cost.

Read anywhere, any place, on any device. Search, copy, and paste code from your favorite technical books directly into your application.

The perks don't stop there, you can get exclusive access to discounts, newsletters, and great free content in your inbox daily

Follow these simple steps to get the benefits:

1. Scan the QR code or visit the link below

https://packt.link/free-ebook/978-1-80323-075-7

2. Submit your proof of purchase

3. That's it! We'll send your free PDF and other benefits to your email directly

Part 1 – Technical Background and Setup

In this part of the book, you will learn the concepts of test-driven development and object-oriented programming in PHP, interpret business requirements as an actionable list, and set up development environments using Docker containers.

This section comprises the following chapters:

1
What Is Test-Driven Development and Why Use It in PHP?

Developing web applications is fun and productive when using the PHP programming language. The learning curve to get started with PHP is relatively shallow, which is a very important trait of a programming language. There are a lot of open source learning materials, frameworks, packages, and full-blown extendable products backed by a very large open source community available for PHP developers. PHP is an enterprise-ready programming language and is widely used as a web-based solution to solve different business problems. Businesses and developers can quickly develop and deploy web applications with PHP. Once these businesses start to succeed and grow, they'll need more features, bug fixes, and improvements to be released on top of the original solution. This is where it starts to get interesting. Maintenance of commercially successful software can be one of the biggest contributing factors to the cost of the software, especially when it's not built to be easily maintainable or testable from the beginning. Implementing **test-driven development** (**TDD**) will improve the maintainability of the software and will help reduce the cost and time to market for a feature.

There's a problem that most of us developers might have already experienced or observed: a feature or a bug fix has been released and it has caused more problems, regressions, or unintended software behavior. If you are coming from a development environment where most or all the **quality assurance** (**QA**) tests are done manually post-, pre-, or even mid-development, then you might have experienced the issues that I have mentioned. This is where implementing TDD can really help. TDD not only helps in implementing automated tests but also guides or even forces us in a way to develop cleaner and more loosely coupled codes. TDD helps developers write and build tests before even writing a single feature code – this helps ensure that whenever a feature or solution code is being written, there will be a corresponding test already written for it. It also helps us developers stop saying "*I'll add my unit tests later.*"

Before writing any codes, it's very important to understand what TDD is, and what it is not. There are some common misconceptions about TDD that we need to clear up to help us stay focused on what TDD really is. In this chapter, we will also try to use a very simple analogy and try to emphasize why we would want to implement TDD as a part of a software project.

In this chapter, we will be covering the following:

- What is TDD?

- Common misconceptions about TDD

- Why should we even consider TDD?

- What are we planning to achieve in this book?

What is TDD?

TDD is a simple way of developing software where we think about and define *what* needs to be the outcome of our programs before we start writing the actual codes that solve a problem.

TDD is a software development process where test cases are developed first before writing the actual code that solves a problem. The test cases will be written as PHP code that will use or call the solution code that developers will be building. The test case code that you build will trigger the development of the solution code that you will write to solve a problem.

From what I've seen, this literal description is what demotivates a lot of developers from applying this process. TDD is a process, and it's a way of thinking. It's not simply about writing unit tests.

The test program you write should always fail the first time you run it because you haven't built the programs the test needs to pass yet. Then, you will basically have to build the solution codes that the test program will use until the test program itself gets the expected results from your solution codes. Literally, the failing test will drive you to write the codes to pass the test – hence the term TDD. Maybe you can even call it failing-TDD. It's like saying "*I wrote a test to fail my code, now I need to fix it.*"

In TDD, I can see four main reasons why it's important to write a failing test first. First, you will write a failing test and make sure your test framework application can recognize it. This ensures that your development environment is properly configured and you can run your test programs. Second, your failing test will help you define what solution or feature code you'd like to write, and what is expected for that test to pass. This will help you as a developer, in setting or focusing your mindset on the purpose of the feature code you are writing. Third, the failing tests you write will serve as reminders to know what other programs you need to complete. Fourth, writing your tests first will help ensure that your solution code is covered by automated tests.

By trying to make your solution code unit-testable, you are sometimes inadvertently making your codes less coupled – it's like a cycle. As you continue to write loosely coupled codes, you will notice that your codes will start to look more organized and less of a tangled mess. As you continue writing solution code following the TDD process, it will continuously help you spot where tight couplings are in your product, sometimes encouraging you to refactor and decouple your code just to make it unit-testable. There are software development principles that will help you further improve your codes, such as the Single-Responsibility Principle, which will be discussed more in *Chapter 8*, *Using TDD with SOLID Principles*.

Now that we have defined and have a brief understanding of what TDD is, let's go through some of the common misconceptions associated with it.

Common misconceptions about TDD

In this section, we'll look at some of the misconceptions that I have personally observed that developers have about TDD. Time and time again, I've encountered people who have a poor understanding of TDD. When I talk to some of them about why they're not a fan of TDD, they sometimes tell me reasons that are not even related to TDD.

Testing software is not my job as a developer; therefore, I don't need TDD

I have said this myself. I used to think that I just needed to churn out solution code as fast as possible, test a little bit manually, and let the testing department ensure that everything is built correctly. This is probably the worst misconception I've ever had about TDD. As software developers, we develop software as solutions to problems. If we developers are the ones causing more problems, then we are not doing our jobs.

Developing with TDD is unnecessarily slow

I would be surprised if this were the first time you are hearing this. I first heard this from a client who had a technical background, not from a developer. I wasn't a fan of TDD myself and willingly agreed with my client back then. Sure, it's slower to write test codes and solution codes together; I would have to type more characters on my keyboard, after all!

When working on enterprise projects, from what I have experienced, TDD is what saved us from months of bugs and regressions. Writing tests and having good test coverage, which is discussed in *Chapter 5*, *Unit Testing*, will help ensure that the next time someone else touches the code or adds new features, no regressions will be introduced. TDD will help you build a lot of automated tests, and running these tests is cheaper and quicker than handing over your untested solution code to a testing team or testing company for manual testing.

Writing automated or unit tests is TDD

TDD is not about writing automated tests or unit tests for existing functionalities. TDD is not about getting your QA department or getting a third-party company to write automated tests for existing software. This is the exact opposite of TDD.

The most common misconception I have observed is that some developers and testers assume that TDD has something to do with testers writing automated tests for the codes that the developers build. I believe that this is a very bad misconception. It's no different from developing a program and sending it to the QA department for manual testing.

Getting testers to write automated functional tests is a very good thing, especially for existing functionalities that do not have automated tests, but this should only be thought of as supplementary test coverage for software and not be confused with TDD.

TDD is a silver bullet

The last misconception that I have encountered is assuming that if we developers have built excellent test coverage by following TDD, we will no longer need input from the software development department and QA department or team. Time and time again, I've proven myself wrong, believing that code that's written via the TDD methodology is bulletproof. I am very fortunate to work with knowledgeable and skilled software engineers and test engineers. Code reviews are critical; always get your codes and test scenarios peer-reviewed. Edge-case tests and functional scenarios that the developers might have overlooked will cause problems – and in my experience, they have caused big problems.

It is very important for the development and testing teams to properly understand the functional and acceptance test cases so that all imaginable scenarios are covered: the different types of tests will be covered in *Chapter 5, Unit Testing*. This is where **behavioral-driven development** (**BDD**) will start to make sense; BDD will be discussed in more detail in *Chapter 6, Applying Behaviour-Driven Development*. I have worked with test engineers and QA personnel who can come up with edge cases that I couldn't have imagined.

We have gone through some common misconceptions I have encountered about TDD. Now let's try to make a case for why we'd want to consider using TDD in our development process.

Why should we even consider TDD?

Why would I want my codes to be driven by tests? I want my codes to be driven by requirements and happy clients! You may have heard about the term TDD and felt uncomfortable with it. When I first heard about the term TDD, I was a bit uncomfortable with it too. Why would you want to waste time writing test code to test solution code that doesn't exist yet? Seriously, I need to write the actual code that solves the business problem, and you want me to write tests first? As a matter of fact, some developers I have trained and worked with have had this same question too – and it's the exact same question that was stopping them from getting interested in TDD!

When I started my software development career, I was working for a small company where we were required to deliver results as soon as possible, in very few iterations. Just thinking about writing automated tests for my super-quickly written codes was a big waste of time! Therefore, when I read about TDD for the first time, I was not interested. I ignored my meatball spaghetti codes; all I cared about was making sure that the client got the intended business results in the shortest amount of time. Solving the regressions that would be caused by the bad codes as a problem for later. I needed to make the client happy as soon as possible – that is, right now. This is probably one of the most short-sighted mistakes I made in my professional career. Most of the time, my colleagues and I had to add features and maintain our own bowl of spaghetti mess. Time and time again, we would hate our past selves when we saw the mess we had made. Early in our careers as software developers, we have a lot of mistakes, inefficiencies, and short-sightedness. Thankfully, we are not the first ones to encounter these problems. There are processes that we can follow to help us improve the quality of the software we produce, and one of them is TDD.

Now, after making so many mistakes, so many failures, and after working on hundreds of business-critical software projects, I can't even imagine living a day without writing tests by following TDD. When working on a project, I don't think I can even sleep properly at night without knowing whether my automated tests have passed or failed; at least I have the tests!

Imagine creating a *clean my home* to-do list on your phone: you only have one item on it and it's *clean the coffee machine*. You write that item down, get distracted and forget about it, and go on with your day. When you check your list again, you will realize that you have not cleaned the coffee machine yet! You then go ahead and clean the machine, and mark the item as completed.

Well, that's a bit like how TDD works. You write a failing test, then you write the codes to pass the test – and with the to-do list, you write out *"clean the coffee machine"*; then after you clean the actual coffee machine, you cross it out from your list.

> **Important note**
>
> Before anything else, I mean right now, you need to understand that it is very normal for a test to fail in the beginning and you need to be very comfortable with it and accept it. It's like writing the coffee machine checklist item on your phone. Once you add that to your to-do list, the to-do list is failing you until you pass it by marking the to-do item as complete. You need to write the failing test first before writing any program to pass that test. This is a part of the **Red, Green, Refactor (RGR)** concept, which will be discussed further in *Chapter 7, Building Solution Code with BDD and TDD*.

Going back to your phone, you add more items to that list: *clean the kitchen, clean the bedroom, clean the bathroom…* You then go to the gym and get distracted. You remember your list and want to know whether you have actually cleaned your home before going out, so you view your to-do list. You realize you only completed one item on the list; you will have to go back and finish the other tasks to fully satisfy the *clean my home* to-do list. When you return home, you can continue cleaning your home and ticking off your to-do list:

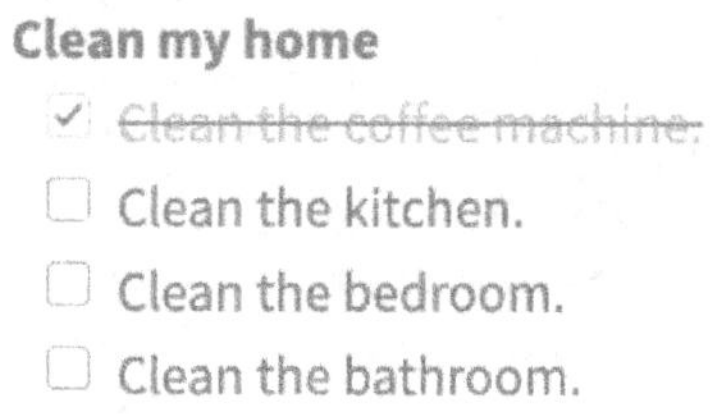

Clean my home

- ☑ ~~Clean the coffee machine.~~
- ☐ Clean the kitchen.
- ☐ Clean the bedroom.
- ☐ Clean the bathroom.

Figure 1.1 – Incomplete to-do list

You can think of the incomplete items on your to-do list as failing tests. The action of cleaning something is writing the codes to satisfy the failing to-do list item. You, finishing the task of cleaning the bedroom or bathroom, is akin to passing a test. Now imagine you have completed all the cleanings and so on, and you've marked all the items as checked on your *clean my home* list on your phone: you're done!

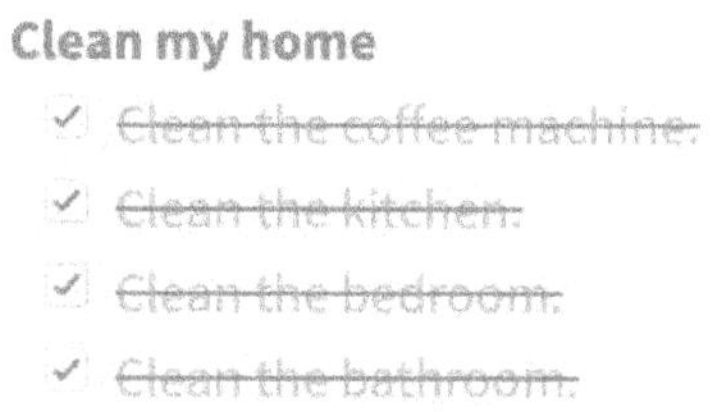

Clean my home

- ☑ ~~Clean the coffee machine.~~
- ☑ ~~Clean the kitchen.~~
- ☑ ~~Clean the bedroom.~~
- ☑ ~~Clean the bathroom.~~

Figure 1.2 – Completed to-do list

Now you can imagine your *clean my home* list as a test as well. Your test is satisfied by the overall completeness of the codes that were built to satisfy your smaller unit and integration tests (the types of tests will be discussed in detail in *Chapter 7, Building Solution Code with BDD and TDD*).

We can consider the *clean my home* list as a test. This test runs through all the processes of cleaning a home. Some objects inside it involve cleaning the bathroom, some the kitchen, and so on. Just as we did when writing the to-do list, you write the failing test that represents the bigger picture first and not the smaller, more detailed tests:

```
// Test Method
public function testCanCleanMyHome()
{

    $isMyHomeClean = $this->getCleaner()->clean();
    $this->assertTrue($isMyHomeClean);

}
```

After writing the failing *clean my home* test, which can only be satisfied by building the programs to clean each part of the house, we can start writing the failing tests for the smaller parts of the solution:

```
// Test Method
public function testCanCleanCoffeeMachine()
{
     $isMyCoffeeMachineClean = $this->getCleaner()->
         clean();
     $this->assertTrue($isMyCoffeeMachineClean);
}
```

Now imagine after cleaning your home, you ended up making a mess of the bedroom and you have unchecked the *clean my bedroom* item on your list. Technically speaking, your *clean my home* to-do list is now incomplete again. The same thing happens when after you have passed all the tests and someone in your team or you modifies the code and changes the expected behavior. If you then run your `testCanCleanMyHome()` test, it will fail. If we then run these automated tests before we deploy our codes to production, we will be able to catch regressions early on! It will be easier to catch code changes that break expected behaviors!

This is an oversimplification, but you will realize as we go along that this is what TDD is like. It's not a bad, time-wasting exercise after all!

We are humans and we tend to make mistakes – at least that's what I believe. Although if you think you don't make mistakes, you might as well just pry the *Delete* key out of your keyboard as you don't need it. I've made so many mistakes, and to help build confidence in my code, I ensure to pass all the tests and get the code peer-reviewed.

Implementing TDD and having a lot of test coverage for your software is a great way of helping you and your team spot mistakes before they cause harm in production. Having all these different types of tests running before deployment helps me sleep better at night.

What are we planning to achieve in this book?

Well, obviously, we want to get a better understanding of TDD – not just with theories but with actual usable and applicable understanding. We want to help ourselves write better codes that will benefit other developers who will work on your own codes as well. We want to be able to lay a foundation for how to write software that will be robust and sturdy, self-diagnosing, and more extensible.

We used a very simple analogy earlier using the *clean my home* to-do list to try to explain what TDD is and how it is done – but this will not be very exciting if it's all just theory. In this book, we will try to implement TDD for real using an example project!

We will be building an example project that will help us do the following:

- Identify what a client or a business wants to achieve
- Translate those requirements into actual tickets
- Learn how to implement TDD and BDD
- Write clean codes following design patterns and best practices
- Automatically run all tests using continuous integration
- Automatically deploy our codes using continuous deployment

Summary

In this chapter, we have defined what TDD is and what it is not. We tried to relate TDD to simple everyday tasks such as cleaning certain parts of your home. By trying to clear up common misconceptions about TDD, hopefully, we will have a clearer understanding of what TDD is. TDD is a process; it's not solely about writing unit tests and automated tests.

We also covered why we would want to use TDD when developing PHP applications. TDD helps us develop cleaner, decoupled, maintainable codes, and it helps us be more confident that we won't introduce regressions whenever we release codes, thanks to the automated test coverage that is inherently built by following TDD.

In the next chapter, we will start building the example project by coming up with a simple hypothetical business challenge first and making sense of what needs to be built to solve the problem.

2
Understanding and Organizing the Business Requirements of Our Project

Before writing a single line of code, we first need to understand the goals of a project and what problems we are trying to solve. We build software to solve problems, and if we do not adequately understand what the client or the business is trying to achieve, we will have problems coming up with the ideal solution—or, worse, we can end up spending months building software that doesn't even address the business requirements.

As software developers, it is great to have a clear list of what needs to be built. It's just like having a simple grocery list. This list will help us determine which features we need to develop or release first. So, before we start building solutions to a problem by writing software, we will try to come up with a simple example where we will try to interpret business problems and goals into a list of software features that we will need to write code for.

In this chapter, we will come up with an example business problem. We will try to analyze what the example business is trying to achieve, and what's stopping it from achieving this goal. We will present a solution to help us define and organize the business requirements into a workable list of *user stories*. These user stories, in turn, will be used to represent our behavior-driven tests. These behavior-driven tests will help us build our test-driven codes. **Behavior-driven development** (BDD) will be discussed in more detail in *Chapter 6, Applying Behavior-Driven Development*.

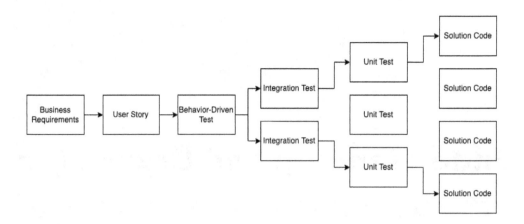

Figure 2.1 – Building with TDD and BDD

In contrast to **test-driven development** (**TDD**) and BDD, developers can also write solution code directly for a user story or a requirement. This is a recipe for future disaster. In fact, this is how I used to develop software:

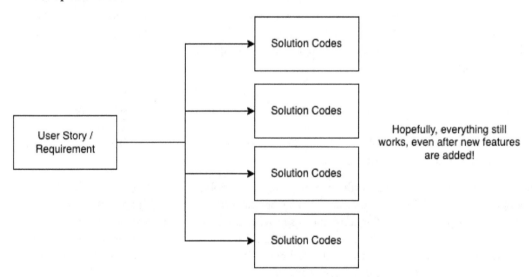

Figure 2.2 – Developing a solution without tests

In this book, we will focus on building solution code based on the business requirements, represented by test programs. So, let's get started with understanding the example business problem and requirements.

In this chapter, we will be covering the following:

- The example business project

- Breaking down the business requirements into software features
- Integrating Jira with Bitbucket

Technical requirements

This chapter requires the reader to have basic knowledge of Git version control.

The example business project

We will be using a simple example—a *motor museum*—to help us go through the process of defining goals and problems and organizing them into workable units.

The business scenario

I was having a catch-up and drinks with my friends from Perth months ago, and they told me that they had volunteered during weekends for fun to help a motor museum organize an inventory of toy car model donations the museum has received. The museum receives big boxes of toy car donations.

As we were drinking, they told me that it's both fun and sometimes challenging as there's no specific tool or process to itemize the toy cars that the museum receives. Sometimes, they open a whole box of toy cars with no information about the toys, and sometimes there are whole boxes containing toy cars properly packaged with all the information in each toy car's box, such as the year of manufacture, the racing driver who drove it, color, and so on. They must itemize these toys and put them in a spreadsheet, and this is where things get interesting.

They said they used a spreadsheet file that they would share around and hand over to the next volunteer. Recording information about a toy car is a bit of a task—for instance, someone records a toy car's color as blue, but someone else might just write down "flames", which obviously is not a color. Sometimes colors are mispelled. So, now, if they want to search for all cars that are blue, it can get complicated as sometimes people might misspell blue when saving the information. They also want to be able to search for model cars a specific racing driver has driven, and they want to discover in which section of the museum the toy car model can be found.

As we were chatting, I couldn't help but start imagining data being entered, submitted, validated, processed, and then persisted. I forgot about my drink for a second, and my mind started to drift away and started imagining code. If you're a software developer, you probably know what I mean!

I thought: I can use this real-life challenge and use it as an example business project. It's simple and it sounds fun, but it will also serve as a good example to demonstrate how to implement TDD and BDD.

I asked my friends if they were okay with me using their example for this project, and they were happy with it. So, from now on, we will refer to them as our clients or the business.

Making sense of the scenario and the problem

By talking to the business or client, we can get some very important information about the problems they have. We can try coming up with a very rough and simple list of problems, constraints, and possible solutions.

What the business is trying to achieve:

- Inventory clerks or volunteers are able to itemize and record toy car model information
- Users are able to search through the records and find in which section of the museum the car model can be viewed

Problems/challenges:

- No system allows different users to record car model data simultaneously
- No system validates the data being stored—for example, for color spelling
- No easy way for visitors to find or search for where a specific car model is being displayed in the museum

Constraints:

- The project is only focused on the toy car model inventory
- Only registered museum staff can enter data into the inventory

Solutions:

- Build a simple inventory system for the toy car models
- Build a simple page with a table for visitors to view the inventory

We were able to come up with a list of very important points about the business scenario. At the end of the day, all the items we have listed will end up satisfying one thing, and that is to address what the business is trying to achieve. This is the most important thing to understand. We are building solutions by first understanding properly what the problems are. And after we solve the problems, we must be sure that we have addressed what the business is trying to achieve.

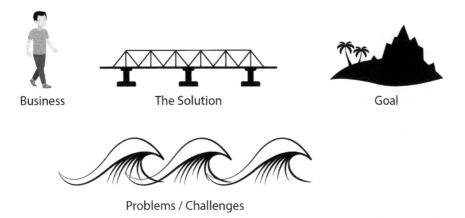

Figure 2.3 – The solution

I had an experience where I saw developers spend a lot of time building software, and when the project got handed over to me, I realized that the direction in which they were going was totally incorrect. So, it doesn't matter how good the software is—it is of no value if it cannot address the real problem and if it cannot help in achieving the business goal.

Now that we have defined what the business is trying to achieve and have identified the problems and challenges the business is facing, we can now start organizing a list of things we need to do to solve the problems.

Breaking down the business requirements into software features

We will need a solution to organize all the tasks we need to work on. We can do this by using a notebook, a scratchpad, post-it notes, or even a simple Kanban board. But since we are planning to develop maintainable software and we want to have visibility into the progress of our development process, it would be great to have a more powerful solution than, say, a notebook.

In this project, we will be using **Atlassian Jira**. Jira is software that we can use to organize all the items that we need to build and work on. We will use it as a turbo-charged notebook to contain our to-do lists of software features.

We will not be focusing deeply on the methodology; instead, we will be using Jira just to help us organize our project so that we can start writing software in an organized sequence.

We want to have the ability to link our Git branches, pull requests, and commits to an issue that we are working on. We want the ability to integrate our **continuous integration** (**CI**) (*Chapter 9, Continuous Integration*) solution into our issues as well. You can think of a *Jira issue* as a list item representing a business problem or a software feature.

We will start breaking down the business requirements into a list of software features represented by user stories, which is an issue type in Jira. But for that, we first need to create a Jira account and initialize our project.

Creating a Jira Cloud account and initializing the Jira Cloud project

To create a Jira Cloud account and initialize the Jira Cloud project, follow these steps:

1. To get started, we first need to create a free Jira account. You can do so by going to the following URL: `https://www.atlassian.com/try/cloud/signup?bundle=jira-software&edition=free`. Then, sign up for an account:

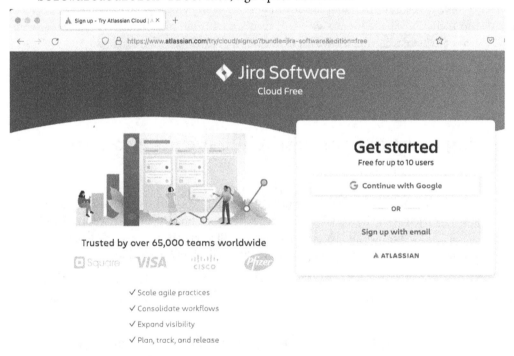

Figure 2.4 – Jira sign-up

2. After signing up for an account, you will be prompted to enter a subdomain name in the **Your site** field. Use any subdomain name you want. After this step, you can skip all other popups until you get to the **Project templates** page:

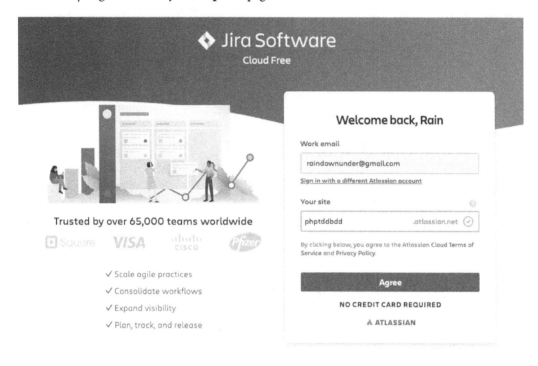

Figure 2.5 – Entering a subdomain name

3. On the **Project templates** page, select **Scrum**:

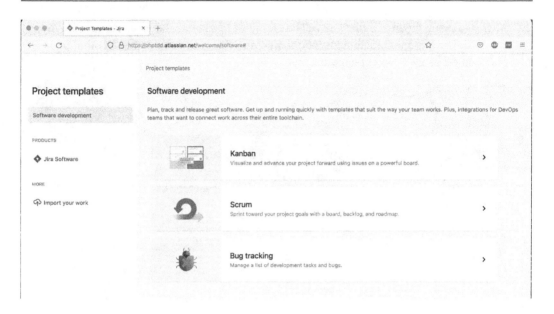

Figure 2.6 – Selecting Scrum

4.   On the **Scrum** page, click on the **Use template** button at the top or bottom right of the screen:

Figure 2.7 – Use template button

5.   On the **Choose a project type** page, click on **Select a team-managed project**:

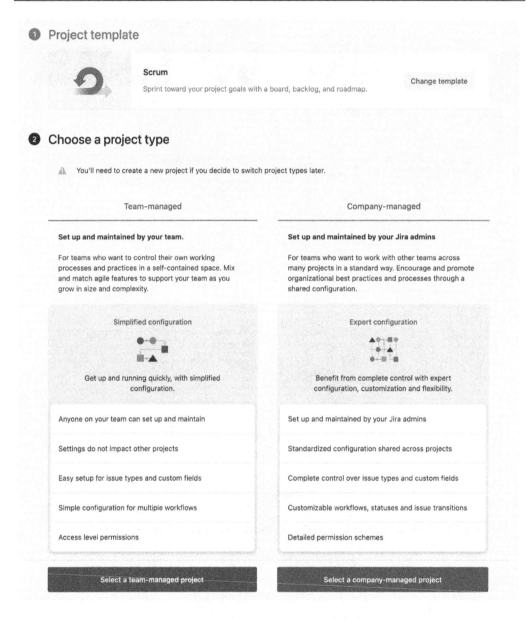

Figure 2.8 – Select a team-managed project

6. On the **Add project details** page, you'll need to enter a project name. Use `toycarmodels` as the name of the project and enter TOYC for the **Key** field:

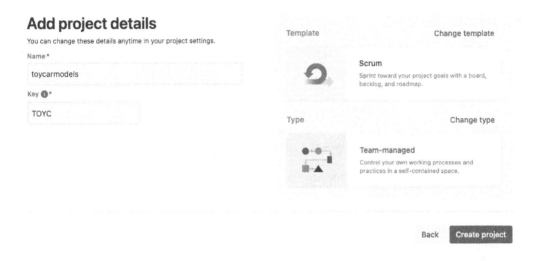

Figure 2.9 – Add project details

7. After these steps, you should end up with an empty **TOYC board** page:

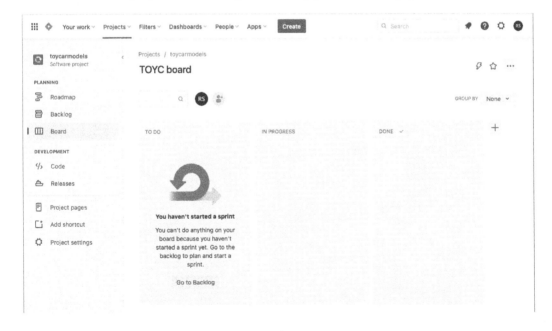

Figure 2.10– Empty TOYC Kanban board

Now that we have a Jira project to play with, we can start creating tickets to represent the things we need to do to help the restaurant business with its online booking system project. We will be using *Jira epics* to group related Jira issues representing software features we want to build.

Creating a Jira epic

If we take a step back and think about the problems and solutions we defined earlier, we can come up with a simple list of things that we can build as features.

We have identified that we want to build a way for inventory clerk volunteers to be able to record donated toy car models in the inventory, and we also identified the need for museum visitors to search through the inventory and locate where the toy car model is being displayed in the museum. Now, we have identified that we will have two types of users:

- Users who need to input and store data (inventory clerks)
- Users who want to view the data (museum visitors)

That means that we can separate the programs we need to build into two separate small projects: one small project for inventory clerks, and another one for visitors. Sometimes, it helps to segregate different parts of a big project into their own smaller projects; this can help in resourcing different developers for different areas of the projects and it can also help focus the developers' efforts.

The inventory clerk-facing solution will probably contain a lot of smaller tasks. We can start defining those tasks into actual Jira tickets, but before thinking about the smaller tickets, let's create an epic first.

Let's go back to the Jira **TOYC board** page from the previous instruction set and let's start creating tickets:

1. On the left menu, click on the **Roadmap** menu item:

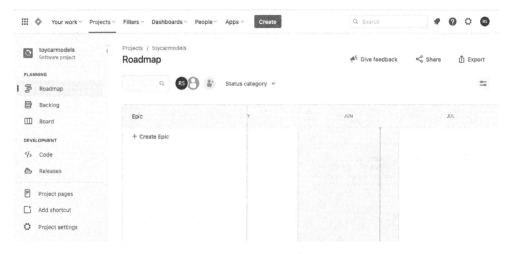

Figure 2.11 – Jira roadmap

2. Within the table, click on the **+ Create Epic** button. A textbox will appear with the text `What needs to be done?:`

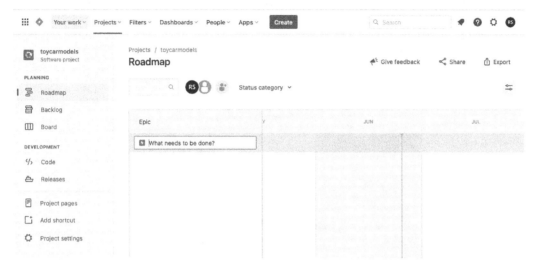

Figure 2.12 – Epic title

3. In the textbox, enter `Inventory Clerk Solution`, then hit *Enter*:

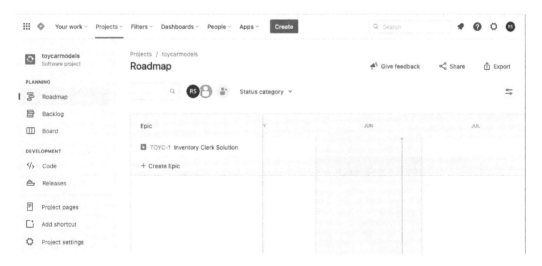

Figure 2.13 – First epic

4.   Click on the epic you just created, and a popup will appear. In the description text area, you can enter any description detailing a summary of things we need to do. In this example, I will just use the following text: `Enable the inventory clerk to be able to input and store toy car model data` and under the **Assignee** field, click on the **Assign to me** link:

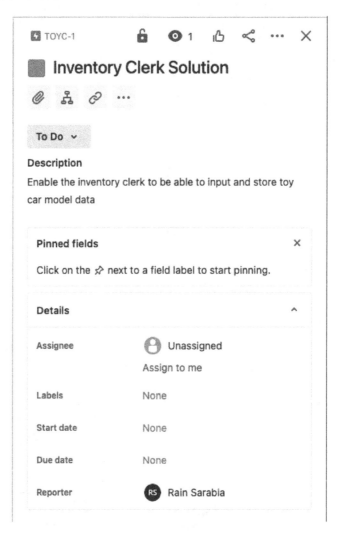

Figure 2.14 – Epic description

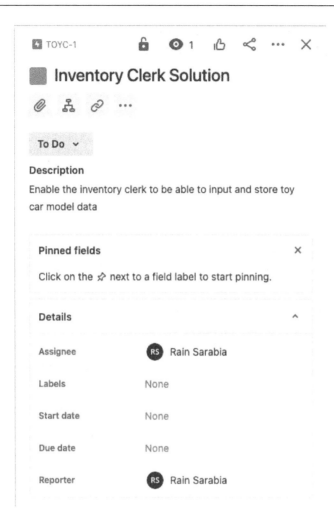

Figure 2.15 – Assignee

5. Close the popup.

Now that we have created a Jira epic, we can add *items* to this epic. The items we will be adding to the epic will be user stories.

Writing user stories

A *Jira user story* is a software feature written informally in a descriptive and expressive way from the perspective of an end user. An end user can be a non-technical customer or a software developer who will end up being the consumer of the software that will be produced.

We created an epic called **Inventory Clerk Solution** in the previous section, which will contain all the things we will need for an inventory clerk to record all information about donated toy car models.

But what would the inventory clerks need to be able to achieve that goal? First, they will need a window or a web page that contains a form. This form will then be used to record the data for a specific toy car model.

But how would an inventory clerk identify themself to the system? It looks like we will need authentication and authorization functionalities, and with these functionalities, we will be able to restrict the data input part of the system to authorized users only.

After inventory clerks have authenticated themselves, they should be able to start inputting and recording toy car model data into the system.

For now, let's stick to these simple features and start writing stories.

We have identified at least three user stories just by thinking about what the inventory clerk needs to be able to do to input and record a toy car model into the system.

We can use the following template to write our own user stories:

As a/an [Actor], [I want to], [so that]

- As an inventory clerk, I want to be able to log in to the system so that I can access the inventory system
- As an inventory clerk, I want to be able to input toy car model data so that I can save the data
- As an inventory clerk, I want to be able to see a table containing the records so that I can review all the toy car model data stored

Now that we have a list of customer user stories we need, let's create tickets for them.

Creating Jira user stories

Follow these steps to create Jira user stories:

1. Mouse over on the **Inventory Clerk Solution** epic and click on the + button on the right. It will then show a text field, What needs to be done?:

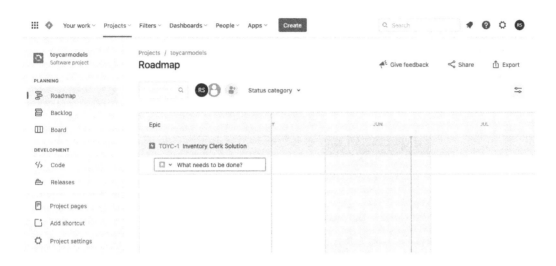

Figure 2.16 – What needs to be done? text: user story title

2. In the dropdown to the left of the text field, make sure **Story** is selected:

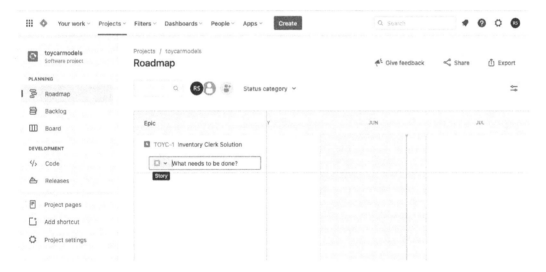

Figure 2.17 – Selecting Story from the dropdown

3. In the text field, enter a title for our first user story, `As an inventory clerk, I want to be able to login to the system, so that I can access the inventory system`, and hit *Enter*:

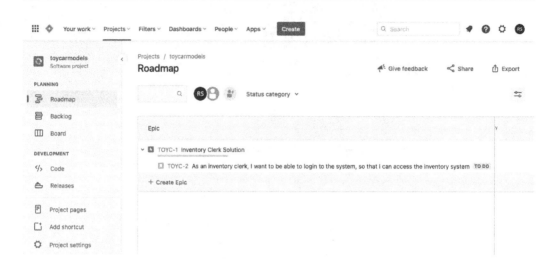

Figure 2.18 – First user story

4.   Repeat the steps to create the three stories we have listed down:

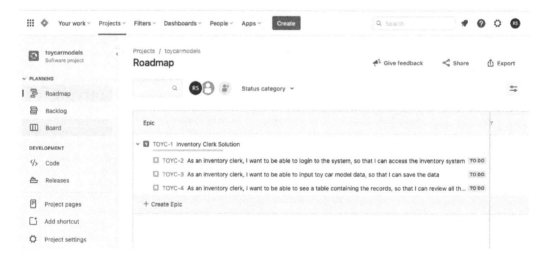

Figure 2.19 – Epic with user stories

These user stories will play a very important role in the behavior-driven tests we are going to be writing in *Chapter 6, Applying Behaviour-Driven Development*.

Now that we have created our first epic and user stories for the **Inventory Clerk Solution** epic, repeat the steps to create visitor epic and user stories. You can use the following epic name and user stories:

Admin epic name: **Visitors Page**

User stories:

- As a visitor, I'd like to see a public page with a table with car model info, so that I can browse through the inventory

- As a visitor, I'd like to be able to filter the table, so that I can narrow down the results:

Figure 2.20 – Epics and user stories

After those steps, we will now have some lists of things we want to achieve as a customer and as an admin. The list of things we want to achieve is called **User Stories**, and we have grouped it by using epics. Before writing code, we want to be able to store and version our code somewhere. We will use Bitbucket as our version control solution.

Integrating Jira with Bitbucket

We will need a Git repository for our code, and it would be great if we could integrate it with the list of tasks (Jira tickets) we need to build. Jira offers a lot of software integration solutions, which is great. Jira can be integrated with our code repository, and with CI solutions, which will be discussed in *Chapter 9, Continuous Integration*.

There is a lot of Git version control hosting software out there, but for this project, we will be using Bitbucket so that we can quickly integrate it with Jira and spend more of our precious time on actual coding.

First, you will need to create a Bitbucket account for this example project. Go to `https://bitbucket.org/product` and sign up for an account. If you have an existing Bitbucket account, that should work too.

There is a lengthy set of instructions for integrating Bitbucket with Jira Cloud; follow the instructions at `https://support.atlassian.com/jira-software-cloud/docs/enable-code/` or `https://support.atlassian.com/jira-cloud-administration/docs/connect-jira-cloud-to-bitbucket/`.

You can also just click on the **Code** link on the left menu:

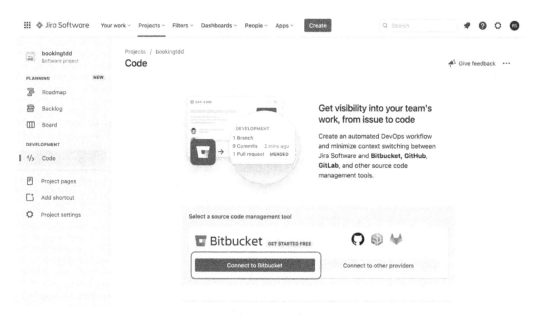

Figure 2.21 – Code page

Click on the **Connect to Bitbucket** button on the main panel. You can then follow the instructions to connect your Jira project to your selected Bitbucket account.

Next, click on the **Project settings** link on the left menu:

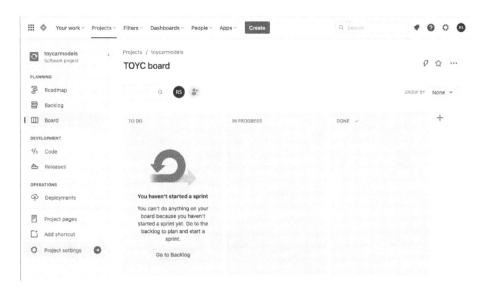

Figure 2.22 – Project settings menu item

While inside the **Project settings** page, click on the **Features** menu item. Once on the **Features** page, in the **Development** group, click on the **Configure…** button inside the **Code** section:

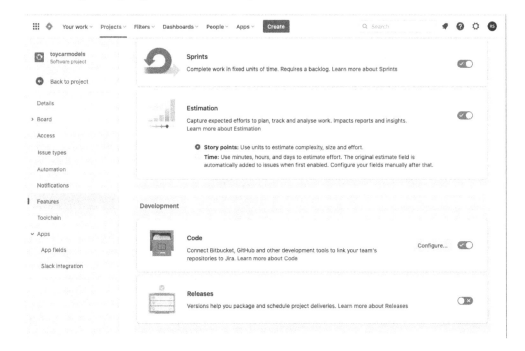

Figure 2.23 – Code Configure… button

After clicking the **Configure…** button, you'll be redirected to a **Toolchain** page; in the **Build** section, click on the **+ Add repository** button:

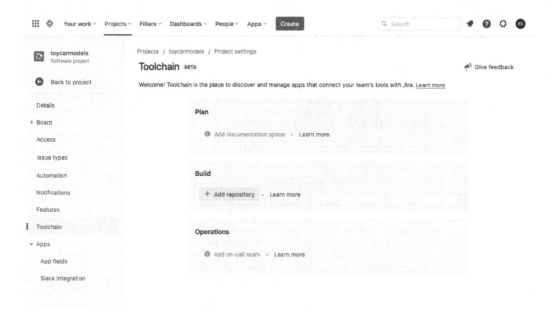

Figure 2.24 – + Add repository button

A popup will appear—select whichever Git solution you want to use with the project. In my case, I'm using a free Bitbucket account:

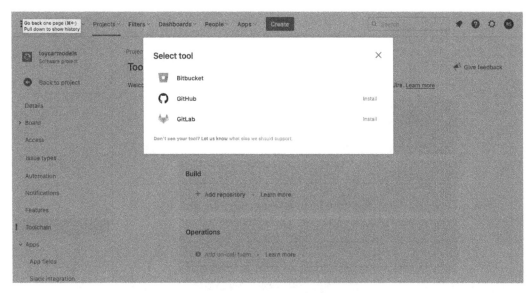

Figure 2.25 – Selecting a Git product

After clicking on **Bitbucket**, you can now enter a new repository name you want to integrate the Jira project with. Or, you can also select a pre-existing repository you have created in your own account. For this example, I'll just create a new repository:

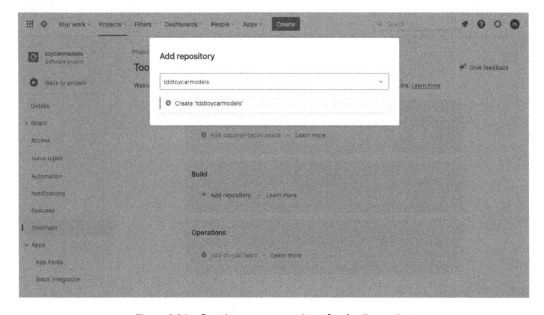

Figure 2.26 – Creating a new repository for the Jira project

Click the **+ Create** button, and your Jira project should now be integrated with your Git repository:

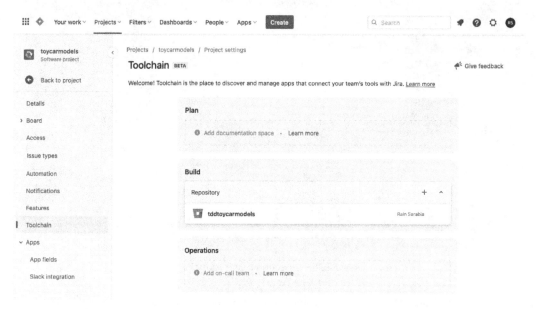

Figure 2.27 – Repository integrated with Jira

Now, you can go back to the project window by clicking the **Back to project** link; then, click on the **Roadmap** link. Click on the **Inventory Clerk Solution** epic we created earlier, and you should see a new **Development** section in our ticket:

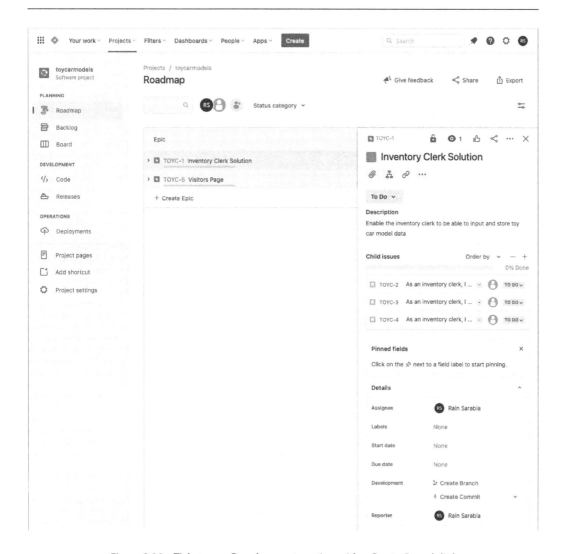

Figure 2.28 – Ticket: new Development section with a Create Branch link

Now that everything is configured, you should be able to create Bitbucket branches from your Jira tickets. In the **Inventory Clerk Solution** popup, click on the **Create Branch** link. You'll be redirected to your Git repository page where you can proceed to create a branch:

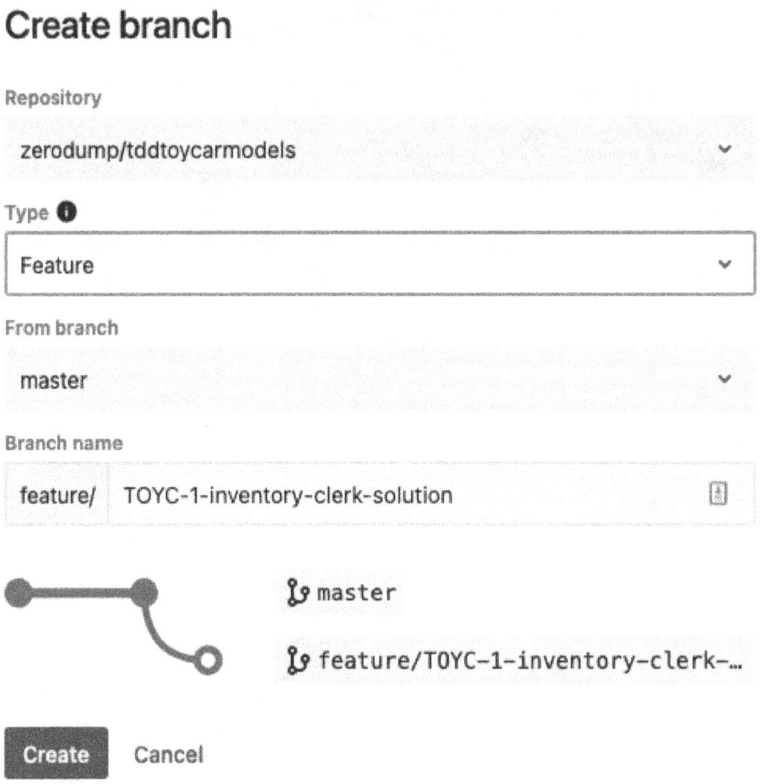

Create branch

Repository

zerodump/tddtoycarmodels   ⌄

Type ⓘ

Feature   ⌄

From branch

master   ⌄

Branch name

feature/   TOYC-1-inventory-clerk-solution   ⎀

⑂ master

⑂ feature/TOYC–1–inventory–clerk–…

Create   Cancel

Figure 2.29 – Creating a new branch for the epic

Go back to the **Roadmap** page, and refresh the page. Open the **Inventory Clerk Solution** epic again, and this time, in the **Development** section, you will see that there is now one branch connected to our Jira epic:

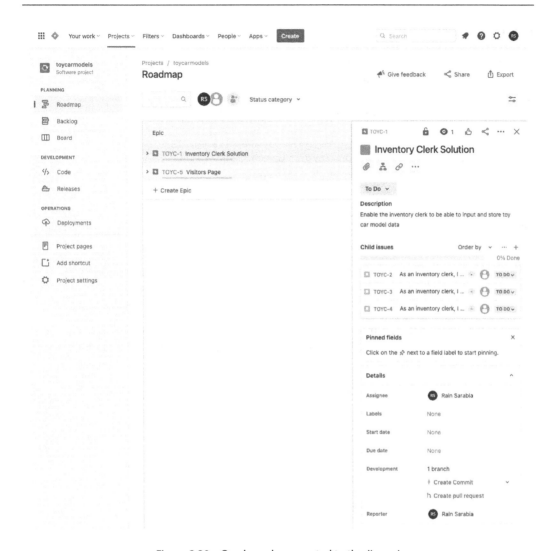

Figure 2.30 – One branch connected to the Jira epic

We now have the ability to create Git repositories using Jira. This will come in handy as we go along in the project because this means that our Git repository is now integrated properly with our ticketing solution.

We will be using BitBucket for this example project, but you are free to choose your own preferred version control system and integrate it with Jira.

Summary

In this chapter, we were able to come up with an example project based on a real-life problem that my friends encountered with a car museum. By trying to understand what the business or client wants to achieve, we were able to identify the problems or challenges that are stopping the business or client from achieving that goal. By analyzing our proposed solution to the problems, we were able to come up with plans for a solution. We listed down the solutions as user stories and grouped them under an epic.

These user stories tell us about behaviors—system behaviors, to be exact. Why are these important? Well, by understanding what we need to build, we developers can plan *how* we build solutions better. I have seen software being built for weeks or months, and after completion, the developers and business analysts realize that the solution does not even solve the problem that is stopping the business or the client from achieving its goal simply because the business analysts and developers did not understand what the business was trying to achieve or solve.

By having a clean list of items that define what needs to be built, we will be able to come up with automated tests that will check whether we have satisfied the desired behavior. We will be building those automated behavior-driven tests in *Chapter 6, Applying Behaviour-Driven Development*.

In the next chapter, we will be introducing *Docker containers* and building our own container. This container will then be used to contain and run the PHP software solution that we will be building to achieve the business's goal.

3

Setting Up Our Development Environment Using Docker Containers

"*It works on my machine*" is a phrase you've probably heard as a software developer; you might even have said it yourself as well. I'm sure I did! And to be fair, my colleague Ben Hansen, who was our test automation engineer at that time, also pointed out that he's also allowed to say, "*It doesn't work on my machine*" in response to us developers. As a developer myself, I've had my fair share of frustrating experiences caused by running the same PHP application across different environments with inconsistent server setups. There were times in my career when I struggled to replicate some production environment bugs from my local development machine. We would find out that the PHP application we were developing would be deployed in staging or production on a different operating system with various libraries installed, which were out of sync with the developers' development environment setups. It was a nightmare!

When we develop PHP applications, we need to ensure that the applications we develop behave consistently across different deployment environments such as staging or production. Also, when a new developer joins your team, it's great if they can set up their local development environments on their development machines easily and quickly. **Containers** can help solve these challenges.

In our example project, we will need a development environment to run our PHP application consistently wherever we deploy it. If our PHP tests and applications pass and run properly from our local machines, they should also pass and run correctly when we deploy them.

We will go through the concept of containers and define what they are. We will learn how to create a Docker image and run Docker containers. Docker containers will help us easily package our application, making it easy to run our application in other server environments more consistently.

In this chapter, we will define and cover the following:

- What is a container?
- Setting up our PHP development container
- Running Docker containers

Technical requirements

This chapter requires you to have access to *Bash*. If you are using a Mac or Linux OS, you can just use *terminal*. If you're on a Windows OS, you will need to install a third-party Bash program.

For the instructions defined in this chapter, you can experiment with the complete Docker setup found in Chapter 3 Git repository at https://github.com/PacktPublishing/Test-Driven-Development-with-PHP-8/tree/main/Chapter%203.

Quick Setup

To run the complete development setup with Docker containers for this chapter, in a macOS development machine, follow the instructions in this chapter to install Docker Desktop, and then simply run the following command from your terminal:

```
curl -Lo phptdd.zip "https://github.com/PacktPublishing/Test-
Driven-Development-with-PHP-8/tree/main/Chapter%203.zip" &&
unzip -o phptdd.zip && cd complete && ./demoSetup.sh
```

What is a container?

A container is a packaging solution that will contain all the software dependencies that your application needs to run correctly. Different container platforms are available, but we will be using Docker in this book. We will be using Docker to build and run our containers for our example project.

Docker is an open source containerization solution that will enable us to package our PHP solution and run it on different development machines and deployment environments, including our **continuous integration (CI) solution**, which will be discussed more in *Chapter 9, Continuous Integration*.

Now that we have defined what containers are and the containerization solution we will be using for our project, let's start setting up our development containers.

Setting up our PHP development container

We will need a development environment for our PHP application. We will be separating our development environment structure into two main parts: the Docker container (server) and the PHP application.

The docker directory will contain the following:

- Dockerfile
- docker-compose.yml
- Server configurations

The codebase directory will serve as the following:

- The root directory for our PHP application
- Vendor directory for composer packages

Now, let us set up our PHP development container:

1. Create the following directory structure in your machine:

Figure 3.1 – Base tree

2. Run the following commands:

```
$ mkdir -p ~/phptdd/docker
$ mkdir -p ~/phptdd/codebase
```

3. Install **Docker Desktop**. Before we create the required Docker files, we will need to download and install Docker Desktop.

   For **macOS** users, Docker can be downloaded from https://docs.docker.com/desktop/mac/install/.

   For **Windows** users, the download link is https://docs.docker.com/desktop/windows/install/.

   Once Docker Desktop has been installed on your macOS machine, we can now organize our development directories.

4. We will need to create a Dockerfile within the phptdd/docker/ directory. Create a phptdd/docker/Dockerfile file, like so:

```
FROM php:8.1.3RC1-apache-buster
RUN docker-php-ext-install mysqli pdo pdo_mysql
```

We declare the base Docker image in the first line using the FROM keyword. Every Dockerfile must start with this keyword. The second line is an instruction to run a command on top of the current image. Since we will also need a database for our project, we can install the **MySQL** extensions we need.

We will need more than just PHP for our example project: we will need a database, a web server, and other tools. Therefore, we need a way to run and organize multiple containers. Let's see how to do that next.

Creating multiple containers

To run multiple containers, let's use the Compose tool that is pre-installed when you install Docker Desktop.

Create a phptdd/docker/docker-compose.yml file, like so:

```
version: "3.7"

services:
  # Web Server
  server-web:
    build:
      dockerfile: ./Dockerfile
      context: .
    restart: always
    volumes:
      - "../codebase/:/var/www/html/"
    ports:
      - "8081:80"

  # MySQL Database
  server-mysql:
    image: mysql:8.0.19
    restart: always
    environment:
      MYSQL_ROOT_PASSWORD: mypassword
    volumes:
      - mysql-data:/var/lib/mysql

  # Optional MySQL Management Tool
```

```
phpmyadmin:
    image: phpmyadmin/phpmyadmin:5.0.1
    restart: always
    environment:
        PMA_HOST: server-mysql
        PMA_USER: root
        PMA_PASSWORD: mypassword
    ports:
        - "3333:80"
volumes:
    mysql-data:
```

In our `docker-compose.yml` file, we have declared and configured three main containers, which are all accessible through different ports:

- **Web server**: `server-web`
- **MySQL DB server**: `server-mysql`
- **phpMyAdmin**: `app-phpmyadmin`

We were able to install Docker Desktop and create the required `Dockerfile` and `docker-compose.yml` files that contain the template to build our containers. Let's try running all the containers and make sure that they are configured correctly and can communicate with each other.

Running Docker containers

Now that we have the two base Docker files that we need, let's create an example PHP program that we can use to make sure that our containers are working as expected.

Create a `phptdd/codebase/index.php` PHP file, like so:

```php
<?php
$dbHost         = "server-mysql";
$dbUsername     = "root";
$dbPassword     = "mypassword";
$dbName         = "mysql";

try {
    $conn = new PDO("mysql:host=$dbHost;dbname=$dbName",
        $dbUsername, $dbPassword);
```

```
    $conn->setAttribute(PDO::ATTR_ERRMODE, PDO::
        ERRMODE_EXCEPTION);

    echo "MySQL: Connected successfully";
} catch(PDOException $e) {
    echo "Connection failed: " . $e->getMessage();
}

// Show PHP info:
phpinfo();
?>
```

At this stage, we have created three files and have the following directory structure:

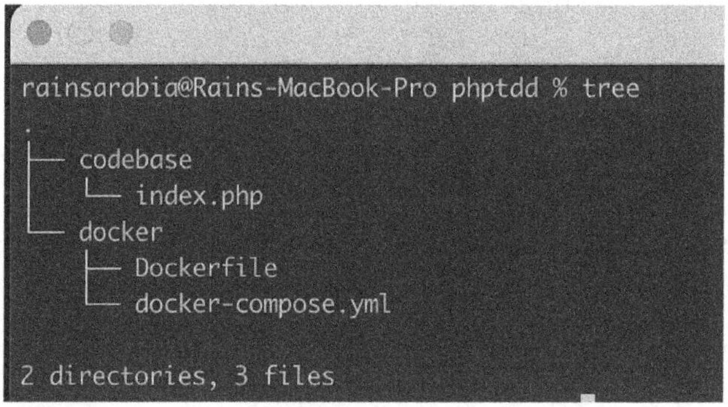

Figure 3.2 – Base files

Let's go through this directory structure:

- `Dockerfile`: The file where we declared which base Docker image to use and added instructions to install MySQL extensions
- `docker-compose.yml`: The file where we added configurations for the three base containers we want to run to serve as our **Linux Apache MySQL PHP (LAMP)** stack
- `index.php`: The test PHP file we created to test if the PHP application was able to connect to the MySQL container and show some details about the PHP server

Before being able to run our containers, we need to build the main image that we need to run the containers first.

Building a Docker image and running containers

Run the following command to download the base image and build our Docker image:

```
$ cd ~/phptdd/docker
$ docker-compose build
```

It will take a few minutes to run on the first try. The command will pull the base image that we have declared inside the Dockerfile from the Docker repository, and it will also execute the RUN command we added in the second line of the Dockerfile.

Once the build is done, we can run the three containers we have configured by using the docker-compose.yml file:

```
$ docker-compose up -d
```

After running the command, you should see all three containers being created:

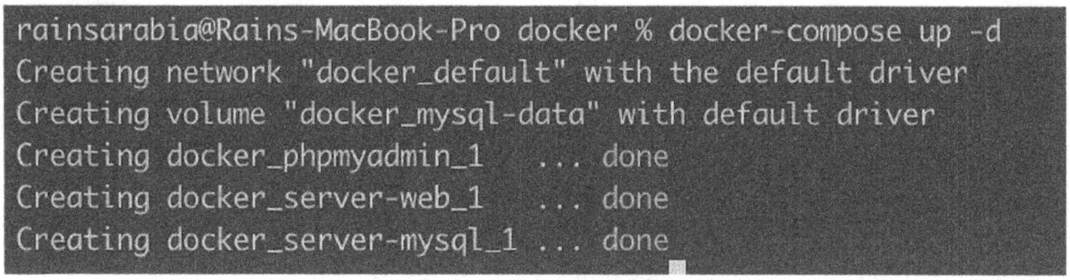

```
rainsarabia@Rains-MacBook-Pro docker % docker-compose up -d
Creating network "docker_default" with the default driver
Creating volume "docker_mysql-data" with default driver
Creating docker_phpmyadmin_1    ... done
Creating docker_server-web_1    ... done
Creating docker_server-mysql_1 ... done
```

Figure 3.3 – Containers created

Now, let's see if the containers are running properly; run the following command:

```
$ docker ps -a
```

You should see the three containers we have created, and the status should indicate that they are running:

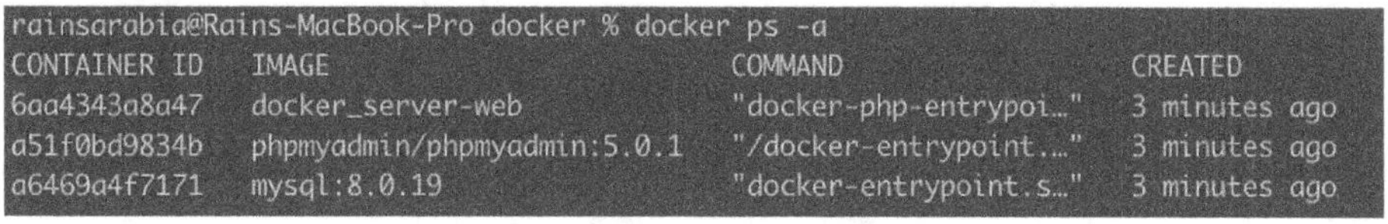

```
rainsarabia@Rains-MacBook-Pro docker % docker ps -a
CONTAINER ID   IMAGE                        COMMAND                CREATED
6aa4343a8a47   docker_server-web            "docker-php-entrypoi…" 3 minutes ago
a51f0bd9834b   phpmyadmin/phpmyadmin:5.0.1  "/docker-entrypoint.…" 3 minutes ago
a6469a4f7171   mysql:8.0.19                 "docker-entrypoint.s…" 3 minutes ago
```

Figure 3.4 – Containers are running

We can see from the list in *Figure 3.4* that the containers are running.

Now, let's try to run the PHP test program we wrote: open a web browser and try to access `http://127.0.0.1:8081`. If you check the `docker-compose.yml` file, you will see we have declared that we want to route port `8081` from your host machine to port `80` of the container. You will also be able to see the port routing for running containers using the `docker ps -a` command.

You should see a **MySQL: Connected Successfully** message and a standard PHP info output. This shows that our PHP application running inside the `server-web` container is connected to the `server-mysql` container:

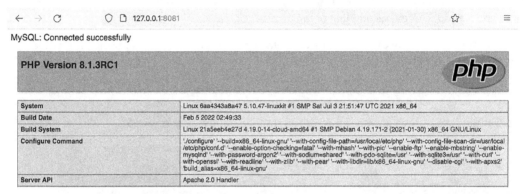

Figure 3.5 – Test script: successful PHP to MySQL connection and PHP info

We have also configured the third container to serve our `phpMyAdmin` application; this is entirely optional. Using your web browser, go to `http://127.0.0.1:3333`:

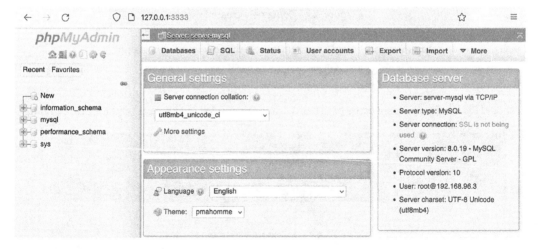

Figure 3.6 – phpMyAdmin screen

You should now see the **phpMyAdmin** main dashboard, with the default databases listed in the left column.

This is all looking good. The three containers we have configured are running correctly and are able to communicate and link to each other. We now have a basic development environment for our PHP application. Next, let's try to stop the containers.

Stopping containers

There are times when you need to stop containers, such as when you want to reload new configurations, or if you just want to stop containers that you no longer need.

To stop running containers, as well as remove their configurations, run the following command:

```
$ docker-compose down
```

Now, if you try to check the status of the containers by running `docker ps`, you will see that our three containers are gone from the list. You can also use `docker kill <container_name>` to stop a specific container.

Summary

In this chapter, we introduced Docker and used it to create and run containers. Containers are instances of packaged applications. Although we have seen that containers are packages and isolated, they can also communicate with each other. For instance, our example PHP program is running inside the `server-web` container and then connects to the `server-mysql` container that runs our MySQL server.

We've seen how simple it is to launch containers. We have two PHP containers running (`server-web` and `app-phpmyadmin`) and one database container (`server-mysql`), and we can run more containers if we need to. We will be using the base containers we have created to build our PHP project; we will continue modifying our containers and will install more libraries and tools as we go along.

In the next chapter, we will start building our base PHP application. We will try to go through the features and reasons why we decided to use PHP in the first place. We will be installing the **Laravel framework** to simplify the process of writing our solution so that we can focus more on **test-driven development** (TDD) itself and not on writing tons of bootstrap code.

4

Using Object-Oriented Programming in PHP

PHP is an open source scripting programming language that has supported **Object-Oriented Programming** (**OOP**) features since PHP 5. PHP is straightforward to learn, and it is very flexible. No wonder it's prevalent. There are a lot of open source PHP learning materials available online, as well as open source libraries and frameworks. If you're planning to build a web application, the chances are that there will be some downloadable PHP libraries and frameworks that will pretty much suit your needs. If you require PHP developers for your project, you'd be glad to know that there are indeed a lot of PHP developers out there.

As a PHP developer, I have worked on many PHP projects ranging from tiny web applications to enterprise applications. I've seen many PHP applications developed by different companies and teams. Some applications I've seen and worked on personally were properly built following best practices and industry standards, but some were made of spaghetti mess glued together by duct tape. There's one thing in common, though; it doesn't matter if the software is well-written or poorly written; successful software will require updates. New features and bug fixes will be required. The more successful the software gets, the more users utilize the software, the more feature requests get submitted, and the more bugs get discovered. It's a cycle, but it's a great problem to have to begin with.

No one wants to see regressions introduced by new features and bug fixes, but it happens. And sometimes, if there are no proper development or release processes involved, regressions happen a lot. New bugs and problems can be introduced after a release, and this is very demoralizing. The business also loses its confidence in releasing more bug fixes or new features. For the developers and the business, releasing codes should be a positive experience, not a cause for anxiety.

Using OOP and **Test-Driven Development** (**TDD**) together helps to improve code quality by making sure that most of the functions and objects are testable, maintainable, reusable, and mockable. Mocks will be discussed more in *Chapter 8, Using TDD with SOLID Principles*.

In this chapter, we'll go through the definition and meaning of OOP in PHP. We'll go through the Four Pillars of OOP: abstraction, encapsulation, inheritance, and polymorphism. We will try to use example codes to explain the OOP concepts, and these concepts will serve as the foundations for the TDD codes we will be writing for our example project later.

In this chapter, we will be going through the following:

- Understanding OOP in PHP

- Classes versus objects

- Abstraction in OOP

- Encapsulation in OOP

- Inheritance in OOP

- Polymorphism in OOP

- **PHP Standards Recommendations (PSRs)**

Technical requirements

The user is expected to have at least basic knowledge of PHP or other OOP languages such as Java or C#. I'm also using the PHPStorm **Integrated Development Environment (IDE)** throughout the book, which can be seen in the screenshots.

Understanding OOP in PHP

Can I use PHP with TDD? Absolutely – and PHP, thanks to its OOP capabilities, works well with TDD. We have previously explained that TDD is a process; it's not a piece of software that you can install. You can install or download tools to implement TDD, and there are a lot of different tools available for other programming languages as well.

Since PHP 5 was released in the early 2000s, classes and objects were supported, allowing OOP to be used for PHP. It would be an advantage if the reader has a good understanding of OOP and has worked on PHP OOP projects, but if not, I'll do my best to introduce OOP to you, as it is an effective and efficient way to write software. We will also be using OOP in our example project, so we need to make sure that the reader understands OOP.

What is OOP, anyway?

OOP is a programming style based on the concept of classes and objects. One of its goals is to let software developers write reusable and extensible codes.

OOP focuses on packaging behaviors, logic, and properties into reusable objects. These objects are instances of classes, and these classes are the files that we software developers have to write to contain logic, routines, and properties. Since objects are based on classes, we can create many instances of objects using a single class. We can also use OOP's inheritance feature to create an object that will also have the capabilities of its parent. Later in this chapter, we will discuss the difference between a class and an object in OOP.

Back when I was a junior developer, my friend, who was a JavaScript developer, told me that he struggled to understand OOP because he had read some OOP explanations that used vehicle and animal metaphors. He said he didn't understand how it related to the actual software he was writing, so for the sake of our younger selves, if I ever travel back in time, I'll try to explain OOP to junior developers such as myself and my friend as if I had never used OOP before. I realized that, at least for me, if I understand the problem and the purpose of a solution, I can understand the concept easier.

I've seen many developers struggle with this concept and fail to take advantage of its incredible power. I learned OOP back in university while using Java and C++ and when I worked professionally as a C# developer after graduating. Back then, I thought OOP was everywhere and was the usual way of writing code in the professional software development world, but when I started my first professional PHP position, I worked on a PHP application with no OOP codes in the code base. With PHP, a developer can create a PHP file and start writing functions and codes directly executed from a CLI or a web browser. It's so easy! However, it's a slippery slope.

I remember telling myself, "I hate OOP, and it's so complicated; why did I waste my time with OOP in Java and C# when I have to write so much code just to return text on a web page?" Sure enough, I ended up writing many files with lots of database queries and lots of business logic intertwined. I basically wrote the user interface, business logic, and persistence codes in a single file. Does that sound familiar? If you're one of the poor souls who may have inherited my spaghetti codes from more than a decade ago, I sincerely apologize. I wrote spaghetti codes with OOP and without OOP in different languages. OOP is not a magic bullet solution to stop messy spaghetti codes, but OOP surely does help. It's not the tool; it's how you use it.

The excitement I felt did not last very long. As a junior PHP developer back then, I ended up writing so many PHP files with so many random functions. It was a nightmare to maintain, and I couldn't even reuse my own codes elsewhere in the application! I told myself that if I only had used OOP, I could at least borrow or reuse some existing codes easily even if I had spaghetti codes. Now, imagine working with a team where you collectively build software and you cannot easily reuse each other's codes. I then hated PHP, but as it turned out, I was not using PHP properly. I did not know that I could use PHP to implement OOP as well. I think the same thing can be said of any other programming language. It doesn't matter how good the language is; the project's success depends on the software engineers, developers, and architects themselves. You can use OOP in any language and still produce spaghetti codes. In this book, we will use TDD and software development best practices to help us write better and less tangled code. We will be talking about some software development principles that will help us a lot in writing better code in *Chapter 8, Using TDD with SOLID Principles*.

It took me a while before I truly understood the real benefits of OOP. Reading OOP explanations with vehicles and animals online are helpful but working on projects and experiencing the pains of not using OOP is what really helped me see the light.

With OOP, a developer can write codes that can be easily borrowed or used by other developers, including yourself.

In the coming sections, we'll go through the fundamental concepts of OOP – abstraction, encapsulation, inheritance, and polymorphism – but before that, we will need to start to define what a class and an object are, as well as their differences and how to distinguish them.

In the following examples, we will not be using TDD yet. We will just be focusing on OOP itself. We will be focusing on the PHP-specific implementation of OOP.

Classes versus objects

A PHP class is a file that contains codes. Your class is a file that physically exists on your drive. If you turn your computer off and turn it on again, the class file is still there. The code it contains is a template to create an object during execution. The class file can contain properties and behaviors. The properties will be able to hold data in memory once the class has been instantiated. The behaviors will be handled by methods or functions. You can use the accessors and mutator methods to change the values of a class's properties.

Dog.php class file

```php
<?php

namespace Animal;

class Dog
{
    public function returnSound(): string
    {
        return "Bark";
    }
}
```

The preceding example class is a PHP file containing the namespace declaration, the class name, and a single method or function called returnSound(), which returns a "Bark" string.

On the other hand, an object is an instance of a class file. The object physically exists in the computer's RAM, which is volatile memory. That means if you turn off your computer or stop the program, you lose the object. The object will only be created if you run your program.

In PHP, when you execute your program, the class file will be loaded by PHP from your hard disk to create an instance of an object that will temporarily exist in your RAM. The class literally is the template for PHP to create the object while your program is running.

We'll use a consumer class that will utilize or consume the Dog.php class, and use a variable to hold an instance of a class, which is an object:

Display.php Class File

```php
<?php

namespace Animal;

class Display
{
    public function outputSound()
    {
        $dog = new Dog();
        echo $dog->returnSound();
    }
}
```

The Display class is another class; you can think of this as a consumer class or the starting point of the example program. In this class, we have an outputSound() method that echoes the value from the object's returnSound() method. Inside the outputSound() method, we have written instructions for PHP to create an instance of the Dog class using the new keyword:

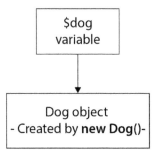

Figure 4.1 – Assigning the Dog object to the $dog variable

When PHP executes the outputSound() method, it will create an object that is based on the Dog.php class file that is stored in your computer's drive and then it will temporarily store the instance or object inside your computer's memory. The $dog variable will be mapped with the Dog class instance or object. Whenever you use an object's method or properties, you are basically accessing the object from your computer's memory, and not from the Dog.php class file. To understand this further, we will need to talk about *References* in PHP, which we will cover in the next subsection.

Now, since we have created a new instance of the Dog.php class file and assigned it to the $dog variable, we will be able to access the Dog object's methods or functions, or properties, depending on their *visibility*. We will talk about visibility in this chapter in the *Encapsulation in OOP* section. Since in our example, we have defined the Dog.php class's returnSound() method as public, we can now access this method from the Display.php class's outputSound() method with the following: $dog->returnSound();.

References and objects in PHP

What is a reference anyway? Well, in PHP, it's an alias or a way for one or more variables to point to specific content. From the Dog object example earlier, we have created an instance of the Dog.php class and assigned it to the $dog variable. The $dog variable itself does not really contain the Dog object or instance's memory address; it simply contains an identifier so that it can point to the Dog object that is stored in the memory. That means that you can have $dog1 and $dog2 variables that point to the same object. Let's modify the Dog.php and Display.php classes to demonstrate the concept.

We will modify the Dog.php class like so:

```php
<?php

namespace Animal;

class Dog
{
    private string $sound;

    public function __construct()
    {
        $this->setSound("Bark");
    }

    public function returnSound(): string
    {
        return $this->getSound();
    }

    /**
     * @return string
```

```
    */
    public function getSound(): string
    {
        return $this->sound;
    }


    /**
     * @param string $sound
     */
    public function setSound(string $sound): void
    {
        $this->sound = $sound;
    }
}
```

And we'll modify the Display.php class as follows:

```php
<?php

namespace Animal;

class Display
{
    public function outputSound()
    {
        $dog1 = new Dog();
        $dog2 = $dog1;

        $dog1->setSound("Barky Bark");

        // Will return "Barky Bark" which was set to $dog1.
        echo $dog2->returnSound();
    }
}
```

We've modified the Dog.php class so that we can change the sound it returns after we instantiate it. In the Display.php class, you'll notice that we have introduced a new variable, $dog2, and assigned

$dog1 to it. We only have one instance of the Dog object, and both the $dog1 and $dog2 variables have the same identifier and are referencing the same thing. Here's a diagram representing this concept:

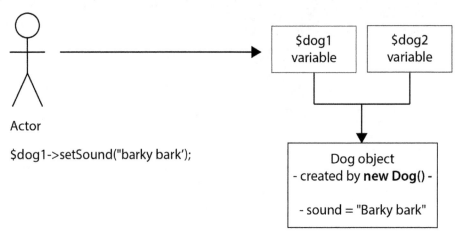

Figure 4.2 – What happens to $dog1's property also happens to $dog2

So, if we run $dog2->returnSound(), it will return the updated string that we have set in $dog1 even if we have mutated the $sound property after we have assigned $dog1 to $dog2.

Well, what if you don't want $dog2 to be affected by what happens to $dog1's properties, but still want to create a copy or a duplicate of that object? You can use PHP's clone keyword like so:

Display.php Class

```php
<?php

namespace Animal;

class Display
{
    public function outputSound()
    {
        $dog1 = new Dog();
        $dog2 = clone $dog1;

        $dog1->setSound("Barky Bark");

        // Will return "Bark".
```

```
        echo $dog2->returnSound();
    }
}
```

This time, $dog2 will return the original Bark string value assigned to the $sound property of $dog1 by its constructor. Here's a diagram for your reference to understand this:

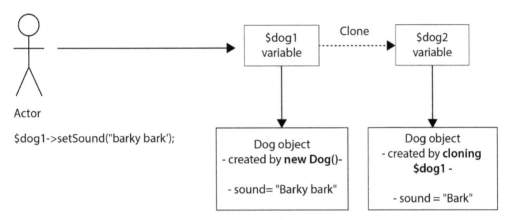

Figure 4.3 – Clone object

Since $dog2 has been cloned before the actor has mutated the $sound property of $dog1, $dog2 will retain the old value. Whatever happens to $dog1 will no longer automatically happen to $dog2, as they are no longer referencing the same object in the memory:

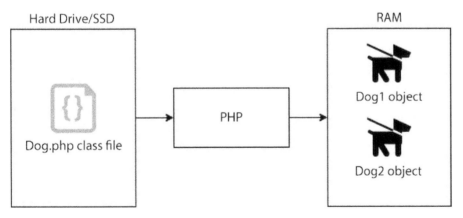

Figure 4.4 – Class versus object

In summary, a PHP class is a file that contains a template for PHP to be able to create an object. When the new keyword is used and executed, PHP takes the class file and generates an instance of the class file, and stores it in the computer's memory, this is what we call an object.

Now that we have clarified and explained the difference between an object and a class in PHP, we can now discuss the Four Pillars of OOP, starting with abstraction.

Abstraction in OOP

Abstraction in OOP is the concept of hiding complexities from the application, user, or developers. You can take a set of complex codes or instructions and wrap them inside a function. That function should use a verb for its name, which will make it easier to understand exactly what the complex instructions inside the function do.

For example, you can have a function called `computeTotal($a, $b, $c)` that contains logic or steps to compute the total based on the requirements. As a developer, you can just use the `computeTotal` method and not think about all the complex operations that are involved in the actual computation of the total, but if you need to fix a bug or understand what's going on, then you can check what's going on inside that `computeTotal` function:

```
public function computeTotal(int $a, int $b, int $c): int
{
    if ($c > 1) {
        $total = $a + $b;
    } else if ($c < 1) {
        $total = $a - $b;
    } else {
        $total = 0;
    }


    return $total;
}
```

What's the benefit of using this concept? Using the preceding example, the developer won't need to worry about the exact sequence of steps inside the function to get the total. The developer only needs to know that there is a `computeTotal` function available to be used, along with hundreds or thousands of other functions each with complex steps in instructions inside them. The developer can focus on the solution and not worry about the fine details inside each function.

An abstract class is a way to implement class abstraction and is a type of class that cannot be instantiated and needs to have at least one method declared as abstract. An abstract class is meant to be extended by other related classes:

```php
<?php

abstract class AbstractPrinter
{
    abstract protected function print(string $message):
        bool;
}

class ConsolePrinter extends AbstractPrinter
{
    protected function print(string $message): bool
    {
        // TODO: Implement print() method.
    }
}

class PdfPrinter extends AbstractPrinter
{
    protected function print(string $message): bool
    {
        // TODO: Implement print() method.
    }
}
```

The method declared as abstract in AbstractPrinter must also exist in the classes that extend this method. Each class that extends the AbstractPrinter abstract class can now have its own specific operations for the print method. A method declared as abstract in an abstract class can only declare the method's visibility, parameters, and return value. It cannot have its own implementation.

Encapsulation in OOP

Encapsulation is a concept where data and methods that access and mutate this data are enclosed in a single unit like a capsule. In PHP, this capsule is the object or class.

The capsule or the object will have the ability to keep its data safe from being read or manipulated, using the concept of visibility.

Visibility in PHP

To be able to control what data or functions the developer can access or use in an object in PHP, the `public`, `protected`, and `private` keywords can be prefixed before the `function` keyword in the function declaration, or before the property name declaration:

- `private` – Only the codes within the object can access this function or property
- `protected` – Any object extending this class will be allowed access to the function or property
- `public` – Any object user is allowed to access the property or method

What benefits do we developers get from this, then? We'll get to know this in a bit.

Let's modify the `Dog.php` class from the earlier example like so:

```php
<?php

namespace Animal;

class Dog
{
    private string $sound;

    private string $color;

    public function __construct()
    {
        $this->setSound("Bark");
        $this->setColor("Black");
    }

    public function makeSound(): string
    {
        $prefix = "Hello ";
        $suffix = " World";

        return $prefix . $this->getSound() . $suffix;
```

```php
    }

    /**
     * @return string
     */
    private function getSound(): string
    {
        return $this->sound;
    }

    /**
     * @param string $sound
     */
    public function setSound(string $sound): void
    {
        $this->sound = $sound . ", my color is: " .
            $this->getColor();
    }

    /**
     * @return string
     */
    protected function getColor(): string
    {
        return $this->color;
    }

    /**
     * @param string $color
     */
    protected function setColor(string $color): void
    {
        $this->color = $color;
    }
}
```

Create a Cavoodle.php class:

```php
<?php

namespace Animal\Dogs;

use Animal\Dog;

class Cavoodle extends Dog
{
    public function __construct()
    {
        parent::__construct();
        // Using the protected method from the Dog class.
        $this->setColor("Chocolate");
    }
}
```

Modify the Consumer.php class like so:

```php
<?php

namespace Animal;

use Animal\Dogs\Cavoodle;

class Consumer
{
    public function sayHello()
    {
        $dog = new Dog();
        $dog->setSound("Wooooof!");

        // Will output Hello Wooooof!, my color is: Black
        $dog->makeSound();
    }
```

```
public function sayHelloCavoodle()
{
    $cavoodle = new Cavoodle();
    $cavoodle->setSound("Bark Bark!");

    // Will output Hello Bark Bark!!, my color is:
        Chocolate
    $cavoodle->makeSound();
}
}
```

In this Dog.php example class, we have declared the following:

- Private:

  - $sound

  - $color

- Protected:

  - getColor()

  - setColor()

- Public:

  - makeSound()

  - setSound($sound)

By doing so, we have protected the values of the Dog object's $sound and $color properties from being modified directly by the object consumer. Only the Dog object can modify these values directly. The value stored inside the $sound property can be modified from the object consumer side by using the $dog->setSound($sound) method, but whatever the object consumer sets in the $dog->setSound($sound) method, the data that will be stored in the Dog object's $sound property will always be suffixed with the value of the $color property. There's nothing the object consumer can do to change that; only the object itself can change its own property's value.

The following is a screenshot of the `Consumer.php` class and as I modify it, my PHPStorm IDE automatically suggests the available methods for the `Cavoodle` object:

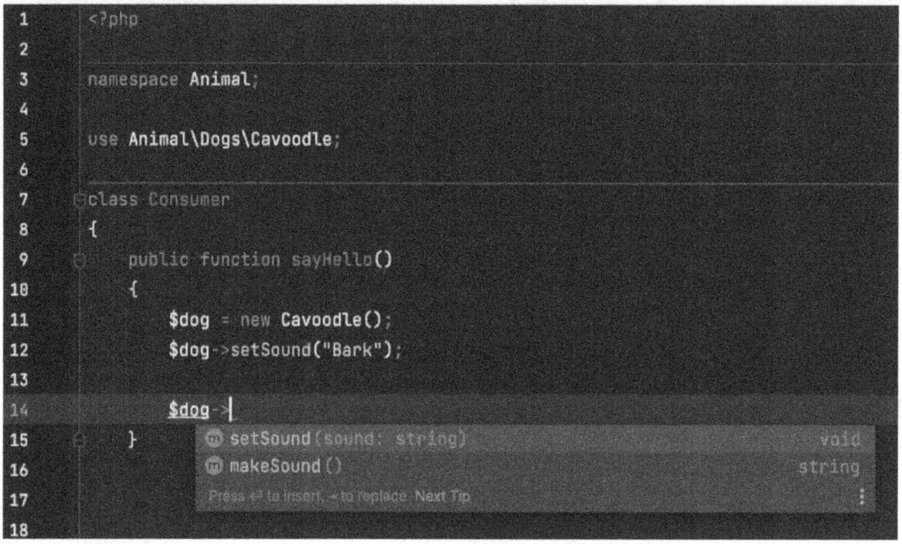

```php
1   <?php
2
3   namespace Animal;
4
5   use Animal\Dogs\Cavoodle;
6
7   class Consumer
8   {
9       public function sayHello()
10      {
11          $dog = new Cavoodle();
12          $dog->setSound("Bark");
13
14          $dog->|
15      }        setSound(sound: string)                    void
16               makeSound ()                                string
17               Press ↵ to insert, → to replace  Next Tip
18
```

Figure 4.5 – Public functions available for Dog

You will notice that in the `Consumer` class, there are only two available functions for us. The `setSound()` and `makeSound()` functions are the functions that we have declared as publicly visible. We have successfully limited or protected the `Cavoodle` (which is an instance of a Dog class) object's other functions and properties.

The following screenshot shows that as we are inside the `Cavoodle.php` class, my IDE automatically suggests the available methods for the `Cavoodle` class itself by using the `$this` key:

```php
1    <?php
2
3    namespace Animal\Dogs;
4
5    use Animal\Dog;
6
7    class Cavoodle extends Dog
8    {
9        public function __construct()
10       {
11           parent::__construct();
12           // Using the protected method from the Dog class.
13           $this->
14       }                   getColor ()                        string
15   }                      setColor (color: string)             void
                            setSound (sound: string)             void
                            makeSound ()                        string
                            Press ↵ to insert, → to replace  Next Tip
```

Figure 4.6 – Cavoodle itself can access more functions than the Consumer class

Inside the Cavoodle.php class itself, you will notice that this Cavoodle object can access the getColor() and setColor() methods. Why is that? It's because the Cavoodle class has extended the Dog.php class, inheriting the Dog.php class's non-private method – and since we have declared the getColor and setColor functions as having protected visibility, these methods are available for the Cavoodle class.

Accessors and mutators

Since we have set the $sound and $color properties to private, how do we let consumers access these properties? For reading data, we can write functions called accessors that return the data stored in the property. To change the value of the property, we can create functions called mutators to mutate the data for the property.

To access the $sound and $color properties in the Dog.php class, we need the following *accessors*:

* getSound
* getColor

To change the values of the $sound and $color properties in the Dog.php class, we need the following *mutators*:

* setSound
* setColor

These functions are declared in the `Dog.php` class – since these are functions, you can add extra validation or logic change the value before storing it into the property or returning it to the user.

When writing properties or functions, it's a good practice to declare their visibility to be as restrictive as possible. Start with `private` and then if you think the child objects need to access the function or property, then set the visibility to `protected`. That way, you can end up having fewer publicly available methods and properties.

This will only allow you and the other developers that use your classes to see the functions that are supposed to be available to the consumers. I've written and seen classes with a lot of methods, only to find out that they are not intended to be used by other objects apart from the main object itself. This will also help preserve the data integrity of the object by preventing consumer objects from modifying properties directly. If you need to let the consumer manipulate the data stored in the property of the object, the user can use mutator methods. To let them read the data from the property, they can use the accessors.

Inheritance in OOP

Inheritance in OOP is a concept in which an object can acquire the methods and properties of another object.

Inheritance can help developers reuse functions for very related objects. You probably heard of the **Don't Repeat Yourself** (**DRY**) principle; inheritance can help with writing less code and fewer repetitions too to help you to reuse codes.

Objects such as `Cavoodle` and `Dog` are related – we know that `Cavoodle` is a type of `Dog`. The functions available for `Dog` and `Cavoodle` should be focused on what `Dog` and `Cavoodle` should be able to do. If you have a `Dog` object and it has a `computeTax` function, for example, that function is not related to the `Dog` object and you're probably doing something wrong – it has low cohesion. Having high cohesion means that your class is focused on doing what your class should really be doing. By having high cohesion, it's easier to decide if an object should be an object that can be inherited, as with the `Dog` and the `Cavoodle` objects. It won't make sense if the `Cavoodle` class extends a `JetEngine` class, but it makes perfect sense for the `Cavoodle` class to extend the `Dog` class:

Cavoodle.php

```php
<?php

namespace Animal\Dogs;

use Animal\Dog;

class Cavoodle extends Dog
```

```
{
    public function __construct()
    {
        parent::__construct();
        // Using the protected method from the Dog class.
        $this->setColor("Chocolate");
    }
}
```

To use the `Cavoodle` class's methods in a consumer class, create a new instance of the `Cavoodle` class:

```
public function sayHelloCavoodle()
{
    $cavoodle = new Cavoodle();
    $cavoodle->setSound("Bark Bark!");

    // Will output Hello Bark Bark!!, my color is:
            Chocolate
    $cavoodle->makeSound();
}
```

The `Cavoodle` object has inherited the `Dog` object using the `extends` keyword. That means that any `public` or `protected` function from `Dog` is now available to the `Cavoodle` object. You will notice that there is no `makeSound` function declared in the `Cavoodle.php` class, but we are still able to use the `$cavoodle->makeSound();` method simply because the `Cavoodle` object has inherited the `makeSound` function from the `Dog` object.

Polymorphism in OOP

Polymorphism means many shapes or many forms. Polymorphism is achieved through the inheritance of a *PHP abstract class*, as well as by implementing *PHP interfaces*.

Polymorphism helps you create a format or a standard for solving a specific problem programmatically, instead of just focusing on a single implementation of a solution.

How do we apply this in PHP and what benefit do we get in using this feature? Let's take the example codes in the following subsections as an example, starting with a PHP abstract class.

Polymorphism with a PHP abstract class

When using abstract classes in PHP, we can implement polymorphism by using abstract functions. The following example is of a PHP abstract class:

AbstractAnimal.php

```php
<?php

namespace Animals\Polymorphism\AbstractExample;

abstract class AbstractAnimal
{
    abstract public function makeSound();
}
```

Every PHP abstract class ideally should start with the `Abstract` prefix, followed by the desired name of the abstract class as suggested by the PSR standards. The PSR standards will be discussed later in this chapter in the *PHP Standards Recommendations (PSR)* section.

The abstract class needs at least one function declared as *abstract*. This can be achieved by adding the `abstract` keyword before the access modifier or visibility declaration of a function, such as `abstract public function makeSound()`. Now, we may notice that there is no actual action or logic inside the `makeSound()` method of the abstract class, and as we have explained earlier, we cannot instantiate abstract classes. We will need child classes to extend the abstract class, where we can declare the specific action or logic to be performed by that child class.

The following is an example of a child `Cat.php` class:

Cat.php

```php
<?php

namespace Animals\Polymorphism\AbstractExample;

class Cat extends AbstractAnimal
{
    public function makeSound(): string
    {
        return "meow!";
```

```php
        }
    }
```

The following is an example of a child Cow.php class:

Cow.php

```php
<?php

namespace Animals\Polymorphism\AbstractExample;

class Cow extends AbstractAnimal
{
    public function makeSound(): string
    {
        return "mooo!";
    }
}
```

Both of these classes have inherited the AbstractAnimal.php class, and since we have declared the makeSound() function as an abstract method, the Cat.php and Cow.php classes are required to have those same methods as well but without the abstract keyword. You will notice that the Cat object's makeSound function returns a meow string, and the Cow object's similar makeSound function returns a moo string. Here, we have achieved polymorphism by having one function signature, and having that function signature implemented uniquely by the child classes.

Next, we will look at implementing polymorphism using a PHP interface.

Polymorphism with a PHP interface

A PHP interface is a simpler version of a PHP abstract class. An interface cannot have properties like a normal class can, and it can only contain publicly visible functions. Each method in an interface must be implemented by any class that uses the interface but without the need to add the abstract keyword. Therefore, we must be very careful when declaring functions to an interface. It's very easy to end up having an interface with too many functions that it doesn't make sense for each implementing class to use. This is where the *Interface Segregation Principle* comes in to help, and this will be discussed more in *Chapter 8, Using TDD with SOLID Principles*.

Imagine that you need a program to return results in different formats, and you'd also like to be able to isolate the logic and dependencies to come up with the desired results. You can use an interface to set a contract that will be followed by your objects. For example, there are different ways and formats in which to return output and in the following example, we will return an XML and a JSON.

We will create a PHP interface, which will serve as a contract that both the JSON and XML classes will implement. The interface will have a single generic print function that accepts a string parameter, and returns a string:

PrinterInterface.php

```php
<?php

namespace Polymorphism\InterfaceExample;

interface PrinterInterface
{
    public function print(string $message): string;
}
```

We will then create the first concrete implementation of `PrinterInterface` and it will have to have a concrete implementation of the `print` function to return a JSON-formatted string:

Json.php

```php
<?php

namespace Polymorphism\InterfaceExample;

class Json implements PrinterInterface
{
    public function print(string $message): string
    {
        return json_encode(['hello' => $message]);
    }
}
```

The second concrete implementation of `PrinterInterface` is the `Xml` class – it will also have to include a `print` function that returns a string, but the string will be formatted as an XML this time:

Xml.php

```php
<?php

namespace Polymorphism\InterfaceExample;

class Xml implements PrinterInterface
{
    public function print(string $message): string
    {
        return "<message>Hello " . $message . "</message>";
    }
}
```

We have declared a `public print(string $message): string` method signature in `PrinterInterface`, and since the `Xml.php` and `Json.php` classes have implemented `PrinterInterface` using the `implements` keyword after the class name declaration, both `Xml.php` and `Json.php` are now required to follow the contract. They must have `public print(string $message): string` functions as well. Each implementing class will have its own unique way of returning an output. One returns an XML and the other returns a JSON – one method, and different forms or shapes. This is how polymorphism is achieved using PHP interfaces.

However, what's the advantage of using polymorphism in the first place? Let's take this consumer class for example:

Display.php

```php
<?php

namespace Polymorphism\InterfaceExample;

class Display
{
    /**
     * @var PrinterInterface
     */
```

```php
    private $printer;

    public function __construct(PrinterInterface $printer)
    {
        $this->setPrinter($printer);
    }

    /**
     * @param string $message
     * @return string
     */
    public function displayOutput(string $message): string
    {
        // Do some additional logic if needed:
        $printerOutput = $this->getPrinter()->print
            ($message);
        $displayOutput = "My Output is: " . $printerOutput;

        return $displayOutput;
    }

    /**
     * @return PrinterInterface
     */
    public function getPrinter(): PrinterInterface
    {
        return $this->printer;
    }

    /**
     * @param PrinterInterface $printer
     */
    public function setPrinter(PrinterInterface $printer):
        void
    {
        $this->printer = $printer;
```

```
    }
}
```

In the `Display.php` class, we have a `displayOutput` method that uses an object that must implement `PrinterInterface`. The `displayOutput` method gets the result from the `PrinterInterface`-implementing object (we don't know what object that is) and appends it as a suffix to a string before returning it.

Now, this is the important bit – the `Display.php` class does not know how the `PrinterInterface`-implementing object comes up with the actual XML or JSON formatting. The `Display.php` class does not care and does not worry about that. We have handballed the responsibility to the `PrinterInterface`-implementing object. Therefore, instead of having one god class that contains all of the logic for returning a JSON or an XML output, resulting in a spaghetti mess, we just use other objects that implement the interface that we need them to implement. The `Display.php` class does not even know what class is being used – it only knows that it is using an object that has implemented `PrinterInterface`. We have now successfully decoupled the `Display.php` class from the job of formatting XML or JSON or any other format to other objects.

Now that we have gone through the fundamentals of OOP in PHP, let's go through some guidelines or standards on how to write PHP codes. These guidelines are not required to build or run a PHP program, but they will help developers write better, more readable, and more shareable codes. The following standards on how to write PHP codes are important when building enterprise-level applications, especially as you are expected to develop codes with a lot of other developers, and your codes can be expected to be used and last for years. Future developers who will eventually take over your project should be able to understand, read, and reuse your codes easily as well. The following standards will help you and your team achieve that

PHP Standards Recommendations (PSRs)

As mentioned earlier, there are a lot of open source libraries and frameworks built for PHP. Each individual developer will have their own preferences in their style of writing codes, and each framework or library can have its own standard or way of doing things. This can start to become problematic for PHP developers, as we tend to use a lot of different libraries and frameworks.

For example, it's no fun transitioning from one framework to another only to end up having different types of service containers, which will require you to change the way you organize the dependencies for your application, and therefore PSR-11 was introduced. Service containers are applications that manage the instantiation of objects including their dependencies—they are very handy when implementing Dependency Injection or DI, which is discussed in *Chapter 8, Using TDD with SOLID Principles*. This is one of the examples of why it is important, although not required, to follow some specific guidelines or standards, and where PSR comes in.

What is a PSR?

A PSR is recommended by the **PHP Framework Interoperability Group** (**PHP-FIG**). They are a group of very kind developers who help us make our PHP coding life way more organized. You can find out more about the PHP-FIG at `https://www.php-fig.org/`.

The following are the currently accepted PSRs:

- PSR-1: Basic Coding Standard
- PSR-3: Logger Interface
- PSR-4: Autoloading Standard
- PSR-6: Caching Interface
- PSR-7: HTTP Message Interface
- PSR-11: Container Interface
- PSR-12: Extending Coding Style Guide (has deprecated PSR-2)
- PSR-13: Hypermedia Links
- PSR-14: Event Dispatcher
- PSR-15: HTTP Handlers
- PSR-16: Simple Cache
- PSR-17: HTTP Factories
- PSR18: HTTP Client

You can find all the currently accepted PSRs at `https://www.php-fig.org/psr/`. Initially, the most important PSRs to get familiar with are PSR-1, PSR-12, and PSR-4. This helps us write codes in a more consistent style, especially when transitioning from one framework to another framework. I used to have a "favorite" PHP MVC framework thinking that I'd use that framework until I grew old – and as usual, I was wrong. I ended up using so many different frameworks that I no longer cared which framework I was using. I now have favorites for each specific job.

The PSRs are just "recommendations." They are not like actual laws that you need to follow, but if you are serious about writing PHP and improving the quality of your own code, then I highly suggest that you follow them. Many people have already experienced the pain of not following standards. I wrote my own dependency injection container once, only to end up having other developers in our team get confused down the road on how to use it. I just reinvented the wheel, the bad way. How I wish there was a standard I could follow! Oh yeah, there is now a PSR-11.

Summary

In this chapter, we defined what OOP is and why we'd want to take advantage of it. Then, we clearly defined what classes and objects are in PHP. We then went through some examples for each of the Four Pillars of OOP. We learned what abstraction, encapsulation, inheritance, and polymorphism are and how they work in PHP. We've also briefly gone through the PSRs because we don't just want to go ahead and invent standards and start writing codes – we want to produce clean PHP code that is easy to understand and maintain, especially in an enterprise environment where you can expect to work with a lot of other developers, and where your codes will have to be very readable and maintainable for years to come.

This chapter should have prepared you to start writing actual object-oriented PHP code – and in our TDD example project, we will take advantage of the OOP capabilities of PHP.

In the next chapter, we will talk about unit testing. We will define what it is, and how unit testing is used in TDD. We will also go through different types of automated tests. After going through the definition of unit testing, we will start writing our first unit tests and start executing those unit tests.

Part 2 – Implementing Test-Driven Development in a PHP Project

In this part of the book, you will achieve the necessary knowledge to utilize test-driven development, behavior development, and automated testing to build a PHP application.

This section comprises the following chapters:

5
Unit Testing

Imagine working on a project without any automated tests with a few other developers, and everything seems to be working fine in production. Then, a bug has been discovered, and one of the developers fixes this bug. The QA department approves the fix and then is pushed to production. A few days later, another bug is reported in production. After investigation, the developers found out that the new bug was introduced by the fix for the other bug. Does that sound familiar?

One small change in the code base can easily change the behavior of software. A single decimal point change can cause millions of dollars worth of incorrect computations. Imagine handballing all these computation checks to the QA department for manual testing – they would have to run these checks every time something had been updated in the code base. It's simply inefficient, stressful, and not sustainable.

One of the solutions to this recurring issue is unit testing. Writing unit test programs will help us developers verify whether our own programs are correct or not. By repeatedly running unit tests, we will also be able to catch problems very early during development if we break other existing tests. If we accidentally change the expected behavior of a function, and if we've written unit tests properly for this function before, then we can be confident that we will break those tests. This, to me, is amazing. I want to know that if I break something, I won't push my code for final verification to the QA or testing department until I am confident that I have not compromised any existing sets of unit tests. For large products, this will save the QA or testing department a lot of man-hours, even if there are automated end-to-end and user interface-to-backend tests.

There are different types of tests that we will be discussing in this chapter as well, but the unit tests are the foundations of those other automated test types.

In this chapter, we will be covering the following topics:

- Defining unit tests
- Writing and running unit tests
- Setting up test coverage monitoring

- What are the different types of tests?
- Utilizing dependency injection and mocking on integration tests

Technical requirements

This chapter requires you to have all the containers we have previously built, and PHPStorm IDE configurations that were defined in *Chapter 3, Setting Up Our Development Environment Using Docker Containers*. You can simply download the development environment setup from GitHub and follow the instructions mentioned in *Chapter 3, Setting Up Our Development Environment Using Docker Containers*: `https://github.com/PacktPublishing/Test-Driven-Development-with-PHP-8/tree/main/Chapter%203`.

In this chapter, it's also required that you understand how to use **Object Relational Mappers** (**ORMs**), and the author assumes that you have experience working with MySQL databases.

It is also required for you to be familiar with PSR-11, and the use of service containers. More information about PSR-11 can be found at `https://www.php-fig.org/psr/psr-11/`.

All the code files related to this chapter can be found at `https://github.com/PacktPublishing/Test-Driven-Development-with-PHP-8/tree/main/Chapter%203`.

Preparing the development environment for the chapter

First, get the base code for *Chapter 5*, found at `https://github.com/PacktPublishing/Test-Driven-Development-with-PHP-8/tree/main/Chapter%203` or simply run the following command:

```
curl -Lo phptdd.zip "https://github.com/PacktPublishing/Test-
Driven-Development-with-PHP-8/raw/main/Chapter%205/base.zip" &&
unzip -o phptdd.zip && cd base && ./demoSetup.sh
```

To run the containers, and execute the commands in this chapter, the reader should be inside the

```
docker-server-web-1 container.
```

To run the containers and execute the commands in this chapter, you should be inside the `docker-server-web-1` container.

Run the following command to confirm the container name for our web server:

```
docker ps
```

To run the containers, run the following command from the `/phptdd/docker` directory from the repository in your host machine:

```
docker-compose build && docker-compose up -d
docker exec -it docker_server-web_1 /bin/bash
```

Once inside the container, run the following commands to install the libraries required through composer:

```
/var/www/html/symfony# ./setup.sh
```

Defining unit tests

A unit test is a program that specifically tests a unit of your solution code. Just think of it as a program that tests a function and does not depend on other objects in your project.

For example, if you have a function called calculateTotal($a, $b, $c), then you can write a unit test function for it called testCanCalculateTotal(). This unit test's job is to verify whether the calculateTotal($a, $b, $c) function is returning the expected result based on the business rules defined by your project's specification.

In this example, let's assume that the expected behavior of the calculateTotal function is to get the summation of the three parameters, $a, $b, and $c.

Let's create an example unit test and solution codes. Create the following file inside our development container:

codebase/symfony/tests/Unit/CalculationTest.php

```php
<?php

namespace App\Tests\Unit;

use App\Example\Calculator;
use PHPUnit\Framework\TestCase;

class CalculationTest extends TestCase
{
    public function testCanCalculateTotal()
    {
        // Expected result:
        $expectedTotal = 6;

        // Test data:
        $a = 1;
```

```
        $b = 2;
        $c = 3;

        $calculator = new Calculator();
        $total       = $calculator->calculateTotal($a, $b,
            $c);

        $this->assertEquals($expectedTotal, $total);
    }
}
```

The test class name needs to be suffixed with `Test`, and it extends the `PHPUnit\Framework\TestCase` class. By doing so, we are now using the PHPUnit library.

Next, let's try to run this unit test and see what happens. Run the following command while inside the container. The instructions on how to do all this are in *Chapter 3, Setting Up Our Development Environment Using Docker Containers*:

```
/var/www/html/symfony# php bin/phpunit -filter
testCanCalculateTotal
```

The result will be an error:

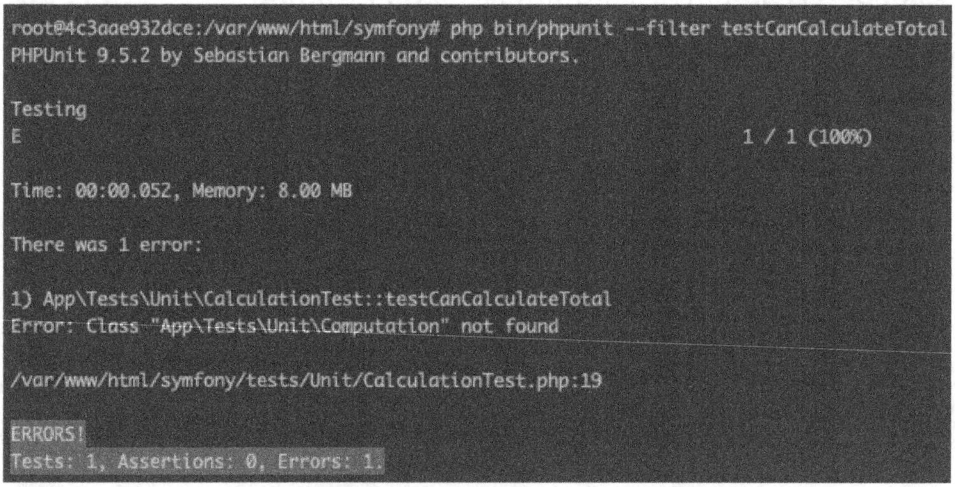

Figure 5.1 – Fail 1 (class not found)

Our unit test has failed as expected – this is good! You'll notice that we tried to instantiate a class that does not exist, so let's now create that class and write the function to do the calculation.

Create the following solution class inside `codebase/symfony/src/Example/` directory that we previously created:

---

codebase/symfony/src/Example/Calculator.php

```php
<?php

namespace App\Example;

class Calculator
{
    public function calculateTotal(int $a, int $b, int $c)
        : int
    {
        return $a + $b - $c;
    }
}
```

After creating the solution class with the `calculateTotal` function, let's try to run the test again by running the following command:

```
/var/www/html/symfony# php bin/phpunit -filter
testCanCalculateTotal
```

We will get the following failing result:

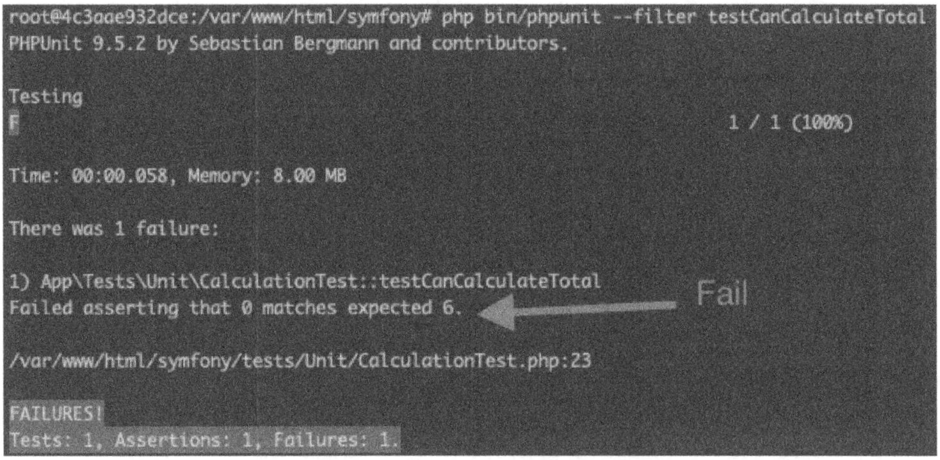

Figure 5.2 – Fail 2 (incorrect result)

PHPUnit will tell us why the test has failed. You'll notice that it says: **Failed asserting that 0 matches expected 6.**. Why is that? Well, this is what happened.

In the `testCanCalculateTotal` unit test, we have declared `$expectedTotal` to be 6. We then called the `calculateTotal` function and sent the following arguments: `$a = 1`, `$b = 2`, and `$c = 3`. If the specification you receive instructs you to get the summation of the three parameters within the `calculateTotal` function, then the expected result is 6.

We then used the `assertEquals` PHPUnit function, where we told PHPUnit that we were expecting that the expected value would be equal to the calculated value with the following line:

```
$this->assertEquals($expectedTotal, $total);
```

Assertions are methods or functions that assert or check whether a condition within a test has been satisfied or not. Like in our example, we used the `assertEquals` method where we tried to compare `$expectedTotal` to the actual `$total` we received from the solution code. There are a lot of different types of PHPUnit assertions, and the documentation can be found here: https://phpunit.readthedocs.io/en/9.5/assertions.html.

The unit test correctly expects the expected result to be 6 – the problem is that in the solution function, we did not follow the expected behavior. We subtracted `$c` instead of adding it to the summation of `$a` and `$b`. If we fix the function to the following, our test should finally pass:

codebase/symfony/src/Example/Calculator.php

```
public function calculateTotal(int $a, int $b, int $c) : int
{
    return $a + $b + $c;
}
```

To get the total, we just need to get the sum of the three parameters. Once you update the `Calculator.php` file, run the following command:

```
php bin/phpunit --filter testCanCalculateTotal
```

We should now see the following result:

```
root@4c3aae932dce:/var/www/html/symfony# php bin/phpunit --filter testCanCalculateTotal
PHPUnit 9.5.2 by Sebastian Bergmann and contributors.

Testing
.                                                                    1 / 1 (100%)

Time: 00:00.053, Memory: 8.00 MB

OK (1 test, 1 assertion)
```

Figure 5.3 – Correct result

Nice! We have finally passed the unit test! The assertEquals function has confirmed that $expectedTotal is now equal to the $total amount returned by the solution codes!

Now, imagine having thousands of these tests. One unintended change in the behavior of the solution codes will cause one or more unit tests to fail. This is very valuable. This will help developers verify the stability of any code change that they implement.

To learn more about PHPUnit, you can visit their documentation page at https://phpunit.readthedocs.io/.

This is one of the most basic examples of the use of a unit test, but we'll be writing more unit tests and utilizing more PHPUnit features as we continue with the project.

The more tests we have for our solution codes, the better it is for the stability of the solution. Therefore, next, we will look into PHPUnit's code coverage analysis solution. This will help us get some metrics about how much test coverage we have for our solution.

Test coverage

It's great having unit tests, but if we only test a few parts of the solution, then there's more chance of breaking the code base unintentionally. Still, having a few unit tests is better than having no unit tests. I'm not aware of a solid industry standard number or percentage of ideal test code coverage. Some say 80% to 95% test coverage is good, but that depends on the project. I still believe that 50% test coverage is better than 0% test coverage, and every project can be very different. The test coverage can be configured to exclude some parts of the code base as well, so having 100% test coverage does not literally mean 100% of all code in the code base is covered by automated tests. Nonetheless, it's still good to know how much test coverage we have for our solution. For developers who are just getting started with unit testing, it's important to point out that having a few tests is better than not writing unit tests at all. Don't be scared or demotivated if your code coverage report gives you a low number; knowing this will at least give you the data or truth about your test coverage.

To let PHPUnit know that a certain test function tests for a specific solution code, we will be using the `@covers` annotation. Annotations in PHP are a type of metadata that is added to classes, functions, properties, and so on. In PHP, we declare annotations within documentation blocks.

Declaring annotations

PHP annotations are just like comments – they are used by PHP libraries to get metadata from a function, property, or class in PHP.

Open the `CalculationTest.php` file and add the following `@covers` annotation right above the `testCanCalculateTotal` function:

codebase/symfony/tests/Unit/CalculationTest.php

```
/**
 * @covers \App\Example\Calculator::calculateTotal
 */
public function testCanCalculateTotal()
```

You'll notice that we have declared the `\App\Example\Calculator::calculateTotal` class and the `calculateTotal` method after the `@covers` annotation. We are basically telling PHPUnit that this specific `testCanCalculateTotal` test function will *cover* the method or function inside the `\App\Example\Calculator` class.

Now, run the following CLI commands to run PHPUnit with test coverage:

```
/var/www/html/symfony# export XDEBUG_MODE=coverage
/var/www/html/symfony# php bin/phpunit --coverage-text --filter
CalculationTest
```

This time around, we added the `--coverage-text` option. We are telling PHPUnit to output the coverage analysis report back to the terminal window. You will now receive the following result:

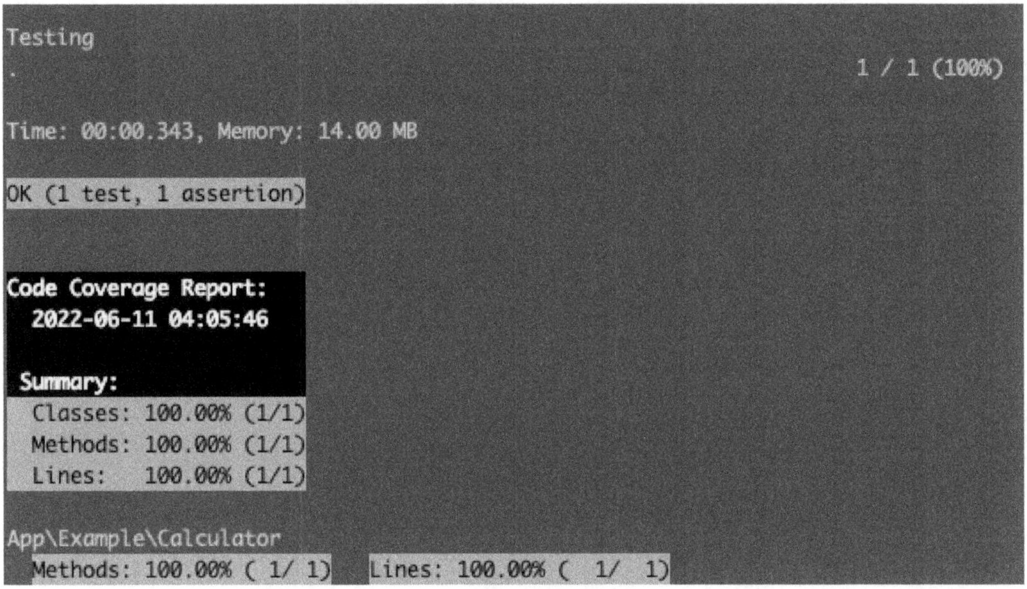

Figure 5.4 – First test coverage

Congratulations! You just received your first test coverage report! This means that the `calculate` method of the `Calculation.php` class is covered by a unit test. However, in real life, we end up having more functions inside a class. What will happen if we start adding functions to the `Calculation.php` class? Well, let's find out.

Adding more functions to the solution class

The `CalculationTest` class we previously created has a test that covers the `calculateTotal` function. When we ran the coverage test, we received a 100% test coverage result. If we add more functions to the solution class, we will no longer get a 100% coverage test result. What does that mean though? In practice, that means that some parts of our solution class are not covered by our automated test. It's not the end of the world, but this will help the developers in a company to identify how much of the system is covered by automated tests. This will affect the business's confidence level with the updates in the code base, and thus also affect the amount of manual testing that needs to be done, or how confident the business is about releasing new code.

Open the `Calculation.php` class and add the following method:

codebase/symfony/src/Example/Calculator.php

```php
<?php

namespace App\Example;

class Calculator
{
    public function calculateTotal(int $a, int $b, int $c)
        : int
    {
        return $a + $b + $c;
    }

    public function add(int $a, int $b): int
    {
        return $a + $b;
    }
}
```

As you can see in the preceding code block, we have added a new function called `add`. This function simply returns the summation of $a and $b. Since we have no unit test for this new function, let's see what will happen when we run our test again. Run the following command:

```
/var/www/html/symfony# php bin/phpunit --coverage-text --filter
CalculationTest
```

After running the preceding command, we'll notice that something has changed in our test coverage result:

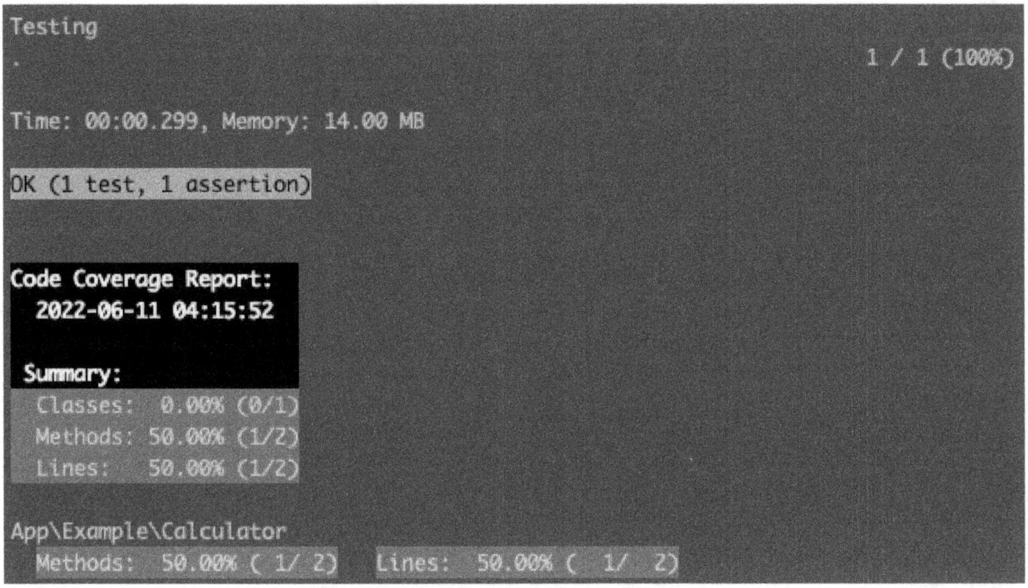

Figure 5.5 – Test coverage has decreased

You will notice that before adding the add function inside the Calculator.php class, we had 100% test coverage. Now, we only have 50% test coverage. Obviously, it's because we don't have a unit test responsible for testing the add function. To improve our test coverage, let's add a unit test for the add function:

codebase/symfony/tests/Unit/CalculationTest.php

```php
<?php

namespace App\Tests\Unit;

use App\Example\Calculator;
use PHPUnit\Framework\TestCase;

class CalculationTest extends TestCase
{
    /**
     * @covers \App\Example\Calculator::calculateTotal
     */
    public function testCanCalculateTotal()
```

```php
    {
        // Expected result:
        $expectedTotal = 6;

        // Test data:
        $a = 1;
        $b = 2;
        $c = 3;

        $calculator = new Calculator();
        $total      = $calculator->calculateTotal($a, $b,
            $c);

        $this->assertEquals($expectedTotal, $total);
    }


    /**
     * @covers \App\Example\Calculator::add
     */
    public function testCanAddIntegers()
    {
        // Expected Result
        $expectedSum = 7;

        // Test Data
        $a = 2;
        $b = 5;

        $calculator = new Calculator();
        $sum        = $calculator->add($a, $b);

        $this->assertEquals($expectedSum, $sum);
    }
}
```

In the preceding code block, we've added the `testCanAddIntegers` test function. By using the `@covers` annotation, we have also declared that this function tests for the `add` function in the `Calculation.php` class.

Let's run the test again and see whether we have improved our test coverage result. Run the following command again:

```
/var/www/html/symfony# php bin/phpunit --coverage-text --filter
CalculationTest
```

Now, we should see the following result:

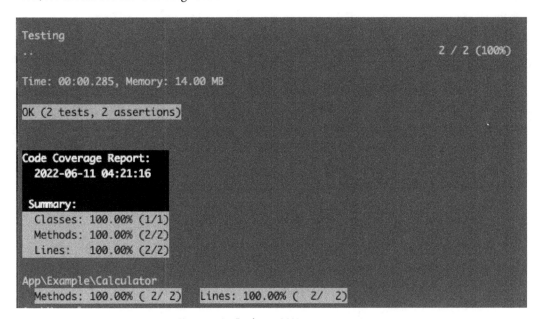

```
Testing
..                                                      2 / 2 (100%)

Time: 00:00.285, Memory: 14.00 MB

OK (2 tests, 2 assertions)


Code Coverage Report:
  2022-06-11 04:21:16

 Summary:
  Classes: 100.00% (1/1)
  Methods: 100.00% (2/2)
  Lines:   100.00% (2/2)

App\Example\Calculator
  Methods: 100.00% ( 2/ 2)   Lines: 100.00% ( 2/ 2)
```

Figure 5.6 – Back to 100% test coverage

Nice! Now, we have 100% test coverage again. We have two functions inside the `Calculation.php` class, and we also have two unit tests that test for each of these functions.

Now, imagine that you're working with other developers on a project, which is very common. If other developers start refactoring a unit-tested class and start adding functions to that class without adding tests to cover them, when your team runs the coverage test, your team will easily and quickly identify that there are new functions or features in that class not covered by the automated tests.

What if you created a `private` function inside the `Calculation.php` class? If you need to test a `private` method, then you can either indirectly test the `private` method by testing the method that calls it or use PHP's reflection feature.

Using PHP's reflection feature to directly test for private methods

Private methods are not supposed to be accessible to external objects, but they can be tested indirectly as will be explained in the next section. If you really want to try testing for a `private` method directly, you can use this method. Open the `Calculator.php` class and add the `private` `getDifference` method:

codebase/symfony/src/Example/Calculator.php

```php
<?php

namespace App\Example;

class Calculator
{
    public function calculateTotal(int $a, int $b, int $c)
        : int
    {
        return $a + $b + $c;
    }

    public function add(int $a, int $b): int
    {
        return $a + $b;
    }

    private function getDifference(int $a, int $b): int
    {
        return $a - $b;
    }
}
```

If you run the test again, you'll see that your test coverage has decreased again, even if you just added a `private` method:

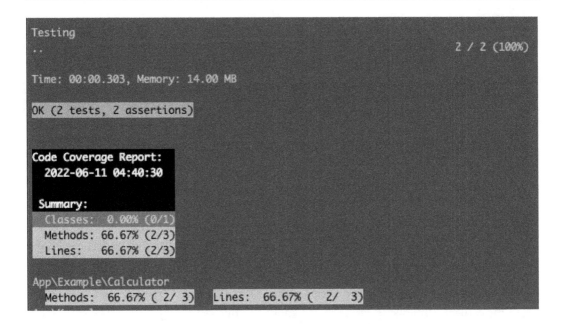

Figure 5.7 – No test for private method

Now, we have untested code, which is also going to be tricky to test as it's a `private` method. To test this, open the `CalculationTest.php` test class and add the `testCanGetDifference` method:

codebase/symfony/tests/Unit/CalculationTest.php

```
/**
 * @covers \App\Example\Calculator::getDifference
 */
public function testCanGetDifference()
{
    // Expected Result
    $expectedDifference = 4;

    // Test Data
    $a = 10;
    $b = 6;

    // Reflection
    $calculatorClass    = new \ReflectionClass
```

```
    (Calculator::class);
$privateMethod        = $calculatorClass->getMethod
    ("getDifference");
$privateMethod->setAccessible(true);

// Instance
$calculatorInstance = new Calculator();

// Call the private method
$difference = $privateMethod->invokeArgs
    ($calculatorInstance, [$a, $b]);

$this->assertEquals($expectedDifference, $difference);
}
```

As with the earlier test methods, we have also annotated this test to signify that it tests for the getDifference method inside the Calculator.php class. Since we are trying to test for a private method that is obviously not accessible if we just instantiate a Calculator object, we need to use PHP's ReflectionClass. We have manually specified the visibility of the getDifference class and indirectly called the private getDifference method. If we run the test again, we'll now see the following:

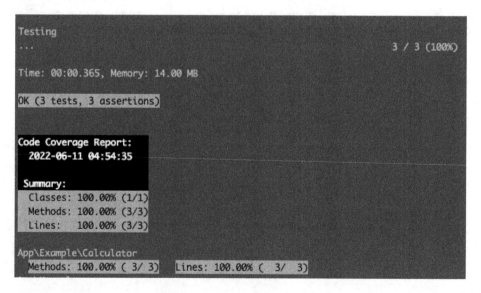

Figure 5.8 – Private method tested

Now, we are back to 100% test coverage, having tested two `public` methods and one `private` method – but is this necessary or practical? I personally think that this is not very practical. If I have a `private` method, I'll obviously use that private method inside another publicly accessible method. What I'd do is test for that publicly accessible method instead. If the instructions inside a `private` method are very complex, I don't think it should be a `private` method inside a class anyway. It might need its own class, or it might need to be broken down more. I've seen a lot of good classes (classes that can do everything) with very complex `private` methods, and it's a headache to maintain these types of classes.

Indirectly testing for private methods

If I have a `private` method, I'd test the public method that uses the `private` method instead of going through the reflection route. If it gets too complex, I will think of moving this test away from the unit test suite altogether. You can read about integration testing later in this chapter to learn more.

Open the `Calculator.php` class and replace the content with the following:

codebase/symfony/src/Example/Calculator.php

```php
<?php

namespace App\Example;

class Calculator
{
    public function calculateTotal(int $a, int $b, int $c)
        : int
    {
        return $a + $b + $c;
    }

    public function add(int $a, int $b): int
    {
        return $a + $b;
    }

    public function subtract(int $a, int $b): int
    {
        return $this->getDifference($a, $b);
```

```
    }

    private function getDifference(int $a, int $b): int
    {
        return $a - $b;
    }
}
```

We have retained the private getDifference method, but we have also added a new publicly accessible method called subtract, which, in turn, uses the getDifference method.

Open the CalculationTest.php file and replace the reflection test with the following:

codebase/symfony/tests/Unit/CalculationTest.php

```
/**
 * @covers \App\Example\Calculator::subtract
 * @covers \App\Example\Calculator::getDifference
 */
public function testCanSubtractIntegers()
{
    // Expected Result
    $expectedDifference = 4;

    // Test Data
    $a = 10;
    $b = 6;

    $calculator = new Calculator();
    $difference = $calculator->subtract($a, $b);

    $this->assertEquals($expectedDifference, $difference);
}
```

In the preceding code block, we have deleted the testCanGetDifference test that uses PHP's ReflectionClass method. It's up to you whether you want to test manually and individually for your private or protected methods using reflection.

In this new `testCanSubtractIntegers` method, you will notice that there are now two @ `covers` annotations. We are explicitly declaring that this specific test method will cover both the public `subtract` method and the private `getDifference` method.

Run the following command to execute the coverage test again and let's see whether we still pass the tests:

```
/var/www/html/symfony# php bin/phpunit --coverage-text --filter
CalculationTest
```

You should see the following 100% coverage result:

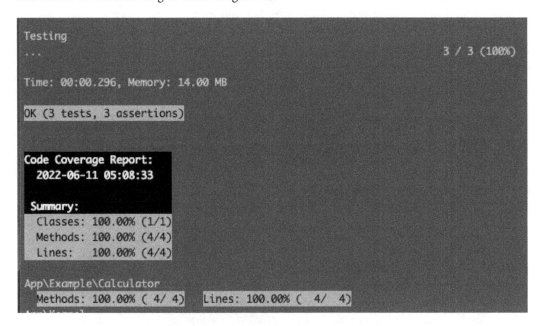

Figure 5.9 – Two methods covered by one test

You'll notice that the coverage report states that we have tested four methods. Technically speaking, we only have three tests inside our `CalculationTest.php` test class that are reported by the test result:

OK (3 tests, 3 assertions)

Since we have declared that the `testCanSubtractIntegers` test will be covering both the `subtract` and `getDifference` methods, we are able to get full test coverage for the `Calculator.php` class:

Methods: 100.00% (4/4)

We were now able to go through running unit tests, using Xdebug to debug with breakpoints and get test coverage results. Next, we will build our own small tools to run tests a little bit easier so that we don't have to write long commands all the time.

Using shell scripts to run tests

We can use shell scripts to run our tests for us, and by doing so, we can add extra configurations to each script. There are different configurations and commands to run when running PHPUnit tests, and there are different goals or intentions in mind when running unit tests. In this chapter so far, we ran tests to trigger Xdebug and go through codes, and we also used PHPUnit to get a report for our test coverage. To simplify the execution of these tests a bit better, we can build some shell scripts to help us encapsulate the commands and configurations to run the tests.

If you go back to your terminal and try to use Xdebug with a breakpoint, you'll probably be disappointed. In PHPStorm, put a breakpoint like so in one of the tests:

```php
<?php

namespace App\Tests\Unit;

use App\Example\Calculator;
use PHPUnit\Framework\TestCase;

class CalculationTest extends TestCase
{
    /**
     * @covers \App\Example\Calculator::calculateTotal
     */
    public function testCanCalculateTotal()
    {
        // Expected result:
        $expectedTotal = 6;
```

Figure 5.10 – Adding a breakpoint

After putting a breakpoint inside the `CalculationTest.php` class on line 16, run the following command:

```
/var/www/html/symfony# php bin/phpunit --filter CalculationTest
```

Did you notice anything? Well, the breakpoint did not get called at all. This is because earlier, we specified that we wanted to use Xdebug in coverage mode by running `export XDEBUG_MODE=coverage`. On the other hand, if we are running the test in debug mode and we want to get the coverage report, then we'll have to run different commands again. There's really nothing wrong with this, but if we are going to be developing a lot of codes and running tests repeatedly with different configurations, it can be helpful to use shell scripts instead.

We will create two scripts to trigger PHPUnit and configure our environment:

- `runDebug.sh` – We'll use this for debugging
- `runCoverage.sh` – We'll use this for test coverage reports

In symfony's root `dir`, create the following file:

codebase/symfony/runDebug.sh

```bash
#!/bin/bash
export XDEBUG_CONFIG="idekey=PHPSTORM"
export PHP_IDE_CONFIG="serverName=phptdd"
export XDEBUG_MODE="debug"

XDEBUGOPT=
if [ "x$NODEBUG" = "x" ]; then
    XDEBUGOPT="-d xdebug.start_with_request=yes"
fi

php $XDEBUGOPT bin/phpunit --color=always --debug $@
```

In the preceding script, we are configuring our environment to run a test with Xdebug. This is important during development as it will let us use breakpoints without having to always think about the configurations.

Make sure that the file you created is executable; run the following command to do so:

```
/var/www/html/symfony# chmod u+x runDebug.sh
```

Now, we can try using this script to execute our `CalculationTest.php` class, and see whether our breakpoint in line 16 gets called:

```
/var/www/html/symfony# ./runDebug.sh
```

After running the preceding command, go back to PHPStorm and make sure that the breakpoint works:

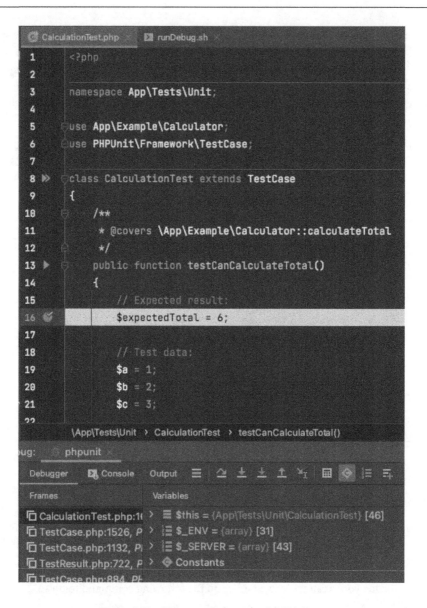

Figure 5.11 – Using runDebug.sh with Xdebug

Great! By using the `./runDebug.sh` script, we can configure our container dynamically and trigger the breakpoint in PHPStorm with Xdebug. Now, if we want to get the test coverage report, we'll need to run a different script to make things easier.

Create a new file called `runCoverage.sh`:

codebase/symfony/runCoverage.sh

```bash
#!/bin/bash
export XDEBUG_CONFIG="idekey=PHPSTORM"
export PHP_IDE_CONFIG="serverName=phptdd"
export XDEBUG_MODE="coverage"

php bin/phpunit --color=always --coverage-text $@
```

The preceding script will configure our environment and attach the `--coverage-text` option so that we can easily get a test coverage report when running this script.

Run the following command:

```
/var/www/html/symfony# ./runCoverage.sh
```

Running the `./runCoverage` script should now generate the respective **Code Coverage Report**:

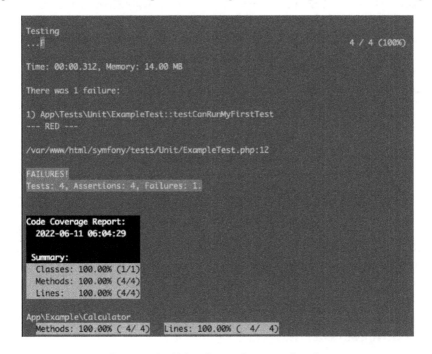

Figure 5.12 – Using the runCoverage.sh script

Great! Now, we can run PHPUnit with different configurations. The last test execution returned a failure because of our previously created `ExampleTest.php` test class, which we deliberately failed.

You can add your own scripts depending on your needs – after all, we are software developers. We can build tools to make things a little bit easier for ourselves. When running **Continuous Integration (CI)**, we won't need the ability to debug nor run code coverage reports all the time, so we can also create a script further down the project for CI usage. CI will be discussed in more detail in *Chapter 9, Continuous Integration*.

We've now learned how to write unit tests, and these tests are focused on testing small programs in our solution codes – but what if we need to test a more complex functionality that uses multiple classes? It would be nice if we could segregate those complex tests that depend on external objects or resources. In the next section, we'll quickly go through the different types of automated tests.

Types of tests

Running PHPUnit tests can be very quick. In my experience, even with tens of thousands of unit tests, it can only take a few minutes to run them completely. This is because they only test small parts or units of the solution.

We can also add tests that will call programs that will interact with external web service APIs or databases. Now, imagine how complex those tests are and how long it would take to execute them. If we combine all the complex tests that use multiple object and unit tests into a single group, it will take a lot of time to run the entire group of tests. I've experienced working with a company where there are thousands of tests that are all grouped into a single suite – you run the suite and wait an hour, only to find out there's one broken unit test. That's very time-consuming and impractical.

Simple tests   Complex tests

Figure 5.13 – Grouping tests

Identifying what a test does and putting it in the right group or basket of tests can help with organizing the tests. There are different types of tests that we can use as "baskets" or groups for our tests. We can simplify these baskets and divide them into two main types. In PHPUnit, these baskets are called test suites.

Basket 1 – unit tests

We've written unit tests earlier in this chapter. If you remember, we created a directory inside the `codebase/symfony/tests` directory called `Unit`. This will be our unit test basket. Every test that specifically tests small parts or units of the solution will be put into this directory, and in turn, the namespace is the following: App\Tests\Unit.

Open up codebase/symfony/phpunit.xml and you'll notice that we have declared a testsuite named Unit in the tests/Unit/ directory. We will use test suites to help group and segregate our tests. This will come in handy when we want to isolate the group of tests we want to run:

```
<testsuites>
    <testsuite name="Project Test Suite">
        <directory>tests</directory>
    </testsuite>
    <testsuite name="Unit">
        <directory>tests/Unit/</directory>
    </testsuite>
</testsuites>
```

This means that if we want to run the Unit test suite, PHPUnit will find all of the tests inside the tests/Unit/ directory.

To run all the tests inside that unit basket or test suite, run the following command:

```
/var/www/html/symfony# ./runDebug.sh --testsuite Unit
```

You'll get the following result:

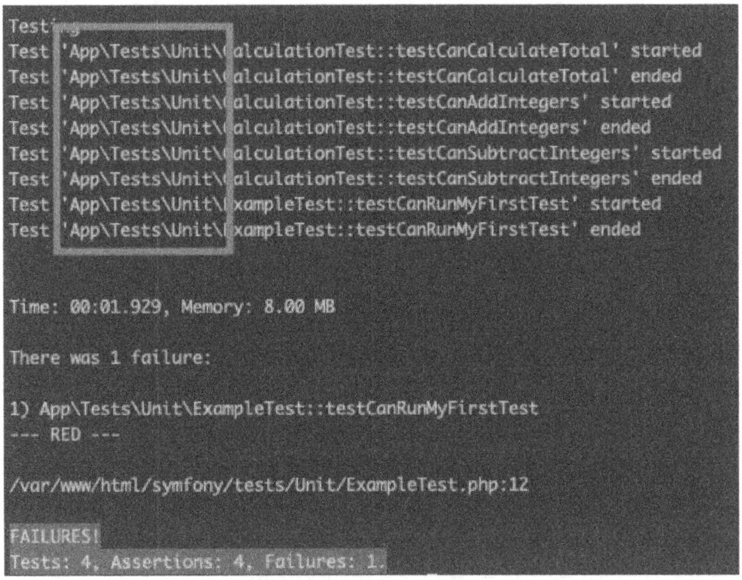

Figure 5.14 – Unit test suite

By adding the `--testsuite` unit option, we ensure that we only run tests inside the `App\Tests\Unit` namespace. This will help us focus our test execution on a specific basket or test suite.

We have covered the first group or basket of tests. We have created a directory called `Unit`, and this is where we will put all the future unit, or simple, tests. Next, we'll need to create a separate group or basket to put the more complex tests.

Basket 2 – integration tests

Integration testing aims to test a bigger part of the solution. Instead of testing a small unit of the application, integration tests aim to cover different parts of the solution in a single test.

Imagine testing an object's method that uses other objects. The success of the test can depend on external factors such as a database connection, an API call, or dependence on other classes that also depend on other classes. It's like a unit test on a slightly bigger scale.

For example, if you have a class that computes some total and then persists it in the database, you'd want to have a test that checks the computation result that is persisted in the database. This is where integration tests can be very useful.

We previously created a directory for our unit tests – now, let's create a directory to contain our integration tests.

Create an `Integration` directory inside the `tests` directory:

```
/var/www/html/symfony# mkdir tests/Integration
```

After creating the `Integration` directory, we need to let PHPUnit know about this directory. We need to add an `Integration` test suite and declare the directory path. Open `codebase/symfony/phpunit.xml` and use the following configuration:

```
codebase/symfony/phpunit.xml      <php>
        <ini name="display_errors" value="1" />
        <ini name="error_reporting" value="-1" />
        <server name="APP_ENV" value="test" force="true" />
        <server name="SHELL_VERBOSITY" value="-1" />
        <server name="SYMFONY_PHPUNIT_REMOVE" value="" />
        <server name="SYMFONY_PHPUNIT_VERSION" value="9.5" />
        <env name="SYMFONY_DEPRECATIONS_HELPER"
            value="disabled" />
    </php>


    <testsuites>
```

```
    <testsuite name="Project Test Suite">
        <directory>tests</directory>
    </testsuite>
    <testsuite name="Unit">
        <directory>tests/Unit/</directory>
    </testsuite>
    <testsuite name="Integration">
        <directory>tests/Integration/</directory>
    </testsuite>
</testsuites>

<coverage processUncoveredFiles="true">
    <include>
        <directory suffix=".php">src</directory>
    </include>
</coverage>

<listeners>
    <listener class="Symfony\Bridge\PhpUnit
        \SymfonyTestsListener" />
</listeners>
```

Now, the `Integration` test suite has been registered. With this, we can still safely run our unit tests by passing the `Unit` argument to the `--testsuite` option when running our tests. To run integration tests, we simply use `--testsuite Integration` instead:

`/var/www/html/symfony# ./runDebug.sh --testsuite Integration`

Since we have no tests, running the preceding command will return the following result:

```
root@0d708cc8ec26:/var/www/html/symfony# ./runDebug.sh --testsuite Integration
PHPUnit 9.5.5 by Sebastian Bergmann and contributors.

No tests executed!
```

Figure 5.15 – Integration test suite

Now that we have a basket to put all our integration tests into, let's start writing our first integration test!

We already have a unit-tested class, the `Calculate.php` class. Now, it would be great if we could use this as a part of our integration test example.

Integration test example

In this section, we will try to do some calculations and then try to store the result in the database. We will create a database called `coffee` and try to create a program that simply calculates the sum of how many coffee cups we had in a day, and then persist it. After persisting, we need to be able to verify whether the persisted sum is correct.

Installing Doctrine with Symfony 6

Since we are using the Symfony framework, which works well with Doctrine, let's just use Doctrine to persist and retrieve data from our database. There are a lot of ways to persist and retrieve data from a database, but for this project, we'll just focus on using Doctrine to simplify our examples so that we can focus on testing rather than reinventing the wheel. Doctrine is an ORM. You can read more about Doctrine at `https://www.doctrine-project.org`.

Let's install Doctrine by running the following commands:

```
/var/www/html/symfony# composer require symfony/orm-pack
/var/www/html/symfony# composer require symfony/maker-bundle
--dev
```

After running the preceding commands, which can take a few minutes, create a local environment file, and save it with the following content:

codebase/symfony/.env.local

```
DATABASE_URL="mysql://root:mypassword@server-mysql/
mydb?serverVersion=8&charset=utf8mb4"
```

In the preceding line, we are telling Symfony that in our local environment, we'd like to use our MySQL container that we created in *Chapter 3, Setting Up Our Development Environment Using Docker Containers*.

You can open up the `docker-compose.yml` file to review the MySQL container details. You can make any further configuration changes there to suit your needs.

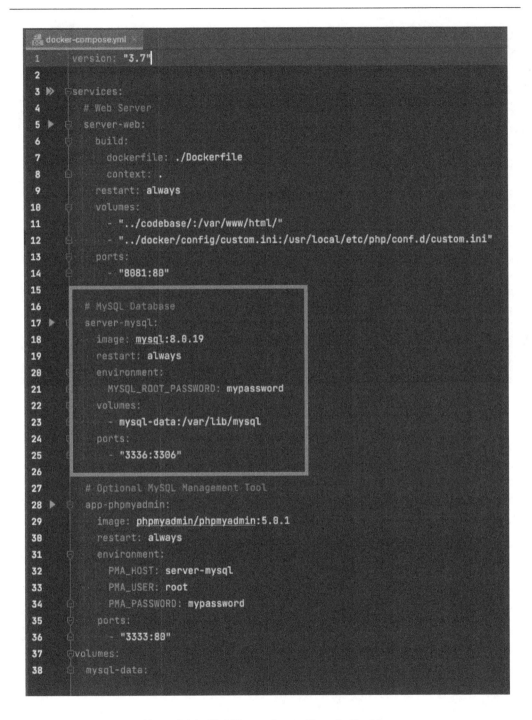

```
docker-compose.yml
1    version: "3.7"
2
3    services:
4      # Web Server
5      server-web:
6        build:
7          dockerfile: ./Dockerfile
8          context: .
9        restart: always
10       volumes:
11         - "../codebase/:/var/www/html/"
12         - "../docker/config/custom.ini:/usr/local/etc/php/conf.d/custom.ini"
13       ports:
14         - "8081:80"
15
16     # MySQL Database
17     server-mysql:
18       image: mysql:8.0.19
19       restart: always
20       environment:
21         MYSQL_ROOT_PASSWORD: mypassword
22       volumes:
23         - mysql-data:/var/lib/mysql
24       ports:
25         - "3336:3306"
26
27     # Optional MySQL Management Tool
28     app-phpmyadmin:
29       image: phpmyadmin/phpmyadmin:5.0.1
30       restart: always
31       environment:
32         PMA_HOST: server-mysql
33         PMA_USER: root
34         PMA_PASSWORD: mypassword
35       ports:
36         - "3333:80"
37   volumes:
38     mysql-data:
```

Figure 5.16 – MySQL container settings for Doctrine

You can change the database password here, or even change the MySQL version to whichever you need. In the `.env.local` file, we have specified that we want to use MySQL8, and we also specified that we want to use the `server-mysql` container, instead of using the IP address of the database server. We also used `coffee` as our database name.

Next, we will use the Doctrine ORM to create a MySQL database for us. We will then be using this new database for our example integration test.

Doctrine and database

We have configured our environment so that it can connect to the MySQL server container we created, and we have specified the database name we want to use for our example. Now, at this stage, we are ready to create a database for our integration test example. Run the following command:

```
/var/www/html/symfony# php bin/console doctrine:database:create
```

By running the preceding command, Doctrine will create a database named `coffee` for us, using the parameters we provided in the `.env.local` file.

```
root@0cb77fcadb5f:/var/www/html/symfony# php bin/console doctrine:database:create
Created database `coffee` for connection named default
root@0cb77fcadb5f:/var/www/html/symfony#
```

Figure 5.17 – Creating a new database

Now, we have our own database to play with. If you have a desktop MySQL client, you can connect to the `server-mysql` container to view the database we just created. If not, to make things look a bit prettier than the unending terminal windows for our automated tests, we have added a `PHPMyAdmin` container for quick and easy DB access back in *Chapter 3*, *Setting Up Our Development Environment Using Docker Containers*.

Open your web browser and go to the following URL: `http://127.0.0.1:3333/index.php`. You will see the following:

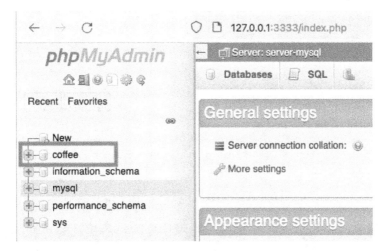

Figure 5.18 – coffee database

Before we write any codes that will utilize the database we just created, first, we need to understand what we want to do with it and create an integration test for it. Next, we'll create our first failing integration test.

Failing our first integration test

We have a solution to persist information, which is Doctrine and MySQL. We also have a way to calculate the sum of some random integers. Now, let's put them to use. We want to be able to pass a string name and three integers to represent the number of cups of coffee we consumed, get the sum, and persist it.

Create the following integration test file:

codebase/symfony/tests/Integration/ConsumptionTest.php

```php
<?php

namespace App\Tests\Integration\Service;

use PHPUnit\Framework\TestCase;

class ConsumptionServiceTest extends TestCase
{
    public function testCanComputeAndSave()
    {
```

```
        $this->fail("--- RED --");
    }
}
```

We created our first integration test inside the App\Tests\Integration namespace, which, in turn, will be a part of our integration test suite. Run the following command to make sure everything works, and that our test fails as expected:

```
/var/www/html/symfony# .runDebug.sh --testsuite Integration
--filter ConsumptionServiceTest
```

You should see the failed test, caused by the $this->fail("--- RED --"); line we have created:

```
root@0cb77fcadb5f:/var/www/html/symfony# ./runDebug.sh --testsuite Integration --filter ConsumptionServiceTest
PHPUnit 9.5.5 by Sebastian Bergmann and contributors.

Testing
Test 'App\Tests\Integration\Service\ConsumptionServiceTest::testCanComputeAndSave' started
Test 'App\Tests\Integration\Service\ConsumptionServiceTest::testCanComputeAndSave' ended


Time: 00:00.096, Memory: 8.00 MB

There was 1 failure:

1) App\Tests\Integration\Service\ConsumptionServiceTest::testCanComputeAndSave
--- RED --

/var/www/html/symfony/tests/Integration/Service/ConsumptionTest.php:14

FAILURES!
Tests: 1, Assertions: 1, Failures: 1.
root@0cb77fcadb5f:/var/www/html/symfony#
```

Figure 5.19 – First failing integration test

Great! We now have a failing Integration test suite test. Now, all we must do is make it pass.

Let's try to break down exactly what we want to do, and what we want to test for:

- We want to be able to track how many cups of coffee a person drinks in a day

- We want to have the number of coffee cups consumed in the morning, afternoon, and night

- We want to get the sum and then persist the total, along with the name of the person

- We want to be able to retrieve the persisted record and check whether it's correct.

Based on the preceding list, we can then update our test with the following:

codebase/symfony/tests/Integration/Service/ConsumptionTest.php

```php
<?php

namespace App\Tests\Integration\Service;

use PHPUnit\Framework\TestCase;

class ConsumptionServiceTest extends TestCase
{
    public function testCanComputeAndSave()
    {
        // Given
        $name              = "Damo";
        $morningCoffee     = 2;
        $afternoonCoffee   = 3;
        $eveningCoffee     = 1;

        // Expected Total:
        $expectedTotal = 6;

        // Persist the data
        $service     = new ConsumptionService();
        $persistedId = $service->computeAndSave($name,
        $morningCoffee, $afternoonCoffee, $eveningCoffee);

        // Verify if the data persisted is correct:
        // TODO:
    }
}
```

As you can see, we have an incomplete test – but for me, this is good. I write a failing test and make sure it fails, but I also try to start writing exactly what I want to test for.

Run the following command to see what happens:

```
/var/www/html/symfony# ./runDebug.sh --testsuite Integration
--filter ConsumptionServiceTest
```

The test tries to instantiate the `ConsumptionService.php` class that does not exist. Therefore, you'll get the following result:

```
There was 1 error:

1) App\Tests\Integration\Service\ConsumptionServiceTest::testCanComputeAndSave
Error: Class "App\Tests\Integration\Service\ConsumptionService" not found

/var/www/html/symfony/tests/Integration/Service/ConsumptionTest.php:21

ERRORS!
Tests: 1, Assertions: 0, Errors: 1.
```

Figure 5.20 – ConsumptionService not found

We deliberately tried to instantiate an object from a class that does not exist, therefore resulting in a test failure. What does this tell us? Remember **Test-Driven Development** (**TDD**), where the development of our solution codes was driven by our failing tests? Well, we might want to start writing the solution code, which is the `ConsumptionService.php` class and the other program it needs to use. We should always fail our test first.

However, before we write the `ConsumptionService.php` class, let's create the Doctrine entity needed by the `ConsumptionService.php` class for our example.

Creating a Doctrine entity

Let's create an entity class to represent our data. A Doctrine entity is just a simple **Plain Old PHP Object** (**POPO**) with some Doctrine-specific annotations that can be mapped to a database table in its most basic usage.

Run the following command to create a `Consumption.php` class:

```
/var/www/html/symfony# php bin/console make:entity
```

After running the preceding command, enter the fields you want to create. For our example, use the following:

```
New property name: name
Field type: string
Field length: 50
```

```
Can this field be null in the database? no
New property name: total
Field type: integer
Can this field be null in the database? no
```

After the command prompts, you should now see a new entity class file in codebase/symfony/ src/Entity/Consumption.php:

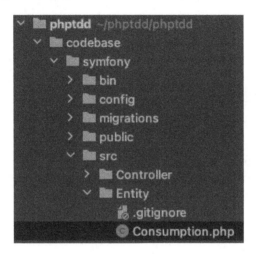

Figure 5.21 – Consumption entity

If you open the file, you'll see the automatically generated Doctrine entity codes:

```php
<?php

namespace App\Entity;

use App\Repository\ConsumptionRepository;
use Doctrine\ORM\Mapping as ORM;

#[ORM\Entity(repositoryClass: ConsumptionRepository::class)]
class Consumption
{
    #[ORM\Id]
    #[ORM\GeneratedValue]
    #[ORM\Column(type: 'integer')]
    private $id;
```

```php
#[ORM\Column(type: 'string', length: 50)]
private $name;

#[ORM\Column(type: 'integer')]
private $total;

public function getId(): ?int
{
    return $this->id;
}

public function getName(): ?string
{
    return $this->name;
}

public function setName(string $name): self
{
    $this->name = $name;

    return $this;
}

public function getTotal(): ?int
{
    return $this->total;
}

public function setTotal(int $total): self
{
    $this->total = $total;

    return $this;
}
}
```

In summary, we only have two fields to play with, the name and total fields. That's going to be perfect for our integration test example.

Next, we'll need the actual database table that our Doctrine entity is going to represent. We will use Doctrine ORM to run the migration tool so that we can generate the database tables we need.

Creating a Doctrine table for the entity

Now that we have an entity, let's also create the database table that the Consumption entity represents.

Run the following commands:

```
/var/www/html/symfony# php bin/console make:migration
/var/www/html/symfony# php bin/console
doctrine:migrations:migrate
```

After running the preceding commands, a new database table should be created for you. If you go back to the **PHPMyAdmin** page, you'll see the new consumption table created, based on the Consumption.php entity class:

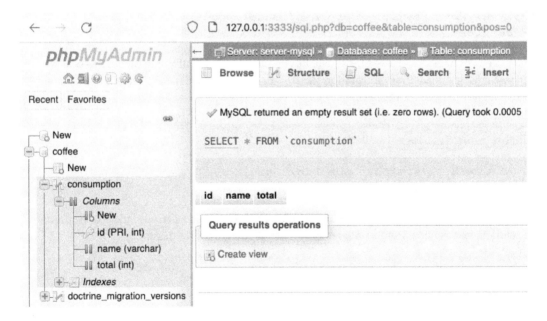

Figure 5.22 – consumption database table

We now have a database table that will be represented by our Consumption.php entity class. This table will be used to persist our coffee drinkers' coffee consumption records!

However, when working on a real project, we don't want to use the main database for running our tests; otherwise, our tests will end up inserting test data into the production database. Next, we'll create the test database. This database will be specifically used by our integration tests and will mirror the structure of the main database.

Creating a test database

Just like in the previous set of instructions, we'll also create a database based on some environment configuration – but this time, this is specifically intended to be used by our tests.

Open the .env.test file and add the following line at the end of the file:

```
DATABASE_URL="mysql://root:mypassword@server-mysql/
coffee?serverVersion=8&charset=utf8mb4"
```

You'll notice that it's identical to the value we used for the .env.local file. Notice that we reused coffee as the database name.

Now, run the following command to create the test database:

```
/var/www/html/symfony# php bin/console doctrine:database:create
--env=test
```

A new database named coffee_test will be created. _test is suffixed to the coffee database name we have specified. Every integration test we run that uses the database will use the coffee_test database to persist and read data.

Next, run the following command so that we can also migrate the Consumption table into our new coffee_test database:

```
/var/www/html/symfony# php bin/console
doctrine:migrations:migrate -n --env=test
```

At this stage, we'll have two almost identical databases. The coffee database that's to be used for the solution, and the coffee_test database that's to be used for our tests.

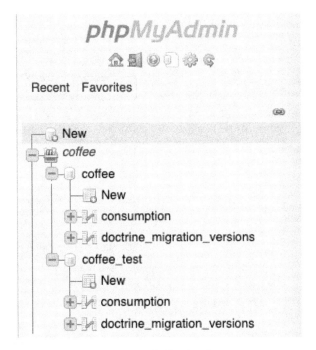

Figure 5.23 – Coffee databases

Now that we have created our databases, and we also have the Doctrine ORM, which will serve as the main tool for communicating with our database from the PHP code base, we will now start building the solution codes to pass our failing integration test.

Putting things together

At this stage, we're now ready to start building the missing solution code that our `ComputationServiceTest.php` integration test keeps on complaining about. Remember this message from our failing test?

```
Error: Class "App\Tests\Integration\Service\ConsumptionService" not found
```

Let's start fixing that error by following these steps:

1. First, open the `services.yaml` file and update it with the following content:

codebase/symfony/config/services.yaml

```
# This file is the entry point to configure your own
services.
```

```
# Files in the packages/ subdirectory configure your
dependencies.

# Put parameters here that don't need to change on each
machine where the app is deployed
# https://symfony.com/doc/current/best_practices.
html#use-parameters-for-application-configuration
parameters:

services:
    # default configuration for services in *this* file
    _defaults:
        autowire: true       # Automatically injects
            dependencies in your services.
        autoconfigure: true # Automatically registers
your services as commands, event subscribers, etc.

    # makes classes in src/ available to be used as
        services
    # this creates a service per class whose id is the
        fully-qualified class name
    App\:
        resource: '../src/'
        exclude:
            - '../src/DependencyInjection/'
            - '../src/Entity/'
            - '../src/Kernel.php'

    App\Service\ConsumptionService:
        public: true

    # add more service definitions when explicit
        configuration is needed
    # please note that last definitions always
        *replace* previous ones
```

Since we are using Symfony for this example, we will use its PSR-11-compliant service container to create instances of the objects we need. Instead of using the *new* PHP keyword to create an instance of the ConsumptionService.php class that we are about to write, we'll use the service container instead.

2. Create the following class with the following content:

codebase/symfony/src/Service/ConsumptionService.php

```php
<?php

namespace App\Service;

use App\Entity\Consumption;
use App\Example\Calculator;
use Doctrine\Persistence\ManagerRegistry;

class ConsumptionService
{
    /**
     * @var Calculator
     */
    private Calculator $calculator;

    /**
     * @var ManagerRegistry
     */
    private $managerRegistry;

    /**
     * @param ManagerRegistry $doctrine
     * @param Calculator $calculator
     */
    public function __construct(ManagerRegistry $doctrine, Calculator $calculator)
    {
        $this->setManagerRegistry($doctrine);
        $this->setCalculator($calculator);
```

```php
    }

    /**
     * @param string $name
     * @param int $morning
     * @param int $afternoon
     * @param int $evening
     * @return int
     */
    public function calculateAndSave(string $name, int
        $morning, int $afternoon, int $evening): int
    {
        $entityManager = $this->getManagerRegistry()->
            getManager();

        // Calculate total:
        $sum = $this->getCalculator()->calculateTotal
            ($morning, $afternoon, $evening);

        // Consumption model or entity:
        $consumption = new Consumption();
        $consumption->setName($name);
        $consumption->setTotal($sum);

        // Persist using the Entity Manager:
        $entityManager->persist($consumption);
        $entityManager->flush();

        return $consumption->getId();
    }

    /**
     * @return Calculator
     */
    public function getCalculator(): Calculator
    {
```

```
        return $this->calculator;
    }


    /**
     * @param Calculator $calculator
     */
    public function setCalculator(Calculator
        $calculator): void
    {
        $this->calculator = $calculator;
    }


    /**
     * @return ManagerRegistry
     */
    public function getManagerRegistry(): ManagerRegistry
    {
        return $this->managerRegistry;
    }


    /**
     * @param ManagerRegistry $managerRegistry
     */
    public function setManagerRegistry(ManagerRegistry
        $managerRegistry): void
    {
        $this->managerRegistry = $managerRegistry;
    }
}
```

Let's quickly go through the things we did in this class before we move back to our integration test class. The ConsumptionService class depends on two objects, ManagerRegistry and CalculationService. The calculateAndSave method will then use these two objects to achieve its goal.

3. Now, let's go back to the `ConsumptionServiceTest.php` class, and replace its content with the following:

codebase/symfony/tests/Integration/Service/ConsumptionTest.php

```php
<?php

namespace App\Tests\Integration\Service;

use App\Entity\Consumption;
use App\Service\ConsumptionService;
use Symfony\Bundle\FrameworkBundle\Test\
    KernelTestCase;

class ConsumptionServiceTest extends KernelTestCase
{
    public function testCanComputeAndSave()
    {
        self::bootKernel();

        // Given
        $name              = "Damo";
        $morningCoffee     = 2;
        $afternoonCoffee   = 3;
        $eveningCoffee     = 1;

        // Expected Total:
        $expectedTotal = 6;

        // Test Step 1: Get the Symfony's service
            container:
        $container = static::getContainer();

        // Test Step 2: Use PSR-11 standards to get an
        instance of our service, pre-injected with the
        EntityManager:
        /** @var ConsumptionService $service */
```

```
$service = $container->get
    (ConsumptionService::class);

// Test Step 3: Run the method we want to test
for:
$persistedId = $service->calculateAndSave
    ($name, $morningCoffee, $afternoonCoffee,
        $eveningCoffee);

// Test Step 4: Verify if the data persisted
    data is correct:
$em              = $service->
    getManagerRegistry()->getManager();
$recordFromDb    = $em->find
    (Consumption::class, $persistedId);

$this->assertEquals($expectedTotal,
    $recordFromDb->getTotal());
$this->assertEquals($name, $recordFromDb->
    getName());
    }
}
```

I have left comments in the code to explain clearly what we did in the test. Let us understand it in more detail:

- **Test step 1**: Since we are using Symfony and are extending the `KernelTestCase` class, we can use the `static::getContainer()` method to get an instance of Symfony's service container. We will use this to create an instance of our `ConsumptionService` instead of manually using the new PHP keyword to instantiate it.

- **Test step 2**: Since we are using Symfony, we can use its PSR-11-compliant service container. We can use this service container to get instances of classes without having to manually instantiate their dependencies. For example, our `ConsumptionService` class expects two objects in its constructor. With the service container being configured for auto wiring, the container will automatically instantiate the dependencies declared in the constructor of `ConsumptionService`. The auto wiring configuration is declared in `codebase/symfony/config/services.yaml` we have modified earlier in this chapter.

- **Test step 3**: This is where it all matters! This is the method we are trying to test. We execute the `calculateAndSave` method. We expect that in this step, the summation of the three integers we provided will be summed up, and then persisted into the database.

- **Test step 4**: If the `calculateAndSave` method succeeded in doing its job, then we can test it for real. We will retrieve a hydrated `Consumption` entity by using the entity manager object inside `ConsumptionService`. We will read the data stored in the database and compare it to the `$expectedTotal` and `$name` values we have declared in the test by using the `assertEquals` method. If all goes well, then we should now be able to pass the test.

4. Now, execute the integration test again by running the following command:

```
/var/www/html/symfony# ./runDebug.sh --testsuite
Integration --filter ConsumptionServiceTest
```

This time around, we should now be able to pass the test!

```
root@0cb77fcadb5f:/var/www/html/symfony# ./runDebug.sh
--testsuite Integration --filter ConsumptionServiceTest
PHPUnit 9.5.5 by Sebastian Bergmann and contributors.

Testing

.

                 1 / 1 (100%)


Time: 00:00.580, Memory: 18.00 MB
OK (1 test, 2 assertions)
root@0cb77fcadb5f:/var/www/html/symfony#
```

5. Great! We finally passed our first integration test! To see the record that we just created in the database, run the following command:

```
/var/www/html/symfony# php bin/console dbal:run-sql
'SELECT * FROM consumption' --env=test
```

You should get the following result:

Figure 5.24 – Database result

Success! We were able to create an integration test, create the solution class, and finally pass the integration test!

Why did we use an integration test in the first place?

Open the `ConsumptionService.php` class and check the `constructor` method.

In the constructor, we have specified two required parameters. We require a `ManagerRegistry` instance and a `Calculator` instance that we ourselves developed earlier in the chapter. These are two objects that our `ComputationService.php` class depends on. Now, this is exactly why we need an integration test and not a unit test.

When we execute the `calculateAndSave` method, we will be using business logic that our `ConsumptionService` does not have. Rather, it depends on other objects to achieve its goal. In contrast with the methods we build unit tests for, those methods do not rely on other objects to do their jobs. That's the main difference between a unit test and an integration test.

Summary

In this chapter, we defined what unit testing is by writing our own examples. We have gone through building and passing unit tests, as well as writing our own shell scripts to help us execute different automated test configurations to make it easier for us to debug or run test coverages. We've gone through what a test coverage report is, and how we can use it.

We've written our first integration test and configured our development environment so that we can also use a MySQL database. We've created a solution class that will perform the business logic that we need to pass the test, and we are also able to verify that what we persist in the database is what we have intended.

In this chapter, we tried to clearly define what a unit test and an integration test are, how they differ, and why we must separate them into their baskets or test suites.

In the next chapter, we will be talking about **Behaviour-Driven Development (BDD)**. We will understand what it is used for, why we need it, and how it is related to TDD.

6

Applying Behavior-Driven Development

In the previous chapter, we learned how to create and use unit tests to our advantage. We used unit tests and integration tests to help ensure the stability of our solution code. That was probably like learning how to do a basic punch on a punching bag. If you go to a boxing class, they'll probably teach you how to use your basic punch more effectively and teach you how to use that basic punch to do combinations of punches, as well as how to defend against them. That's akin to what **behavior-driven development** (BDD) and **test-driven development** (TDD) are. We first need to start with the basics: unit and integration testing. Now that we have those basics, we can start applying processes or techniques so that we can use them more effectively.

A lot of developers know how to write unit tests and integration tests—after all, these tests are just programs that we developers write. From my personal experience, what I've noticed is that a lot of developers won't know how to utilize their unit tests and integration tests effectively on their projects. Some developers know how to write unit tests but could not even write one for their project. So, merely having basic or technical knowledge of how to write a unit test is not enough to help improve a project. Applying and using it effectively is what counts.

With BDD and TDD, that's what we'll try to do. We will utilize those testing skills by following a process to help us build our example project.

In this chapter, we will go through the following topics:

- What is BDD?
- Applying BDD using Behat and Gherkin
- Writing PHP code based on Gherkin
- Browser emulators and Mink
- Why bother with Gherkin, then?

By the end of the chapter, you will be able to write behavior-driven features, scenarios, and solution code.

Technical requirements

This chapter requires you to have all the containers, configurations, and testing tools we have utilized in *Chapter 5, Unit Testing*. You can download the source files from this URL and run the containers: `https://github.com/PacktPublishing/Test-Driven-Development-with-PHP-8/tree/main/Chapter%205`.

Preparing the development environment for the chapter

First, get the base code for Chapter 6, found in `https://github.com/PacktPublishing/Test-Driven-Development-with-PHP-8/tree/main/Chapter%206/base/phptdd` or simply run the following command:

```
curl -Lo phptdd.zip "https://github.com/PacktPublishing/Test-
Driven-Development-with-PHP-8/raw/main/Chapter%206/base.zip" &&
unzip -o phptdd.zip && cd base && ./demoSetup.sh
```

To run the containers and execute the commands in this chapter, you should be inside the `docker-server-web-1` container.

Run the following command to confirm the container name for our web server:

```
docker ps
```

To run the containers, run the following command from the `/phptdd/docker` directory from the repository in your host machine:

```
docker-compose build && docker-compose up -d
docker exec -it docker_server-web_1 /bin/bash
```

Once inside the container, run the following command to install the libraries required through Composer:

```
/var/www/html/symfony# ./setup.sh
```

What is BDD?

BDD is a way or a process to develop software where the intended behavior of a solution is first defined by the business and then translated into automated test scenarios, before starting the actual development of the solution code.

This development process promotes collaboration among the different departments or teams in a software company. It might sound ridiculous, but in my experience, understanding exactly "what" needs to be built and what is the actual goal of the project is what I always see as the most elusive part when starting a project.

There are times when the business or a client doesn't even know what it wants, or maybe the business or client does not know how to express or relay those goals effectively. Now, imagine being a software developer for a company—your job is to develop solutions to problems to achieve a goal. What if that goal is not defined clearly? Or, what if the goal was defined by the business but not relayed properly to the software developers? Basically, the developers will end up developing the wrong solution and— worse—for the wrong problem! That's why collaboration among different departments in a software company is very important.

Business analysts, project managers, architects, and developers can define what the goals are for a project, and why the project is needed in the first place. The test engineers and software developers can then coordinate, debate, and discuss with the business analysts to come up with expected or intended behaviors of a solution, then break them down into smaller pieces. This is the first step that's needed in BDD: knowing exactly what the goal is, what needs to be built, and knowing which behaviors are expected from a solution.

Now that we know what BDD is, we can start applying it to our example project.

Applying BDD using Behat and Gherkin

To help us easily understand what BDD is and how it is used, we will try to apply it to example scenarios in a project.

Going back to *Chapter 2, Understanding and Organizing the Business Requirements of Our Project*, we have created some Jira tickets to help us break down the features that we need to build. Within the **Inventory Clerk Solution** epic, we have created a user story with the following title:

As an inventory clerk, I want to be able to log in to the system so that I can access the inventory system.

With this user story, we can deduce that we will need a user for the application and that user will need to be able to authenticate themself so that they can access a restricted feature.

So, usually, as software developers, we'll then go ahead and start building the solution code for that– write code, then check the results from the controller or web page we just created. We won't be doing that.

With BDD, we'll first start with a failing scenario. Sounds familiar? Yes—from the previous chapter, it's just like writing our failing unit test before we write the solution code to pass that failing test.

Before we start writing our BDD test, we'll need to use some PHP packages to let us do this. We'll use the Behat testing framework to help us build and organize our BDD tests.

What is Behat?

Behat is a PHP framework built for implementing BDD in PHP. It's a framework to help us PHP developers write behavior-driven tests and programs. This will help us write better behavior-driven programs quicker so that we won't have to reinvent the wheel in coming up with bootstrap code or skeleton code to write these behavior-driven tests. Behat uses Gherkin to describe the actual features we want to test.

What is Gherkin?

Gherkin is a language used to define business scenarios and goals. It's in plain English text, so anyone in the company—even non-technical staff—will be able to understand the business scenario being described.

What is Mink?

This is where it gets very interesting, at least for a PHP developer like me. Mink is a PHP library that will serve as an emulator for a web browser. We web application developers develop PHP applications; our users will be using our web applications through a web browser. So, it will be very beneficial for us if we automate the process of testing our application through a web browser. Instead of manually clicking on buttons or filling out forms, and so on, we can just use some programs to do this for us. So, think about a robot version of yourself testing your program for you through a web browser.

In the next section, we will be installing Behat.

Installing Behat and Mink

Before we start writing our first behavior-driven test programs, we'll first need to install all the libraries and dependencies we need. Let's get started:

1. Create a new directory named `behat` under the `codebase` directory so that we can have a separate installation directory from our Symfony application:

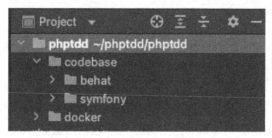

Figure 6.1 – Behat root directory

    After creating the new directory, we can go ahead and start installing the Behat PHP package through Composer.

2. Using your terminal, inside the `behat` directory, run the following command:

```
/var/www/html/behat# composer require --dev behat/behat
```

3. After the installation, you can verify whether Behat was successfully installed by running the following command:

```
/var/www/html/behat# ./vendor/bin/behat -V
```

Once done, you should then see the Behat version that you just installed:

```
root@0cb77fcadb5f:/var/www/html/behat# ./vendor/bin/behat -V
behat 3.11.0
```

Figure 6.2 – Behat installed

Now, we also need to install Mink so that we can do some frontend testing.

Run the following command to install Mink:

```
/var/www/html/behat# composer require --dev behat/mink-
extension -W
/var/www/html/symfony# composer require --dev behat/mink-
goutte-driver
```

Great! Now, we need to let Behat create some skeleton files to help us get started. Run the following command:

```
/var/www/html/behat# ./vendor/bin/behat --init
```

You should now see a new directory called `features`. This is where we will be putting our business feature scenarios.

Creating a Behat feature

Now that we have installed Behat and initialized it, we can create our first example feature file. We will use the Gherkin language to define the feature's story. It's literally like telling a story.

In the `features` directory, create a new file called `home.feature` and add the following content:

/var/www/html/behat/features/home.feature

```
Feature: Home page
  In order to welcome visitors
  As a visitor
  I need to be able to see the Symfony logo


  Scenario: See the Symfony logo
```

```
Given I have access to the home page URL
When I visit the home page
Then I should see the Symfony Logo
```

We have created `feature` and `scenario` files using the Gherkin language. They are descriptive and very easy to understand. You don't need a programmer to understand what they mean. So, showing them to your colleagues such as business analysts or test engineers won't be an issue; they'll even be able to help you fine-tune or improve your features and scenarios.

Next, we'll focus on the `Feature` keyword itself and its content.

Feature keyword

As you can see in the preceding code snippet, we have written three sections below the `Feature` keyword. The three sections below it are set out here:

- `In order to` <business goal>
- `As a/an` <actor>
- `I need to be able to` <what the actor defined previously should be able to do>

In the `In order to` section, we define what the business wants to achieve in this feature. In our example, we want our site visitors to feel welcomed when they land on our home page.

In the `As a/an` section, we define who is performing the action. In our example, this is the site visitor who is accessing the home page.

And lastly, in the `I need to be able to` section, we define what the actor should be able to do or achieve so that the business can achieve its end goal. In our example, we just want the actor or visitor to see the Symfony logo and the welcome message.

Next, as a part of a feature, we will need to add scenarios using the `Scenario` keyword.

Scenario keyword

Inside a feature, we can have one or more scenarios. In the `home.feature` file we created, you'll notice that the `Scenario` tag is indented compared to the `Feature` tag above it. A scenario is written in plain English; it is just a written outline of a sequence of events. In Gherkin, we will divide a scenario into three sections as well:

- `Given`: Used to declare the existing or current state or value of the system
- `When`: Used to define verbs or actions performed on the system
- `Then`: The expected result after performing the verbs or actions declared in the `When` section

Now that we have defined both an example feature and scenario, let's try to run Behat and see what we get.

Run the following command:

```
/var/www/html/behat# ./vendor/bin/behat
```

You should then see the following result:

```
root@0cb77fcadb5f:/var/www/html/behat# ./vendor/bin/behat
Feature: Home page
  In order to welcome visitors
  As a visitor
  I need to be able to see the Symfony logo and welcome message

  Scenario: See the Symfony logo                    # features/home.feature:6
    Given I have access to the home page URL
    When I visit the home page
    Then I should see the Symfony Logo

1 scenario (1 undefined)
3 steps (3 undefined)
0m0.06s (8.79Mb)

 >> <snippet_undefined><snippet_keyword>default</snippet_keyword> suite has undefined steps. Please ch
oose the context to generate snippets:</snippet_undefined>

  [0] None
  [1] FeatureContext
 > 0

--- Use --snippets-for CLI option to generate snippets for following default suite steps:

    Given I have access to the home page URL
    When I visit the home page
    Then I should see the Symfony Logo

root@0cb77fcadb5f:/var/www/html/behat#
```

Figure 6.3 – Missing snippets

You'll notice that Behat tried to look for some PHP code that represents the scenario we declared earlier, but we did not do that. So, that means that we also have to write some PHP code for Behat to execute in relation to the actual `Given`, `When`, and `Then` definitions we have created.

Next, we'll write the PHP code needed to support the features and scenarios we just created.

Writing PHP code based on Gherkin

We will need PHP programs to represent the features and scenarios we created using Gherkin. The Behat framework will follow the features and scenarios we created in the previous section, but it will also look for PHP code that represents each feature and scenario. Within this PHP code, we can add any custom logic we want to interpret the features and scenarios into programs. Create the following files that the Behat framework needs to run our features and scenarios:

1. First, we need to create a new context class. A context class is what Behat uses to represent Gherkin features into PHP programs.Create the following file with the content shown:

codebase/behat/features/bootstrap/HomeContext.php

```php
<?php

use Behat\Behat\Tester\Exception\PendingException;

class HomeContext implements \Behat\Behat\Context\Context
{


}
```

2. Then, after creating the `HomeContext.php` class, we also need to tell Behat that we have a new context class. We can do this by creating a configuration file. Create the following file with the content shown:

codebase/behat/behat.yml

```yaml
default:
  suites:
    default:
      contexts:
        - FeatureContext
        - HomeContext
```

Here, we can declare more PHP context classes. By default, you can use the `FeatureContext.php` file that's been automatically created earlier in this chapter, but if we keep on adding different steps inside the `FeatureContext.php` class, we'll end up with a mess.

3. Now, let's try running Behat again, but this time, we'll use the following command to automatically generate the missing snippets for our `Given`, `When`, and `Then` steps:

```
/var/www/html/behat# ./vendor/bin/behat features/home.
feature --append-snippets
```

You'll then be prompted to enter which specific context class you want to use:

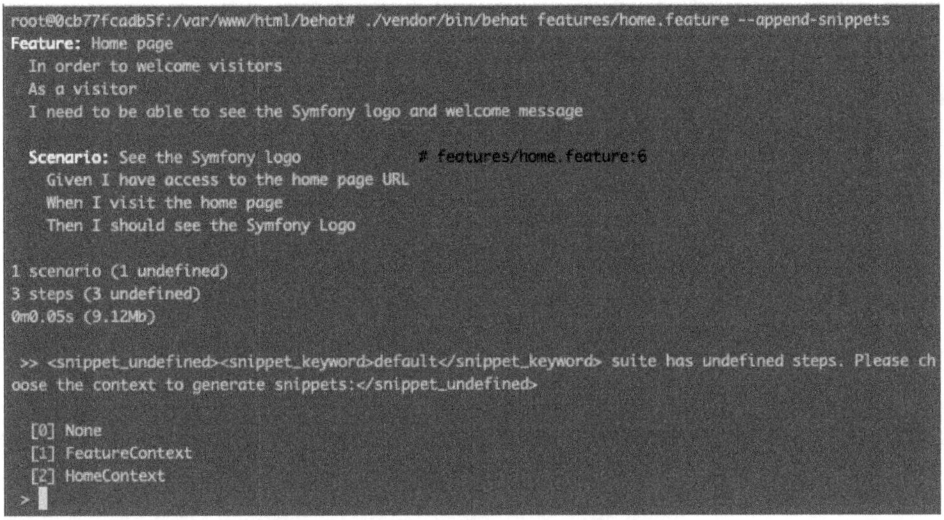

```
root@0cb77fcadb5f:/var/www/html/behat# ./vendor/bin/behat features/home.feature --append-snippets
Feature: Home page
  In order to welcome visitors
  As a visitor
  I need to be able to see the Symfony logo and welcome message

  Scenario: See the Symfony logo                # features/home.feature:6
    Given I have access to the home page URL
    When I visit the home page
    Then I should see the Symfony Logo

1 scenario (1 undefined)
3 steps (3 undefined)
0m0.05s (9.12Mb)

 >> <snippet_undefined><snippet_keyword>default</snippet_keyword> suite has undefined steps. Please ch
oose the context to generate snippets:</snippet_undefined>

  [0] None
  [1] FeatureContext
  [2] HomeContext
 > 
```

Figure 6.4 – Selecting a context class

4. Enter 2 into the CLI, then press *Enter*. Now, you should get the following result:

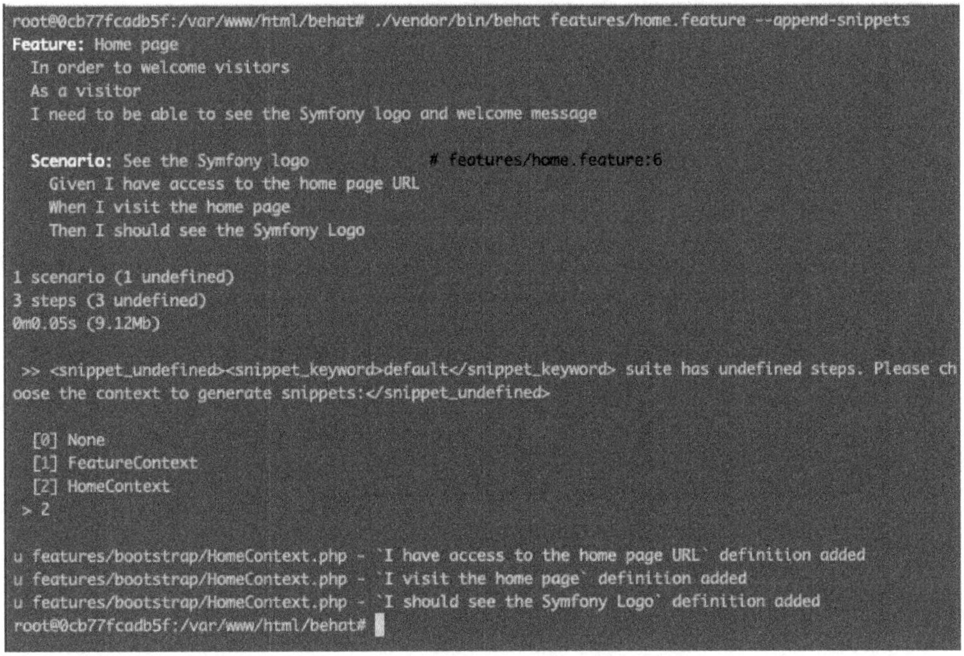

```
root@0cb77fcadb5f:/var/www/html/behat# ./vendor/bin/behat features/home.feature --append-snippets
Feature: Home page
  In order to welcome visitors
  As a visitor
  I need to be able to see the Symfony logo and welcome message

  Scenario: See the Symfony logo                # features/home.feature:6
    Given I have access to the home page URL
    When I visit the home page
    Then I should see the Symfony Logo

1 scenario (1 undefined)
3 steps (3 undefined)
0m0.05s (9.12Mb)

 >> <snippet_undefined><snippet_keyword>default</snippet_keyword> suite has undefined steps. Please ch
oose the context to generate snippets:</snippet_undefined>

  [0] None
  [1] FeatureContext
  [2] HomeContext
 > 2

u features/bootstrap/HomeContext.php - `I have access to the home page URL` definition added
u features/bootstrap/HomeContext.php - `I visit the home page` definition added
u features/bootstrap/HomeContext.php - `I should see the Symfony Logo` definition added
root@0cb77fcadb5f:/var/www/html/behat#
```

Figure 6.5 – Automatically generated snippets

Behat has automatically generated the PHP snippets needed to represent the `Given`, `When`, and `Then` steps we have defined inside the `home.feature` file.

5. Open the `HomeContext.php` class we created earlier, and there you should see the new automatically generated methods:

```php
<?php

use Behat\Behat\Tester\Exception\PendingException;

class HomeContext implements \Behat\Behat\Context
    \Context
{
    /**
     * @Given I have access to the home page URL
     */
    public function iHaveAccessToTheHomePageUrl()
    {
        throw new PendingException();
    }

    /**
     * @When I visit the home page
     */
    public function iVisitTheHomePage()
    {
        throw new PendingException();
    }

    /**
     * @Then I should see the Symfony Logo
     */
    public function iShouldSeeTheSymfonyLogo()
    {
        throw new Exception();
    }
}
```

6. In the `iShouldSeeTheSymfonyLogo()` method, replace the `PendingException` class with just an `Exception` class.

7. Great! Now, let's run Behat again, and see what we get:

```
/var/www/html/behat# ./vendor/bin/behat features/home.
feature
```

Since the automatically generated snippets return a `PendingException` object, we'll get the following result from Behat:

```
root@0cb77fcadb5f:/var/www/html/behat# ./vendor/bin/behat features/home.feature
Feature: Home page
  In order to welcome visitors
  As a visitor
  I need to be able to see the Symfony logo and welcome message

  Scenario: See the Symfony logo              # features/home.feature:6
    Given I have access to the home page URL  # HomeContext::iHaveAccessToTheHomePageUrl()
    When I visit the home page                # HomeContext::iVisitTheHomePage()
    Then I should see the Symfony logo        # HomeContext::iShouldSeeTheSymfonyLogo()
      (Exception)

--- Failed scenarios:

    features/home.feature:6

1 scenario (1 failed)
3 steps (2 passed, 1 failed)
0m0.06s (9.23Mb)
root@0cb77fcadb5f:/var/www/html/behat#
```

Figure 6.6 – Behat with automatically generated PHP snippets

We should now see the warm and comforting failed test message. So far, we were able to use Gherkin to define our feature. Then, we created a separate context class to house the methods that Behat will execute in relation to each of the `Given`, `When`, and `Then` steps we have defined using Gherkin. Then, we used Behat to automatically generate those methods. Now, how do make all these tests pass? Well, we can remove the exception we are throwing from the `iShouldSeeTheSymfonyLogo()` method! As you can see, this is all happening inside PHP land. But to really pass the test, we have to let Behat fire up a browser, visit the home page URL, and verify whether it can see the Symfony logo.

So, how do we do that? Remember when we installed Mink earlier? We will now have to use Mink and a browser emulator to do the browser work for us.

Browser emulators and Mink

Browser emulators are programs that emulate or mimic the functionalities and behaviors of a web browser. These emulators can then be used by another program, such as Behat or Codeception, to simulate what a real user would do on a web browser while using your application.

There are two types of browser emulators:

- **Headless**: These types of emulators fire HTTP requests and simply listen for the returned DOM or response from the web application. They will be best suited for lightweight testing, without the need for complicated checks such as checking for an AJAX response after a mouseover event.

- **Controllers**: These types of emulators use real browsers, and they basically act like a person who controls a real browser. The good thing about using these types of emulators, in my experience, is that we can set the type of browser we want to test with. We can also check for the JavaScript and AJAX results on a page.

In our example, we will use the headless browser as we won't need to do any JavaScript/AJAX actions. If you need to use a real browser emulator for your project, I highly recommend using Selenium2. You can read more about Selenium from the Selenium website at `https://www.selenium.dev`.

Next, to let our Behat application start interacting with a browser emulator, in place of a real user, create the following program files:

1. Open the `HomeContext.php` class we created earlier and replace it with the following content:

codebase/behat/features/bootstrap/HomeContext.php

```php
<?php

use Behat\Mink\Mink;
use Behat\Mink\Session;
use Behat\Mink\Driver\GoutteDriver;
use Behat\MinkExtension\Context\MinkContext;
use Behat\MinkExtension\Context\MinkAwareContext;

class HomeContext extends MinkContext implements
MinkAwareContext
{
    public function __construct()
    {
        $mink    = new Mink([
```

```
            'goutte'      => new Session(new
                GoutteDriver()), // Headless browser
        ]);


        $this->setMink($mink);
        $this->getMink()->getSession('goutte')->start
            ();
    }
}
```

In the constructor, we have instantiated an instance of Mink, which we injected with a `Session` object. We have injected a driver object into the session with an instance of the Goutte headless emulator. Mink supports different types of browser emulators; you can read more about them here: `https://mink.behat.org/en/latest/at-a-glance.html`.

Next, add the following functions inside the same class. These methods represent each of the steps you have defined in your scenarios:

```
    /**
     * @Given I have access to the home page URL
     */
    public function iHaveAccessToTheHomePageUrl()
    {
        return true;
    }


    /**
     * @When I visit the home page
     */
    public function iVisitTheHomePage()
    {
        // Using the Goutte Headless emulator
        $sessionHeadless = $this->getMink()->getSession
            ('goutte');
        $sessionHeadless->visit("symfony/public");
        $sessionHeadless->getPage()->clickLink('Create
your
            first page');
    }
```

```
/**
 * @Then I should see the Symfony Logo
 */
public function iShouldSeeTheSymfonyLogo()
{
    // Headless emulator test:
    $assertHeadless = $this->assertSession('goutte');
    $assertHeadless->elementExists('css', '.logo');
    $assertHeadless->pageTextContains('Welcome To
        Symfony 6');
}
```

Within the `iVisitTheHomePage()` method, we retrieved the Goutte-injected session we just created, and then we let the emulator visit the URL and click on a link.

2. Now, let's run the test and see whether it works! Run the following command:

    /var/www/html/behat# ./vendor/bin/behat

    You should then see the following result:

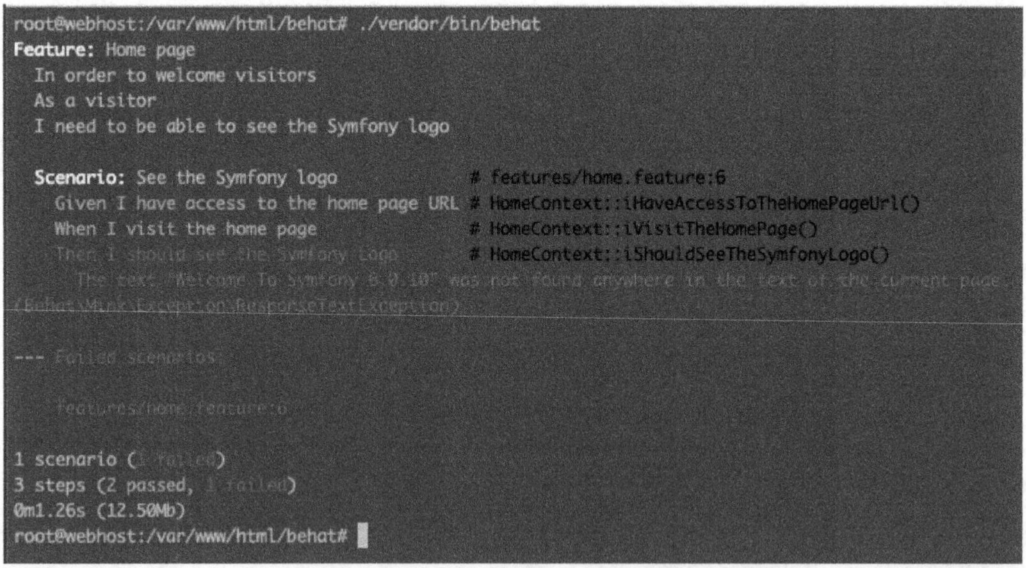

Figure 6.7 – Failed headless browser assertion

We failed the test again, but why is that? Notice that inside the `iVisitTheHomePage()` method, we have this line:

```
$sessionHeadless->getPage()->clickLink('Create your first page');
```

This line tells the emulator to click on the **Tutorials** option on the home page, which uses the **Create your first page** anchor text:

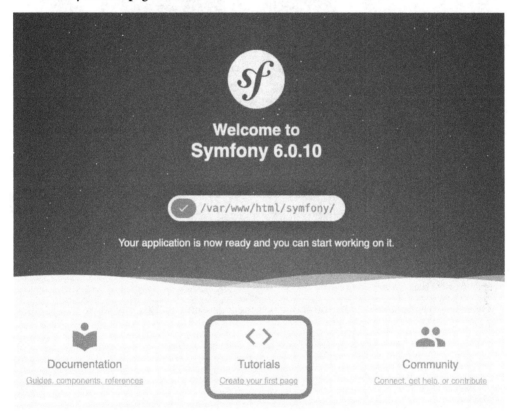

Figure 6.8 – Create your first page link

What happened was the emulator successfully loaded the Symfony home page, and then clicked on the tutorial link, and therefore the browser was redirected to a different page! That's why we failed the test. So, if we update the `iVisitTheHomePage()` method and remove the offending line, we should now be able to pass the test!

3. Run the test again by running the following command:

```
/var/www/html/behat# ./vendor/bin/behat
```

We should then see the following result:

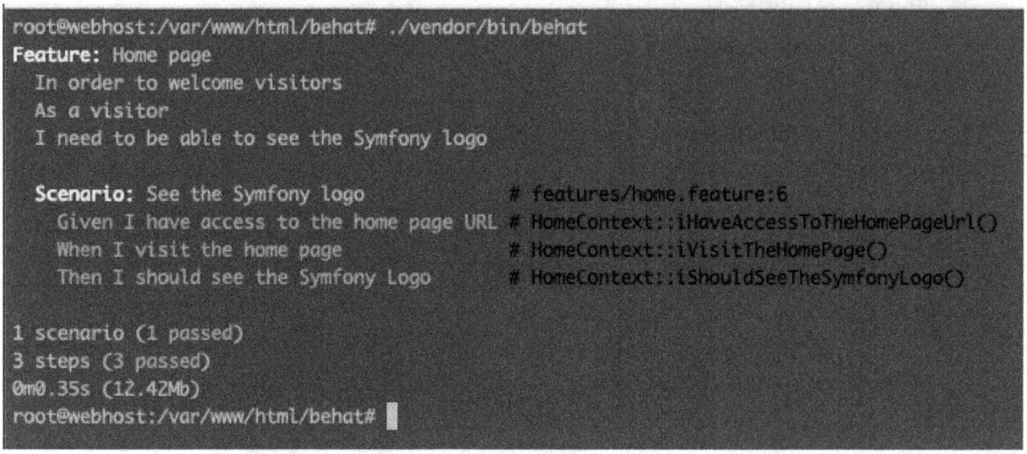

```
root@webhost:/var/www/html/behat# ./vendor/bin/behat
Feature: Home page
  In order to welcome visitors
  As a visitor
  I need to be able to see the Symfony logo

  Scenario: See the Symfony logo                    # features/home.feature:6
    Given I have access to the home page URL        # HomeContext::iHaveAccessToTheHomePageUrl()
    When I visit the home page                      # HomeContext::iVisitTheHomePage()
    Then I should see the Symfony Logo              # HomeContext::iShouldSeeTheSymfonyLogo()

1 scenario (1 passed)
3 steps (3 passed)
0m0.35s (12.42Mb)
root@webhost:/var/www/html/behat#
```

Figure 6.9 – The first Behat test passed

Great! We finally passed our first Behat test! In the `iShouldSeeTheSymfonyLogo()` method, you'll notice that we have two assertions. In the first assertion, we wanted to check whether an element exists in the returned DOM, which is the *logo* element. We then added another assertion to check for the **Welcome to Symfony 6** text.

4. Open your web browser and visit the following page: `http://127.0.0.1:8081/ symfony/public/`.

5. Open your element inspector; you should see the logo element. This is what we told Mink to look for:

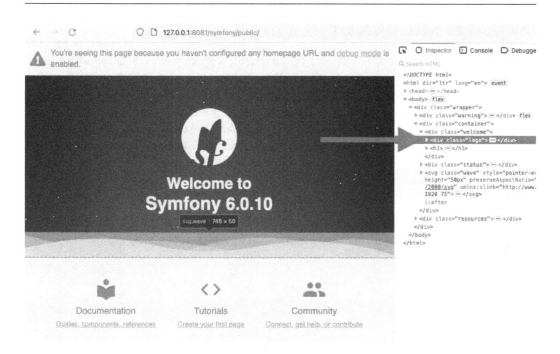

Figure 6.10 – Logo element

Since both the *logo* element and **Welcome to Symfony 6** text exists when the browser emulator visited the home page, it finally passed the test!

Now, I think you'll have an idea of how useful and powerful these tools can be. This can save you and your team hours of manual testing.

At this stage, you can start writing behaviors represented by features and scenarios using the Gherkin language, then use Behat to execute those tests, then develop features using PHP to satisfy those tests. If you follow this process, your development will be driven by the behaviors that were defined before writing a single line of code. Now, your development is behavior driven!

Why bother with Gherkin, then?

The example we used in this chapter is very simple, but you might be tempted to think that we can just skip the features written in the Gherkin language. Well, I did that too. I thought: it's not that useful. But when I started working on bigger projects, with bigger teams, with different companies working collaboratively on the same project and goal, I thought to myself: I wish there were a common format that we could share so that we all understand what the business is trying to achieve. I was working collaboratively with a third-party company, and I wanted to ask them whether I could borrow or get a copy of their test cases, but the thing is, they wrote down their test cases directly into their application, which is not written in PHP. I then realized how important it is to have some sort of a common language that we can use to understand the intended behavior of a system that is programming-language agnostic!

The following diagram represents how useful the Gherkin language is in being a platform-agnostic, intermediary language to represent how the intended software solution should behave:

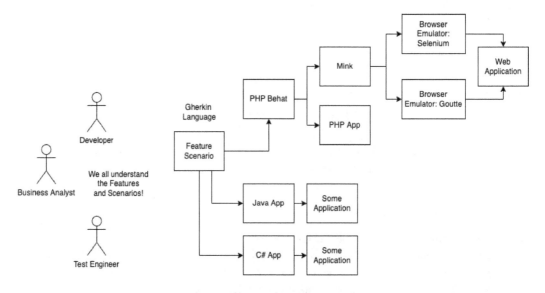

Figure 6.11 – Gherkin features and scenarios

By using a common language to define the intended features and scenarios in a project, we can easily coordinate with different teams that do not do any software programming at all. This is very important for a business. People across different teams will be able to collaborate and understand each other easier and quicker, and by doing so, the developers can also be more confident and certain that what they are building is correct. It might sound ridiculous, but I've seen a lot of projects go wrong simply because of a breakdown in communication between different teams in a business.

Summary

In this chapter, we defined and explained what BDD is and why we need it. By implementing BDD, we will be able to develop our solutions better to properly address the actual business goal. We can start defining these business goals using features and scenarios, written in the Gherkin language, which is just plain English. By doing so, different people from different teams in the company will be able to coordinate and understand each other better in defining the system's intended behavior. This will help bridge the gap and language barrier between different teams.

We created a feature and a scenario, then used Behat, Mink, and Goutte to define the intended system behavior, open a headless browser, visit the web application, and verify the content of the home page.

This is just the tip of the BDD iceberg. In the next chapter, we will start writing solution code while making sure that our code is maintainable and testable by using BDD and TDD together.

Building Solution Code with BDD and TDD

Now that we have gone through the fundamentals of writing test programs using **test-driven development (TDD)** and **behavior-driven development (BDD)**, we can start using both processes in developing our example application. When working on commercially successful and large-scale applications, one thing is common: they all need maintenance. There will always be room for improvement in terms of the product's functionality. There could be some bugs that were missed, and—more commonly—more features to improve the product will continuously be added to the application. This is usually how badly written code gets worse. A nicely written class can end up being a god class: a class that can do everything with a few thousand lines of code. A developer can start writing additional functions inside the god class while another developer is using that class, therefore changing the class's behavior. You can guess what happens next! A new bug is introduced.

There are a lot of times during development when a developer may start working on a feature that will depend on other features that are not written yet. So, how do we write tests for these types of features? We'll need to start mocking those dependencies. In this chapter, we will learn how to use mock objects and we will also start writing our code so that it will be cleaner and easier to maintain by following the SOLID principles. We will also be using the Red-Green-Refactor pattern to help us lay down the tests and features that we need to build. But before all that, we'll first create a Behat feature to kickstart all of the tests and code we'll be writing.

In this chapter, we will go through the following topics:

- Implementing the Red-Green-Refactor pattern
- Writing tests and solution code for the example project
- Creating a Behat feature based on a Jira ticket
- Passing the Behat registration feature

Technical requirements

In this chapter, you are advised to use the following base code from this code repository: `https://github.com/PacktPublishing/Test-Driven-Development-with-PHP-8/tree/main/Chapter%207/base/phptdd`. After completing the chapter, the resulting solution code can be found at `https://github.com/PacktPublishing/Test-Driven-Development-with-PHP-8/tree/main/Chapter%207/complete` for reference.

Preparing the development environment for the chapter

First, get the base code for this chapter found at `https://github.com/PacktPublishing/Test-Driven-Development-with-PHP-8/tree/main/Chapter%207/base` or simply run the following command:

```
curl -Lo phptdd.zip "https://github.com/PacktPublishing/Test-
Driven-Development-with-PHP-8/raw/main/Chapter%207/base.zip" &&
unzip -o phptdd.zip && cd base && ./demoSetup.sh
```

To run the containers and execute the commands in this chapter, you should be inside the `docker-server-web-1` container.

Run the following command to confirm the container name for our web server:

```
docker ps
```

To run the containers, run the following command from the `/docker` directory from the repository in your host machine:

```
docker-compose build && docker-compose up -d
docker exec -it docker-server-web-1 /bin/bash
```

Once inside the container, run the following commands to install the libraries required through Composer:

```
/var/www/html/symfony# ./setup.sh
/var/www/html/behat# ./setup.sh
```

Implementing the Red-Green-Refactor pattern

The Red-Green-Refactor pattern is a type of programming approach to implementing TDD. It's a cycle where you first deliberately write a failing test, in which you see a red-colored failing message when you execute the test. Then, you write solution code to pass that test, in which you will see a green-colored passing message. After passing the test, you can then go back to clean up and refactor your test and solution code.

If you open the `codebase/symfony/runDebug.sh` file that we created earlier in this book in *Chapter 5, Unit Testing*, you'll notice that we are running PHPUnit by adding the `--color=always` parameter. Then, whenever we run PHPUnit and we get a failing test, you will notice that we always get a red error or failed test message.

To demonstrate the pattern clearly, let's go through an example:

1. Create a new file called `HelloTest.php`:

---

codebase/symfony/tests/Unit/HelloTest.php

```php
<?php

namespace App\Tests\Unit;

use PHPUnit\Framework\TestCase;

class HelloTest extends TestCase
{
    public function testCanSayHello()
    {
        $this->fail("--- RED ---");
    }
}
```

2. After creating the new unit test, run the following command to make sure that PHPUnit can execute a `testCanSayHello` test:

```
/var/www/html/symfony# php bin/phpunit --filter
testCanSayHello --color=always
```

You should then see the following result:

```
root@webhost:/var/www/html/symfony# php bin/phpunit --filter testCanSayHello --color=always
PHPUnit 9.5.5 by Sebastian Bergmann and contributors.

Testing
F                                                                    1 / 1 (100%)

Time: 00:00.063, Memory: 10.00 MB

There was 1 failure:

1) App\Tests\Unit\ExampleTest::testCanSayHello
--- RED ---

/var/www/html/symfony/tests/Unit/ExampleTest.php:20

FAILURES!
Tests: 1, Assertions: 1, Failures: 1.
```

Figure 7.1 – Red highlighted failed message

In TDD, we always start by writing a test that will have no implementations to support or pass it. We then need to run the test to make sure that PHPUnit recognizes the test and that it can execute it. We also want to confirm that we've created the test class in the correct test suite and the correct directory and that it uses the correct namespace.

After running the command stated previously, this newly created test will fail as expected and PHPUnit will show a red colored error or fail message. This is the *Red* in the Red-Green-Refactor pattern!

Once we are sure that we can use PHPUnit to run a test, we can then move on to start writing code to pass our failing test. Remember TDD? Our test will start or drive the creation of the solution code to solve a problem, hence test-driven. So, now, to quickly pass the failing test, we will write some code to pass the failing test by following these steps:

1. Modify the test and add a new class:

Codebase/symfony/tests/Unit/HelloTest.php

```php
<?php

namespace App\Tests\Unit;

use App\Speaker;
use PHPUnit\Framework\TestCase;

class HelloTest extends TestCase
```

```
{
    public function testCanSayHello()
    {
        $speaker = new Speaker();
        $this->assertEquals('Hello' $speaker->
            sayHello());
    }
}
```

2. Create a new class:

codebase/symfony/src/Speaker.php

```php
<?php

namespace App;

class Speaker
{
    public function sayHello(): string
    {
        return 'Hello';
    }
}
```

In the `HelloTest` class, we have modified the `testCanSayHello()` method so that it will create an instance of the new `Speaker` class we created, and then, in the assertion line, we directly compare the expected word `Hello` to the string returned by the `sayHello()` method. Now, if we run the test again, we should no longer see the red failure message.

3. Run the same test by using the following command:

```
/var/www/html/symfony# php bin/phpunit -.-filter
testCanSayHello --color=always
```

We should now see the following result from PHPUnit:

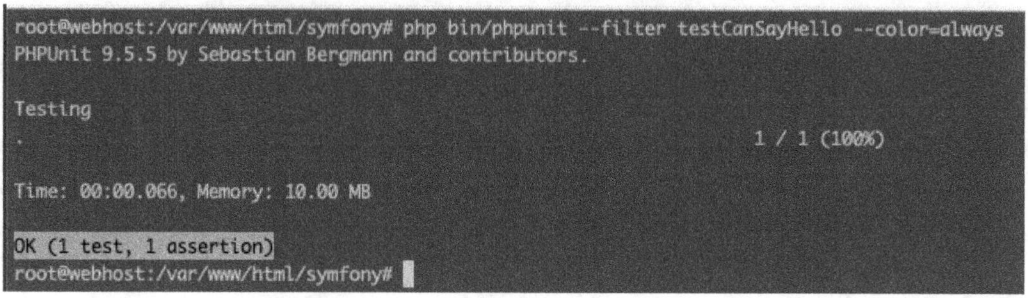

```
root@webhost:/var/www/html/symfony# php bin/phpunit --filter testCanSayHello --color=always
PHPUnit 9.5.5 by Sebastian Bergmann and contributors.

Testing

.                                                                    1 / 1 (100%)

Time: 00:00.066, Memory: 10.00 MB

OK (1 test, 1 assertion)
root@webhost:/var/www/html/symfony#
```

Figure 7.2 – Green highlighted message

We passed the test! Now, our testCanSayHello() test no longer returns a red error/failure message. We did the minimum work to pass the test, and we can now see a green **OK (1 test, 1 assertion)** message instead. This is the *Green* in the Red-Green-Refactor pattern.

When you're working on your own project, at this stage after passing a test, you can either move on to the next test or next problem in your list of things to do or you can try improving both the test and the solution code to make it cleaner and easier to read.

In this example, we'll go ahead and improve both the test and solution code to let it support more test scenarios.

Follow these steps:

1.   Modify the HelloTest class with the following content:

codebase/symfony/tests/Unit/HelloTest.php

```php
<?php

namespace App\Tests\Unit;

use App\Speaker;
use PHPUnit\Framework\TestCase;

class HelloTest extends TestCase
{
    /**
     * @param \Closure $func
     * @param string $expected
     * @dataProvider provideHelloStrings
```

```php
         */
        public function testCanSayHello(\Closure
            $func, string $expected)
        {
            $speaker        = new Speaker();
            $helloMessage   = $speaker->sayHello($func);

            $this->assertEquals($expected, $helloMessage);
        }


        /**
         * @return array[]
         */
        private function provideHelloStrings(): array
        {
            return [
                [function($str) {return ucfirst($str);},
                    'Hello'],
                [function($str) {return strtolower($str)
                    ;}, 'hello'],
                [function($str) {return strtoupper($str)
                    ;}, 'HELLO'],
            ];
        }
    }
```

2. Modify the `Speaker.php` class with the following content:

codebase/symfony/src/Speaker.php

```php
<?php

namespace App;

class Speaker
{
    /**
```

```
    * @return string
    */
    public function sayHello(\Closure $func): string
    {
        return $func('Hello');
    }
}
```

We have refactored the test so that we can add more flexibility to the `Speaker.php` class. We have also refactored the `HelloTest.php` test class itself to be more flexible as well. If we run the test again, we should still pass the test.

3.   Run the test again by running the following command:

```
/var/www/html/symfony# php bin/phpunit --filter
testCanSayHello --color=always
```

Now, we should see the following result:

```
root@webhost:/var/www/html/symfony# php bin/phpunit --filter testCanSayHello --color=always
PHPUnit 9.5.5 by Sebastian Bergmann and contributors.

Testing
...                                                               3 / 3 (100%)

Time: 00:00.065, Memory: 10.00 MB

OK (3 tests, 3 assertions)
root@webhost:/var/www/html/symfony#
```

Figure 7.3 – Still green after the refactor

You will notice that instead of getting **OK (1 test, 1 assertion)** because we only executed one test, we are now getting **OK (3 tests, 3 assertions)** instead. This is because we have refactored the test so that it can use `@dataProvider`. We then created a new function called `provideHelloStrings()` that returns an array of closures and strings. Each array set will be used as parameters for the `testCanSayHello()` test method. At this stage, we still pass the test, even after we have done the refactors. This is the *Refactor* phase of the Red-Green-Refactor pattern.

It will be very common in a real-world enterprise project to write programs that rely on someone else's project that is not readily available to you or your team. Should this stop you from developing your program that relies on something that is not complete yet? Probably not! Next, we'll need a way to focus on testing a specific part of our application, even if it depends on other objects that are not built yet. For this, we will need to use mock objects.

Writing tests and solution code for the example project

Back in *Chapter 2, Understanding and Organizing the Business Requirements of Our Project*, we used Jira as a tool to organize the list of things we need to build for the project. Aside from using Jira, there is other project tracking software out there too, or we can just simply use a notepad or a piece of paper and write down the tasks we want to write programs for. But we just want to be a bit more organized, and if you're working with a team of software developers and with other teams in the company, it's easier to collaborate if you use issue-tracking software, rather than a piece of physical paper.

We have grouped the Jira user stories into two groups: the **Inventory Clerk Solution** group and the **Visitors Page** group. These groups are called epics. We will start working on the **Inventory Clerk Solution** epic first. This is to allow the car museum inventory clerk to enter that valuable data into the system for the visitors to view.

Up to this point, as we were going through BDD and TDD, we were playing with our development environment setup as an example. Now, we can use it to build our example project too. Download the base code from `https://github.com/PacktPublishing/Test-Driven-Development-with-PHP-8/tree/main/Chapter%207/base/phptdd`. You can use the base code and push it into your master branch that is linked to your Jira project. Then, all subsequent tickets that we will be working on moving forward will branch off and get merged from and into that master branch.

Let's start with the first ticket, `TOYC-2`. Go back to your Jira **Roadmap** page and click on the `TOYC-2` story, then click on the **Create branch** link from the popup:

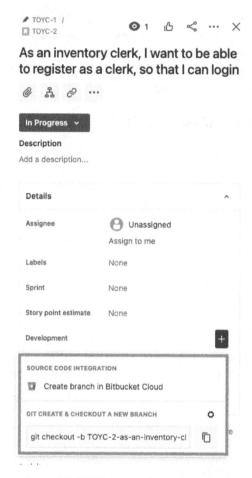

Figure 7.4 – TOYC-2 story: Create branch link

We'll need to create a new Bitbucket branch for this feature. This is where we will commit all additional code we will be building for this specific ticket. Ideally, you'll need to develop a branch that is branched off the master branch. We will then branch off the develop branch, and after we finish a feature, we will merge it back into the develop branch.

Create a new feature branch from the develop branch. Let's call this the TOYC-1 branch, which represents our **Inventory Clerk Solution** epic. Then, branch off the TOYC-1 branch and create a new feature branch—let's call it TOYC-2. Check out the TOYC-2 branch into your local development environment, and at this stage, you should have all the base files cloned into your local machine.

We will need to make sure that our containers are running. Run the following commands to build and run the containers.

Using your terminal, within the `docker` directory, run the following command:

```
$ docker-compose build && docker-compose up -d
```

After successfully running the containers, execute the following command, and make sure you can go inside the web container:

```
$ docker exec -it docker_server-web_1 /bin/bash
```

At this point, you should now see our main `behat` and `symfony` directories:

```
rainsarabia@Rains-MacBook-Pro docker % docker exec -it docker_server-web_1 /bin/bash
root@webhost:/var/www/html# ls -lap
total 12
drwxr-xr-x  5 root root  160 Aug 28 02:45 ./
drwxr-xr-x  1 root root 4096 Jan 26  2022 ../
-rw-r--r--  1 root root 6148 Aug 28 02:46 .DS_Store
drwxr-xr-x  6 root root  192 Aug 28 02:30 behat/
drwxr-xr-x 20 root root  640 Aug 28 02:45 symfony/
root@webhost:/var/www/html#
```

Figure 7.5 – behat and symfony root directories

At this stage, our development environment is running properly again. Next, we will create a Behat feature that will help us start the development of the software solution for the `TOYC-2` ticket.

Creating a Behat feature based on a Jira ticket

In the previous chapter, we learned how to create a simple Behat feature. In this section, we will create a new Behat feature that will represent the `TOYC-2` Jira ticket we created earlier, in *Chapter 2, Understanding and Organizing the Business Requirements of Our Project*. This will then help drive the development of the integration and unit tests that will help us build the actual solution code. Let's get started with the steps.

Create a Behat feature file, name it `inventory_clerk_registration.feature`, and save it with the following feature content:

codebase/behat/features/inventory_clerk_registration.feature

```
Feature: Inventory Clerk Registration
  In order to access the inventory system
  As an Inventory Clerk
  I need to be able to create a clerk account
```

```
Scenario: Access Registration Page
  Given I am in the home "/" path
  When I click the "Register" link
  Then I should be redirected to the registration page

Scenario: Register
  Given I am in the register "/register" path
  When I fill in Email "Email" with
      "clerk_email@phptdd.bdd"
  And I fill in Password "Password" with "password"
  And I check the "AgreeTerms" checkbox
  And I click on the "Register" button
  Then I should be able to register a new account
```

If you read through the Behat feature we just created, it is going to be very self-explanatory about what we are trying to achieve. These steps are the steps that a real-life user would do to be able to register to our system. At this point, we won't be building the solution code yet but will create Behat registration test code first.

Creating a Behat registration feature

Since we are using the base code for this chapter, we will have to make sure that we have all the libraries installed for us to be able to run Behat.

We need to install the Composer package again to be able to use Behat. Run the following command to reinstall the libraries needed:

```
/var/www/html/behat# composer install
```

This will then pull and install all the libraries we were using in the previous chapter. After the installation, let's see whether we can generate a Behat PHP class for our login feature:

1. Update the behay.yml file with the following content:

codebase/behat/behat.yml

```
default:
  suites:
    default:
      contexts:
        - FeatureContext
        - HomeContext
        - InventoryClerkRegistrationContext
```

2. After updating the behat.yml file, let's now try running this command to generate a PHP context class:

```
/var/www/html/behat# ./vendor/bin/behat --init
```

After running the command, we should have been able to generate a new PHP class in codebase/behat/features/bootstrap/InventoryClerkRegistrationContext.php.

3. Now, let's try to automatically generate PHP methods inside the InventoryClerkRegistrationContext.php class based on the inventory_clerk_registration.feature file.

Run the following command:

```
/var/www/html/behat# ./vendor/bin/behat features/
inventory_clerk_registration.feature --append-snippets
```

After running the command, you should see the following result:

```
root@webhost:/var/www/html/behat# ./vendor/bin/behat features/inventory_clerk_registration.feature --append-sn
ippets
Feature: Inventory Clerk Registration
  In order to access the inventory system
  As an Inventory Clerk
  I need to be able to create a clerk account

  Scenario: Access Registration Page                      # features/inventory_clerk_registration.feature:6
    Given I am on /
    When I click the "Register" link
    Then I should be redirected to the registration page

  Scenario: Register                                      # features/inventory_clerk_registration.feature:11
    Given I am on /register
    When I fill in "Email" with "clerk_email@phptdd.bdd"  # HomeContext::fillField()
    And I fill in "Username" with "clerk"                 # HomeContext::fillField()
    And I fill in "Password" with "password"              # HomeContext::fillField()
    And I check the "AgreeTerms" checkbox
    And I click on the "Register" button
    Then I should be able to register a new account

2 scenarios (2 undefined)
10 steps (7 undefined, 3 skipped)
0m0.23s (10.18Mb)

>> <snippet_undefined><snippet_keyword>default</snippet_keyword> suite has undefined steps. Please choose the
context to generate snippets:</snippet_undefined>

  [0] None
  [1] FeatureContext
  [2] HomeContext
  [3] InventoryClerkRegistrationContext
 > 3

u features/bootstrap/InventoryClerkRegistrationContext.php - `I am on /` definition added
u features/bootstrap/InventoryClerkRegistrationContext.php - `I click the "Register" link` definition added
u features/bootstrap/InventoryClerkRegistrationContext.php - `I should be redirected to the registration page`
 definition added
u features/bootstrap/InventoryClerkRegistrationContext.php - `I am on /register` definition added
u features/bootstrap/InventoryClerkRegistrationContext.php - `I check the "AgreeTerms" checkbox` definition ad
ded
u features/bootstrap/InventoryClerkRegistrationContext.php - `I click on the "Register" button` definition add
ed
u features/bootstrap/InventoryClerkRegistrationContext.php - `I should be able to register a new account` defi
nition added
root@webhost:/var/www/html/behat# ./vendor/bin/behat features/inventory_clerk_registration.feature --append-sn
ippets
```

Figure 7.6 – Autogenerating context methods

After running the preceding command, if you open the `codebase/behat/features/bootstrap/InventoryClerkRegistrationContext.php` class, you should be able to see the newly added methods. Now, if we run Behat, we'll probably get a failing result.

4. Run the following command:

```
/var/www/html/behat# ./vendor/bin/behat
```

You should see the following result:

```
root@webhost:/var/www/html/behat# ./vendor/bin/behat
Feature: Home page
  In order to welcome visitors
  As a visitor
  I need to be able to see the Symfony logo

  Scenario: See the Symfony logo                    # features/home.feature:6
    Given I have access to the home page URL # HomeContext::iHaveAccessToTheHomePageUrl()
    When I visit the home page                # HomeContext::iVisitTheHomePage()
    Then I should see the Symfony Logo        # HomeContext::iShouldSeeTheSymfonyLogo()
      Element matching css "img.logo" not found. (Behat\Mink\Exception\ElementNotFoundException)

Feature: Inventory Clerk Registration
  In order to access the inventory system
  As an Inventory Clerk
  I need to be able to create a clerk account

  Scenario: Access Registration Page                        # features/inventory_clerk_registration.feature:6
    Given I am on /                                          # InventoryClerkRegistrationContext::iAmOn()
      TODO: write pending definition
    When I click the "Register" link                         # InventoryClerkRegistrationContext::iClickTheLink()
    Then I should be redirected to the registration page # InventoryClerkRegistrationContext::iShouldBeRedirec
tedToTheRegistrationPage()

  Scenario: Register                                         # features/inventory_clerk_registration.feature:11
    Given I am on /register                                  # InventoryClerkRegistrationContext::iAmOnRegister()
      TODO: write pending definition
    When I fill in "Email" with "clerk_email@phptdd.bdd" # HomeContext::fillField()
    And I fill in "Username" with "clerk"                    # HomeContext::fillField()
    And I fill in "Password" with "password"                 # HomeContext::fillField()
    And I check the "AgreeTerms" checkbox                    # InventoryClerkRegistrationContext::iCheckTheCheckbo
x()
    And I click on the "Register" button                     # InventoryClerkRegistrationContext::iClickOnTheButto
n()
    Then I should be able to register a new account          # InventoryClerkRegistrationContext::iShouldBeAbleToR
egisterANewAccount()

--- Failed scenarios:

    features/home.feature:6

3 scenarios (1 failed, 2 pending)
13 steps (2 passed, 1 failed, 2 pending, 8 skipped)
0m0.22s (12.20Mb)
root@webhost:/var/www/html/behat#
```

Figure 7.7 – Behat failures

You will notice that we have failed the home feature, have skipped the pending tests, and at this stage, we can't even visit the home page. This is because we also must install the missing libraries for the Symfony application. Like what we did for Behat, let's install the missing Composer packages for the Symfony app.

5. Run the following command:

```
/var/www/html/symfony# composer install
```

6. After installing the missing Symfony packages, let's modify the InventoryClerkRegistrationContext.php class so that we throw an exception on the iAmOn method:

codebase/behat/features/bootstrap/InventoryClerkRegistrationContext.php

```
/**
 * @Given I am on \/
 */
public function iAmOn()
{
    throw new \Exception();
}
```

Now, let's try running Behat again and see whether we can at least pass the home page feature test.

7. Run Behat again by running the following command:

```
/var/www/html/behat# vendor/bin/behat
```

We should now be able to pass the **home page** feature test and still continue to fail the inventory clerk feature test:

```
root@webhost:/var/www/html/behat# ./vendor/bin/behat
Feature: Home page
  In order to welcome visitors
  As a visitor
  I need to be able to see the Symfony logo

  Scenario: See the Symfony logo                   # features/home.feature:6
    Given I have access to the home page URL  # HomeContext::iHaveAccessToTheHomePageUrl()
    When I visit the home page                 # HomeContext::iVisitTheHomePage()
    Then I should see the Symfony Logo         # HomeContext::iShouldSeeTheSymfonyLogo()

Feature: Inventory Clerk Login
  In order to access the inventory system
  As an Inventory Clerk
  I need to be able to login

  Scenario: Access Login Page                      # features/inventory_clerk_login.feature:6
    Given I am on /                            # InventoryClerkLoginContext::iAmOn()
      TODO: write pending definition
    When I click the "Login" link              # InventoryClerkLoginContext::iClickTheLink()
    Then I should be redirected to the login page # InventoryClerkLoginContext::iShouldBeRedirectedToTheLogi
nPage()

  Scenario: Authenticate                           # features/inventory_clerk_login.feature:11
    Given I am on /login                       # InventoryClerkLoginContext::iAmOnLogin()
      <Exception>
    When I fill in "Username" with "clerk"     # HomeContext::fillField()
    And I fill in "Password" with "password"   # HomeContext::fillField()
    And I click on the "Login" button          # InventoryClerkLoginContext::iClickOnTheButton()
    Then I should be able to access the Inventory system # InventoryClerkLoginContext::iShouldBeAbleToAccess
TheInventorySystem()

--- Failed scenarios:

    features/inventory_clerk_login.feature:11

3 scenarios (1 passed, 1 failed, 1 pending)
11 steps (3 passed, 1 failed, 1 pending, 6 skipped)
0m0.34s (12.60Mb)
root@webhost:/var/www/html/behat# █
```

Figure 7.8 – Home page feature passing, login failing

Because we have installed the missing Symfony packages, the home page test now passes. But since we have not built any solution code to pass the login test yet, it will continue to fail.

By following the Red-Green-Refactor pattern, now that we have a failing test, which is the Red phase, we can now move on to writing the solution code needed to pass this failing test, which is the Green phase.

Passing the Behat registration feature

Now that we have a couple of failing Behat tests for the login feature, let's try to do the minimum amount of work to complete the feature, and pass the tests. Luckily, Symfony makes it easy to implement security. We can use the `symfony/security-bundle` Composer package to add authentication and authorization to our application, without having to build everything from scratch.

You can read more about Symfony's security documentation at `https://symfony.com/doc/current/security.html`.

To pass the failing Behat registration feature, as Behat simulates a user using a web browser, we will have to create all the programs needed for a real user to be able to register an account in our application from the web browser, which then hits the controllers, the services, and then down to the database persistence process. Let's start with the controllers.

Writing failing controller tests

Before passing our main Behat feature tests, which can also be considered functional tests, let's write some controller tests inside our Symfony application itself. Although the Behat tests will also run tests against the controllers, these Symfony controller tests will be less complex than the Behat feature tests.

By reading the Behat registration feature we created earlier, we can easily identify that we need two controllers at the very least: a home page controller and a registration page controller. The home page is where the user starts the journey, and the registration page is where the clerk registers for a new account.

Create home page test classes with the following content:

codebase/symfony/tests/ Integration /Controller/HomeControllerTest.php

```php
<?php

namespace App\Tests\Integration\Controller;

use Symfony\Bundle\FrameworkBundle\Test\WebTestCase;

class HomeControllerTest extends WebTestCase
{
    public function testCanLoadIndex(): void
    {
        $client = static::createClient();
        $client->request('GET', '/');

        $this->assertResponseIsSuccessful();
    }
}
```

Next, create a registration page test class with the following content:

codebase/symfony/tests/ Integration /Controller/RegistrationControllerT-est.php

```php
<?php

namespace App\Tests\Integration\Controller;

use Symfony\Bundle\FrameworkBundle\Test\WebTestCase;

class RegistrationControllerTest extends WebTestCase
{
    public function testCanLoadRegister(): void
    {
        $client = static::createClient();
        $client->request('GET', '/register');

        $this->assertResponseIsSuccessful();
        $this->markTestIncomplete();
    }
}
```

Now that we have tests for the main controllers that we'll be using to pass the Behat feature tests, let's first see whether we pass these Symfony tests.

Run the following command:

```
/var/www/html/symfony# php bin/phpunit --testsuite Functional
```

After running the tests, you should get two failing tests. We used the --testsuite parameter so that we only execute the two controller tests we just created.

Now we know that we will have to pass these two tests, we can continue working on the solutions to pass them. At this stage, we are in the "Red" phase of the Red-Green-Refactor pattern we discussed earlier in the chapter.

We can now start working on the registration and registration solution first.

Implementing a registration solution using Symfony

The great thing about using open source frameworks is that there is a big chance of a lot of the software we developers need to build for our own projects having already been built as an open source library or package. And to pass our failing registration test, let's use Symfony's `security-bundle` package instead of writing everything from scratch.

Remember—as software developers, we don't simply develop code alone. We develop solutions. And if there are existing packages or libraries that can help you speed up the development of your solution, and if they fit your specifications, you can consider using them instead. Otherwise, you'll have to build the code from scratch.

You can read about Symfony's security solution on its official documentation page at `https://symfony.com/doc/current/security.html`.

We can use Symfony's security solution by running the following command:

```
/var/www/html/symfony# php bin/console make:user
```

Read the prompts and enter the default values suggested.

Next, we need to set up the databases we need. Remember—we are not only using one database, but we also need a separate test database as well. You can read more about this in *Chapter 5, Unit Testing*.

Database setup

We will need to create two databases: `cars` and `cars_test` databases. The `cars` database will serve as our main database, and the `cars_test` database will be like a replica database that our automated tests will use. After all, you don't want to run data mutation tests against your production database.

Run the following commands to set up our databases:

```
/var/www/html/symfony# php bin/console doctrine:database:create
--env=test
/var/www/html/symfony# php bin/console doctrine:database:create
/var/www/html/symfony# php bin/console make:migration
/var/www/html/symfony# php bin/console
doctrine:migrations:migrate -n --env=test
/var/www/html/symfony# php bin/console
doctrine:migrations:migrate -n
```

As we did in *Chapter 5, Unit Testing*, we have created our MySQL databases and tables based on the Doctrine entity found in the `codebase/symfony/src/Entity` directory.

Next, let's create a registration form using Symfony's `security-bundle` package.

Using Symfony's registration form

Next, we can use Symfony's registration form. The base solution code already has all the dependencies declared in the composer.json file, so you can just run the following command to generate the registration code:

```
/var/www/html/symfony# php bin/console make:registration-form
```

The preceding command will generate a few files—one of them is the RegistrationController. php class. If you open that class, you'll see that it has a register method. We also created a test for this controller and method. Let's see whether it now works.

Run the following command:

```
/var/www/html/symfony# php bin/phpunit --filter
RegistrationControllerTest
```

After running the test, we should now be able to pass this test:

```
root@webhost:/var/www/html/symfony# php bin/phpunit --filter RegistrationControllerTest
PHPUnit 9.5.5 by Sebastian Bergmann and contributors.

Testing
.                                                                    1 / 1 (100%)

Time: 00:00.924, Memory: 28.00 MB

OK (1 test, 1 assertion)
root@webhost:/var/www/html/symfony#
```

Figure 7.9 – Passing the register route test

At this stage, we are in the "Green" phase of the Red-Green-Refactor pattern. Does that mean we are done with the registration feature? Absolutely not. Since we are not completed with this test yet, usually I use PHPUnit's $this->markTestIncomplete(); method and add it to the test class. This can help remind developers that the test is written and the solution is partially there but is still incomplete. Go ahead and add the $this->markTestIncomplete(); method inside the testCanLoadRegister method in the codebase/symfony/tests/Functional/Controller/RegistrationControllerTest.php test class.

Now, run the test again:

```
/var/www/html/symfony# php bin/phpunit --filter
RegistrationControllerTest
```

You should see the following result:

```
root@webhost:/var/www/html/symfony# php bin/phpunit --filter RegistrationControllerTest
PHPUnit 9.5.5 by Sebastian Bergmann and contributors.

Testing
I                                                                    1 / 1 (100%)

Time: 00:00.071, Memory: 10.00 MB

OK, but incomplete, skipped, or risky tests!
Tests: 1, Assertions: 0, Incomplete: 1.
root@webhost:/var/www/html/symfony#
```

Figure 7.10 – Incomplete register route test

Now the test is marked as incomplete, and we can go back to it later. It's up to you whether you want to use this feature, but I find it useful when working on large projects. The only thing I don't like about this is that sometimes it doesn't grab my attention as much as a failing test would. For now, let's remove the **Incomplete** mark.

Creating a home controller

Now let's create a home controller where the users usually land first. Here, we will also find the **Register** link that the user will click to get redirected to the **Registration** page.

Create a home controller by running the following command:

```
/var/www/html/symfony# php bin/console make:controller
HomeController
```

After running that command, we should now have a new Symfony controller in `codebase/symfony/src/Controller/HomeController.php`. Edit the route inside the controller and replace `/home` with just a forward slash (`/`).

Now, let's see whether our controller tests now pass. Run the Symfony functional tests again:

```
/var/www/html/symfony# php bin/phpunit --testsuite Functional
--debug
```

You should now see the following result:

```
root@webhost:/var/www/html/symfony# php bin/phpunit --testsuite Functional --debug
PHPUnit 9.5.5 by Sebastian Bergmann and contributors.

Testing
Test 'App\Tests\Functional\Controller\HomeControllerTest::testCanLoadIndex' started
Test 'App\Tests\Functional\Controller\HomeControllerTest::testCanLoadIndex' ended
Test 'App\Tests\Functional\Controller\RegistrationControllerTest::testCanLoadRegister' started
Test 'App\Tests\Functional\Controller\RegistrationControllerTest::testCanLoadRegister' ended


Time: 00:00.971, Memory: 28.00 MB

OK (2 tests, 2 assertions)
root@webhost:/var/www/html/symfony#
```

Figure 7.11 – Passing controller tests

Since our controller tests are very simple, we are basically just testing whether the page response for the route is successful; we can now be sure that both tests pass. This will not satisfy the Behat registration feature test, though. So, let's continue working on it!

Let's modify the home controller's twig template content. Open the following file and replace the entire `example-wrapper` div content with the following:

codebase/symfony/templates/home/index.html.twig

```
<div class="example-wrapper">
    <h1>{{ controller_name }}</h1>
    <ul>
        <li><a href="/register" id="lnk-register">
            Register</a> </li>
    </ul>
</div>
```

We just added a link to the registration page. If you try to access the home page through the browser, you'll see something like this:

HomeController

- Register

Figure 7.12 – HomeController

Next, let's go back to our BDD test in the behat directory. Let's try to write some test code and see whether we can finally register a new user.

Passing the Behat feature

Our Behat registration feature simulates a user visiting the home page, clicking on the registration link, getting redirected to the registration page, filling up the registration form, clicking on the **Register** button, and then getting redirected to some elected page.

This is exactly like what a manual tester would do to test the registration feature. Instead of doing these steps manually using a browser, let's just use Behat to do all these steps for us.

Open the following Behat context file, and replace the content with the following:

codebase/behat/features/bootstrap/InventoryClerkRegistrationContext.php

```php
<?php

use Behat\Mink\Mink;
use Behat\Mink\Session;
use Behat\Mink\Driver\GoutteDriver;
use Behat\MinkExtension\Context\MinkContext;
use Behat\MinkExtension\Context\MinkAwareContext;

/**
 * Defines application features from the specific context.
 */
```

```php
class InventoryClerkRegistrationContext extends MinkContext
implements MinkAwareContext
{
    /**
     * Initializes context.
     *
     * Every scenario gets its own context instance.
     * You can also pass arbitrary arguments to the
     * context constructor through behat.yml.
     */
    public function __construct()
    {
        $mink = new Mink([
            'goutte'    => new Session(new GoutteDriver()), //
Headless browser
        ]);

        $this->setMink($mink);
        $this->getMink()->getSession('goutte')->start();
    }
}
```

In the preceding snippet, we started with the constructor. We declared the emulator and session objects we will use in the class.

Next, add the following code:

```php
/**
 * @Given I am in the home :arg1 path
 */
public function iAmInTheHomePath($arg1)
{
    $sessionHeadless = $this->getMink()->getSession
        ('goutte');
    $sessionHeadless->visit($arg1);

    // Make sure the register link exists.
    $assertHeadless = $this->assertSession('goutte');
```

```
        $assertHeadless->elementExists('css', '#lnk-register');
}


/**
 * @When I click the :arg1 link
 */
public function iClickTheLink($arg1)
{
    $sessionHeadless = $this->getMink()->getSession
        ('goutte');
    $homePage = $sessionHeadless->getPage();
    $homePage->clickLink($arg1);

}
```

The preceding code will simulate a user being on the home page, then clicking on the **Register** link.

In the next snippet, Behat will try to confirm that it got redirected to the register controller page:

```
/**
 * @Then I should be redirected to the registration page
 */
public function iShouldBeRedirectedToTheRegistrationPage()
{
    // Make sure we are in the correct page.
    $assertHeadless = $this->assertSession('goutte');

    $assertHeadless->pageTextContains('Register');
    $assertHeadless->elementExists('css', '#registration_form_
email');
}
```

You can easily check whether you're on the right page by checking the route, but the preceding snippet shows that you can inspect the DOM itself, returned by the controller.

Next, add the following code to mimic a user inputting values into input forms:

```
/**
 * @When I fill in Email :arg1 with :arg2
 */
public function iFillInEmailWith($arg1, $arg2)
```

```
{
    $sessionHeadless = $this->getMink()->getSession
        ('goutte');
    $registrationPage = $sessionHeadless->getPage();
    $registrationPage->fillField($arg1, $arg2);
}


/**
 * @When I fill in Password :arg1 with :arg2
 */
public function iFillInPasswordWith($arg1, $arg2)
{
    $sessionHeadless = $this->getMink()->getSession
        ('goutte');
    $registrationPage = $sessionHeadless->getPage();
    $registrationPage->fillField($arg1, $arg2);
}
```

In the preceding snippet, the code mimics entering text into the Email and Password fields. Next, we will simulate checking a checkbox and clicking on the **Submit** button. Add the following code:

```
/**
 * @When I check the :arg1 checkbox
 */
public function iCheckTheCheckbox($arg1)
{
    $sessionHeadless = $this->getMink()->getSession
        ('goutte');
    $registrationPage = $sessionHeadless->getPage();
    $registrationPage->checkField($arg1);
}


/**
 * @When I click on the :arg1 button
 */
public function iClickOnTheButton($arg1)
{
```

```
    $sessionHeadless = $this->getMink()->getSession
        ('goutte');
    $registrationPage = $sessionHeadless->getPage();
    $registrationPage->pressButton($arg1);
}
```

In the preceding code, we have checked the **Agree terms** checkbox, then clicked on the **Register** button.

Next, add the following code to complete the test:

```
/**
 * @Then I should be able to register a new account
 */
public function iShouldBeAbleToRegisterANewAccount()
{
    $sessionHeadless = $this->getMink()->getSession
        ('goutte');
    $thePage = $sessionHeadless->getPage()->getText();

    if (!str_contains($thePage, 'There is already an
        account with this email')) {
    $assertHeadless = $this->assertSession('goutte');
    $assertHeadless->addressEquals('/home');
}
```

Since, in the Symfony app, we are redirecting the user back to the home controller when successful, we can check whether we got redirected to the home page. You'll notice that it also checks whether the user already exists; you can break down this test further as much as you want so that you can separate scenarios like this.

What we did in the preceding code block is break down the scenarios inside the `codebase/behat/features/inventory_clerk_registration.feature` file into PHP methods. We then wrote PHP code to click links and buttons, populate text fields, check a checkbox, and more.

But let's see whether this works. Run the following command to run this test:

```
/var/www/html/behat# ./runBehat.sh --suite=suite_a features/
inventory_clerk_registration.feature
```

It will take a few seconds to execute, but you should get the following result:

Figure 7.13 – Registration feature test

By running the Behat test, we can replace a manual testing process usually done from a browser. But we need to confirm whether we were really able to register, and persist the data into our MySQL database using Doctrine ORM! At this point, we are in the "Refactor" phase of the Red-Green-Refactor pattern, and I personally think that the "Refactor" phase can be a bit more open-ended and open to interpretation.

You can use your own MySQL client or the phpMyAdmin app that we configured earlier, in *Chapter 3, Setting Up Our Development Environment Using Docker Containers*, to verify the data.

You will get the following result using the command line in the MySQL container:

Figure 7.14 – User successfully registered: view from the CLI

And this is the result using the phpMyAdmin application we configured, which can be accessed with a local browser at `http://127.0.0.1:3333`:

Figure 7.15 – User successfully registered: view from phpMyAdmin

We can see from the database that we were able to persist the registration details. At this stage, we can say that our registration functionality works! And we were able to test it without manually opening a desktop browser to enter form details.

We now have a PHP program doing the registration feature testing for us, but we also need to build the login feature and the most important part: the inventory system itself. We have a lot of other features to build, but this is a great start!

Summary

In this chapter, we started by creating an easy-to-understand list of features and scenarios detailing what needs to be built, based on a Jira ticket. Before working on the solution code, we first started with a Gherkin feature called **Inventory Clerk Registration**. This feature can be read by anyone—even non-developers will be able to understand it. This feature explains how our system should behave. We then took that behavior and created simple and failing functional tests inside the Symfony application. Creating these failing tests gave us a list of things we need to build. We then proceeded to develop the solution to pass these failing functional tests. And finally, we wrote code to tell Behat the intricate steps to click a link or a button, and fill up fields. BDD and TDD are not just about writing automated tests—it's about using them as a process to develop our solutions.

In the next chapter, we will continue building tests and solution code. We will go through the SOLID principles to help us structure our own code to make sure it is more maintainable and testable.

8
Using TDD with SOLID Principles

When I first started programming, I instantly got addicted to it. I felt so excited about the thought of coming up with a solution to a problem using programs and my own imagination. Back in school, there was a time when the instructor gave us the task of solving some simple algebraic challenges using Turbo-C. I had goosebumps and felt very excited as I quickly realized I could just write programs to solve these types of challenges repeatedly. Write the program once, pass different arguments, and get different results. I loved it. I remember a challenge to compute the height of a bridge if someone is standing on it, drops a ball, and hears a sound after several seconds. Easy! Now, I can just use my program to compute the height of the bridge for me repeatedly. Now, I don't have to keep remembering that the Earth's gravitational acceleration is at around 9.8 m/s2 – I can just declare it in the program! I learned that in programming, I can follow my own rules to get from point A to point B. Give me a task, and I can come up with a solution using my own imagination to finish the task. This, for me, is the best thing about programming. I was one proud spaghetti-code-writing machine. I didn't care about how clean my code was – I just needed to solve problems using code! Learning about other programming languages made me even more excited, and I thought the possibilities were endless – if the task or challenge did not defy the laws of physics, I thought it could be solved using programming! I did not pay attention to code cleanliness or maintainability. What are those? I don't need those!

When I started working professionally as a software developer, I continued with my mindset of just enjoying solving problems using programming. I didn't care how disorganized my solutions were – they solved the problems, and my employers and clients were happy. Done, I'm out of here. Too easy. I thought I knew everything and that I was unstoppable. Oh boy, I was so wrong. The more I learned, the more I realized how little I knew how to program.

As I continued working on more complex projects with other developers while having to maintain these projects, I learned the hard way how difficult I had made my life by writing code I couldn't easily maintain myself. I'm probably not the only developer on the planet to have experienced this problem. I was sure other people had encountered these issues before, and I was sure there were solutions out there. One of the solutions that helped make my life a lot easier was by trying to follow the **SOLID** principles by *Robert C. Martin*. They really helped change my programming life, and using these principles with **Test-Driven Development (TDD)** made my programming life even easier! There are more principles and architectural design patterns out there to help make your application more maintainable, but in this chapter, we will be focusing on the SOLID principles one by one while doing TDD.

We'll go through the process of interpreting a Jira ticket into a BDD test, which, in turn, will help us in creating our integration tests, down to the development of the solution code. Then, one by one, we will go through each of the SOLID principles by using TDD as you would do in a real project.

In this chapter, we will go through the following topics:

- Jira to BDD to TDD
- TDD with the Single-Responsibility Principle
- TDD with the Open-Closed Principle
- TDD with the Liskov Substitution Principle
- TDD with the Interface Segregation Principle
- TDD with the Dependency Inversion Principle

Technical requirements

In this chapter, the reader needs to use the base code from the repository found at https://github.com/PacktPublishing/Test-Driven-Development-with-PHP-8/tree/main/Chapter%208.

Preparing the development environment for the chapter

First, get the base code for this chapter found at https://github.com/PacktPublishing/Test-Driven-Development-with-PHP-8/tree/main/Chapter%206/base/phptdd or simply run the following command:

```
curl -Lo phptdd.zip "https://github.com/PacktPublishing/Test-
Driven-Development-with-PHP-8/raw/main/Chapter%208/base.zip" &&
unzip -o phptdd.zip && cd base && ./demoSetup.sh
```

To run the containers and execute the commands in this chapter, you should be inside the docker-server-web-1 container.

Run the following command to confirm the container name for our web server:

```
docker ps
```

To run the containers, run the following command from the /docker directory from the repository in your host machine:

```
docker-compose build && docker-compose up -d
docker exec -it docker-server-web-1 /bin/bash
```

Once inside the container, run the following commands to install the libraries required through composer:

```
/var/www/html/symfony# ./setup.sh
/var/www/html/behat# ./setup.sh
```

Jira to BDD to TDD

The SOLID principles, as defined by Robert C. Martin, are a set of coding guidelines or standards that help developers write more organized, decoupled, maintainable, extensible software. In this chapter, we'll go through them one by one, but we will try to simulate the process by working on a real project and then implementing each of the principles.

In this chapter, we will be writing solution code that will try to adhere to the SOLID principles, but before that, we need an example problem to solve. As we did in *Chapter 7, Building Solution Code with BDD and TDD*, we'll start with a Jira ticket, write some Gherkin features, write Behat tests, write integration and unit tests, and then write the SOLID-adhering solution code as depicted in the following flowchart:

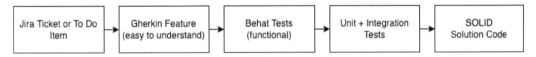

Figure 8.1 – Development flow

Let's use one of the Jira tickets we created in *Chapter 2, Understanding and Organizing the Business Requirements for Our Project*. We created a story to let a logged-in user input and save some toy car model data. This will be a nice simple feature to use to demonstrate the SOLID principles:

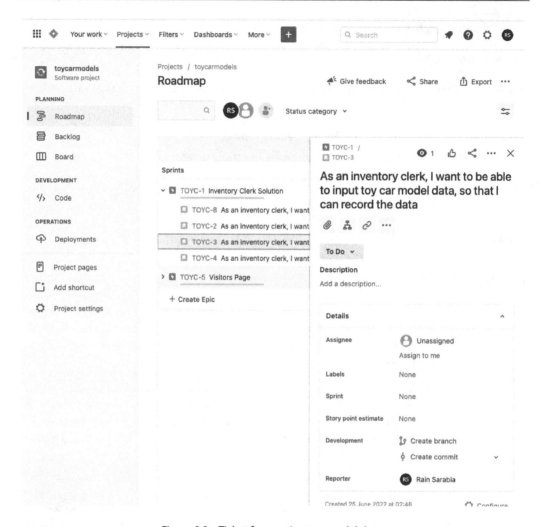

Figure 8.2 – Ticket for creating toy model data

As we did in *Chapter 7, Building Solution Code with BDD and TDD,* create a new git branch for your Jira ticket. Check out the git branch from the repository you set up in *Chapter 2, Understanding and Organizing the Business Requirements for Our Project,* and let's start writing some tests and programs!

Before we start learning about the SOLID principles, first, we need to work on the BDD tests that will drive us to write the solution code while trying to follow the SOLID principles. Remember, we always need to start with failing tests. Next, to start with BDD, we need to write a Gherkin feature first.

Gherkin feature

Let's start by writing a Gherkin feature to describe what behavior we expect to build. Create the following feature file with the following content inside the `behat` directory:

codebase/behat/features/create_toy_car_record.feature

```
Feature: Clerk creates new toy car record
   In order to have a collection of toy car model records
   As an Inventory Clerk
   I need to be able to create a single record


   Scenario: Create new record
      Given I am in the inventory system page
      When I submit the form with correct details
      Then I should see a success message
```

Now that we have our feature, let's generate the Behat PHP context class for it.

Behat context

We will now take the Gherkin feature and make a PHP context class for it. Follow these steps:

1. First, update the `behat.yml` file:

codebase/behat/behat.yml

```
default:
  suites:
    default:
      contexts:
          - FeatureContext
          - HomeContext
    suite_a:
      contexts:
          - InventoryClerkRegistrationContext
    suite_create:
```

```
contexts:
    - CreateToyCarRecordContext
```

2. After updating the main behat.yml file, run the following commands to create the PHP context class:

```
/var/www/html/behat# ./vendor/bin/behat --init
/var/www/html/behat# ./vendor/bin/behat features/
    create_toy_car_record.feature --append-snippets -
        suite=suite_create
```

3. There should now be a new class created in features/bootstrap/ CreateToyCarRecordContext.php. Refactor the iAmInTheInventorySystemPage method so that it throws \Exception.

4. Next, let's make sure we can execute this feature test by running the following command:

```
/var/www/html/behat# ./vendor/bin/behat features/
    create_toy_car_record.feature --suite=suite_create
```

You should then see the following test result:

```
root@webhost:/var/www/html/behat# ./vendor/bin/behat features/create_toy_car_record.feature --suite=suite_crea
te
Feature: Clerk creates new toy car record
  In order to have a collection of toy car model records
  As an Inventory Clerk
  I need to be able to create a single record

  Scenario: Create new record                    # features/create_toy_car_record.feature:6
    Given I am in the inventory system page       # CreateToyCarRecordContext::iAmInTheInventorySystemPage()
      (Exception)
    When I submit the form with correct details   # CreateToyCarRecordContext::iSubmitTheFormWithCorrectDetails(
)
    Then I should see a success message           # CreateToyCarRecordContext::iShouldSeeASuccessMessage()

--- Failed scenarios:

    features/create_toy_car_record.feature:6

1 scenario (1 failed)
3 steps (1 failed, 2 skipped)
0m0.07s (8.98Mb)
root@webhost:/var/www/html/behat#
```

Figure 8.3 – Failed test

Good – now, we know that the Behat test for this feature can be executed and fails as expected, so let's move on to the Symfony application.

Functional test

The Behat test we created is already a functional test – do we still have to create a functional test inside the Symfony directory? I think this is optional, but it will help us to quickly run basic smoke tests – for example, if we want to quickly check whether our controller loads and doesn't encounter a fatal error. We don't need to run the bigger and slower Behat test to find that out:

1. Create the following test class with the following content:

codebase/symfony/tests/Functional/Controller/InventoryAdminControllerTest.php

```php
<?php

namespace App\Tests\Functional\Controller;

use Symfony\Bundle\FrameworkBundle\Test\WebTestCase;

class InventoryControllerTest extends WebTestCase
{
    public function testCanLoadIndex(): void
    {
        $client      = static::createClient();
        $client->request('GET', '/inventory-admin');
        $this->assertResponseIsSuccessful();
    }
}
```

2. After creating our controller test class, let's run the following command to make sure that PHPUnit can execute this test and that it fails:

```
/var/www/html/symfony# ./vendor/bin/phpunit --filter
    InventoryAdminControllerTest
```

After running the test, make sure that you get a test failure. Remember the red phase?

Great – we can forget about creating the controller for now. Let's move on to the integration tests. These tests will be used to develop the mechanism to persist the toy car model in the database.

Integration test

We will now need to start writing integration tests that will help us write the code to persist or create a new toy car model. After passing these tests, then we can go back to the Behat tests we created earlier and make sure they pass:

1. Create the following test class, with the following content:

codebase/symfony/tests/Integration/Processor/ToyCarProcessorTest. php

```php
<?php

namespace App\Tests\Integration\Repository;

use Symfony\Bundle\FrameworkBundle\Test\
    KernelTestCase;

class ToyCarProcessorTest extends KernelTestCase
{
    public function testCanCreate()
    {
        $this->fail("--- RED ---");
    }
}
```

2. After creating the test class, make sure that PHPUnit can recognize the new test class by running the following command:

```
/var/www/html/symfony# ./vendor/bin/phpunit --filter
ToyCarRepositoryTest
```

3. After running the command, you should see the familiar and soothing PHPUnit failure result:

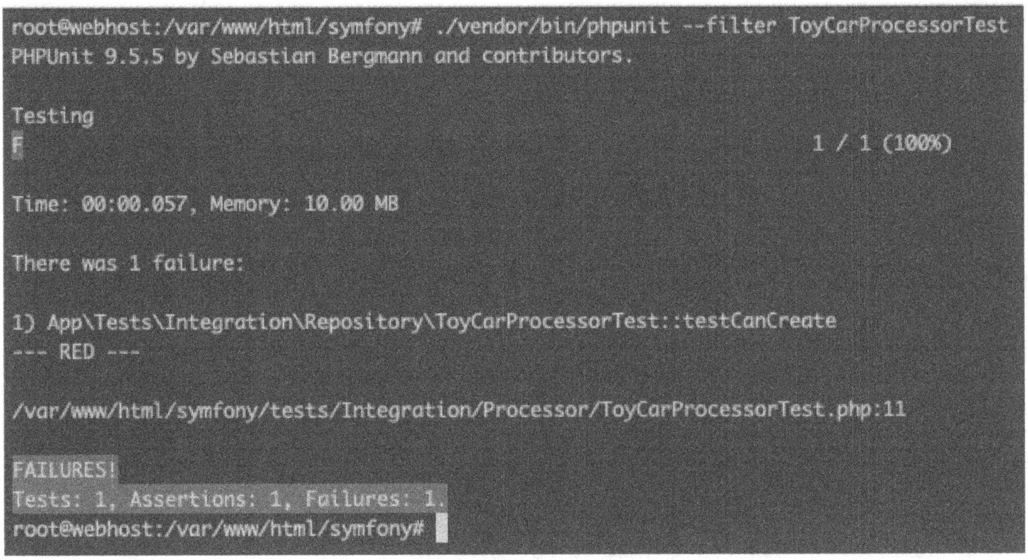

```
root@webhost:/var/www/html/symfony# ./vendor/bin/phpunit --filter ToyCarProcessorTest
PHPUnit 9.5.5 by Sebastian Bergmann and contributors.

Testing
F                                                                    1 / 1 (100%)

Time: 00:00.057, Memory: 10.00 MB

There was 1 failure:

1) App\Tests\Integration\Repository\ToyCarProcessorTest::testCanCreate
--- RED ---

/var/www/html/symfony/tests/Integration/Processor/ToyCarProcessorTest.php:11

FAILURES!
Tests: 1, Assertions: 1, Failures: 1.
root@webhost:/var/www/html/symfony#
```

Figure 8.4 – Failing processor test

Now that we have a failing integration test, let's build the code to pass it. We want to be able to persist a new toy car model into the persistence layer which is our database. Do we even have a DB table for it? Nope, not yet. But we don't care. We can continue working on the solution code. Next, we will be trying to follow the **Single-Responsibility Principle** (**SRP**) to write our solution code.

TDD with the Single-Responsibility Principle

Let's start with what I think is one of the most important principles in the SOLID principles. Are you familiar with god classes or objects – where one class can do almost everything? A single class for login, registration, displaying registered users, and so on? If there are two developers working on the same god class, can you already imagine how challenging that can be? And what happens after you deploy it to production and then an issue is found in the part where you display a list of registered users? You will have to change or fix that god class, but now the same class for login and registration has been modified and these processes may be compromised too. You run a bigger risk of introducing regressions to your login and registration functionalities by just trying to fix the list of registered users. You fix one feature, and there's a greater risk of breaking other features.

This is where the SRP will start to make sense. The SRP mandates that a class should only have one main responsibility, and one reason to be changed. Is it that simple? Sometimes not. A `Login` class should only know about letting a user log in, and not have the program responsible for displaying a list of registered users or checking out a shopping cart, but sometimes where to draw the line can become very subjective.

Next, we'll start writing the actual solution code while trying to implement the SRP.

Writing the solution code

We have a failing test that tests whether our application can create a toy car model and persist it in the database, but we don't even have a database table for it yet. It's okay – we will only focus on the PHP side of things for now.

Model class

It's better for our processor PHP class to deal with objects and not to directly know about database table rows and so on. Let's create a **Plain Old PHP Object** (**POPO**) that will represent what a toy car model is, without caring about the database structure:

1. Create the following file with the following content:

codebase/symfony/src/Model/ToyCar.php

```php
<?php

namespace App\Model;

class ToyCar
{
    /**
     * @var int
     */
    private $id;

    /**
     * @var string
     */
    private $name;

    /**
     * @var CarManufacturer
     */
    private $manufacturer;
```

```
    /**
     * @var ToyColor
     */
    private $colour;

    /**
     * @var int
     */
    private $year;
}
```

After declaring the properties, it's best to generate the accessors and mutators for all of these properties, rather than accessing them directly.

As you can see, this is just a POPO class. Nothing fancy. No information whatsoever about how to persist it in our database. Its responsibility is just to be a model that represents what a toy car is.

2. Let's also create the `CarManufacturer` and `ToyColor` models. Create the following classes with the following content:

codebase/symfony/src/Model/ToyColor.php

```php
<?php

namespace App\Model;

class ToyColor
{
    /**
     * @var int
     */
    private $id;

    /**
     * @var string
     */
    private $name;
}
```

After declaring the properties, generate the accessors and mutators for the class.

3. See the following for the car manufacturer:

codebase/symfony/src/Model/CarManufacturer.php

```php
<?php

namespace App\Model;

class CarManufacturer
{
    /**
     * @var int
     */
    private $id;

    /**
     * @var string
     */
    private $name;
}
```

Now, generate the accessors and mutators for this class as well.

Now, we have the main `ToyCar` model, which is also using the `ToyColor` and `CarManufacturer` models. As you can see, as with the `ToyCar` model, these two classes are not responsible for persisting or reading data either.

As you remember, we are using the Doctrine ORM as a tool to interact with our database. We can also use Doctrine entities directly in our processor class if we want to, but that would mean that our processor class would now be using a class that has a dependency on Doctrine. What if we need to use a different ORM? To keep things a little bit less coupled, we will just use `codebase/symfony/src/Model/ToyCar.php` in the processor class we will be creating next.

Processor class

For us to create and persist a toy car model, we will need a class that will need to process it for us. The thing is, we still don't have a database at this stage – where do we persist the toy car model? For now, nowhere, but we can still pass the test:

1. Create the following interface with the following content:

codebase/symfony/src/DAL/Writer/WriterInterface.php

```php
<?php

namespace App\DAL\Writer;

interface WriterInterface
{
    /**
     * @param $model
     * @return bool
     */
    public function write($model): bool;
}
```

We created a very simple interface that our data-writer objects can implement. We'll then use this interface for our processor class.

2. Now, let's create the toy car workflow or processor class. Create the following class with the following content:

codebase/symfony/src/Processor/ToyCarProcessor.php

```php
<?php

namespace App\Processor;

use App\DAL\Writer\WriterInterface;
use App\Model\ToyCar;
use App\Validator\ToyCarValidationException;

class ToyCarProcessor
{
    /**
     * @var WriterInterface
     */
    private $dataWriter;
```

```php
/**
 * @param ToyCar $toyCar
 * @return bool
 * @throws ToyCarValidationException
 */
public function create(ToyCar $toyCar)
{
    // Do some validation here
    $this->validate($toyCar);

    // Write the data
    $result = $this->getDataWriter()->
        write($toyCar);

    // Do other stuff.

    return $result;
}

/**
 * @param ToyCar $toyCar
 * @throws ToyCarValidationException
 */
public function validate(ToyCar $toyCar)
{
    if (is_null($toyCar->getName())) {
        throw new ToyCarValidationException
            ('Invalid Toy Car Data');
    }
}

/**
 * @return WriterInterface
 */
public function getDataWriter(): WriterInterface
```

```
    {
        return $this->dataWriter;
    }


    /**
     * @param WriterInterface $dataWriter
     */
    public function setDataWriter(WriterInterface
        $dataWriter): void
    {
        $this->dataWriter = $dataWriter;
    }
}
```

We have created a processor class that has a `create` method that accepts the toy car model we created previously, and then tries to write the model using an instance of a writer class that doesn't exist. What if another developer in your company is working on the data-writer class and it will take him 2 weeks to complete it? Do you wait for 2 weeks to pass your integration test?

If your processor class must validate the data and do other things after the data has been written into the database, should those programs be delayed too just because you are waiting for the other developer to complete their work? Probably not! We can use test doubles to replace the missing dependencies for now.

Test doubles

Most of the time, it's just difficult or impractical to be able to run a test against a feature with all its dependencies already built. Sometimes, we need to have a solution to be able to test the specific feature we want, even if we have not built the other dependencies yet, or simply want to isolate or only focus our test on a certain feature. Here, we can use test doubles. You can read more about test doubles for PHPUnit at `https://phpunit.readthedocs.io/en/9.5/test-doubles.html`.

Mock and Stub

The processor class we just created needs a concrete instance of `ToyValidatorInterface` and `WriterInterface`. Since we have not created those classes yet, we can still proceed in passing the test just by using a `Mock` object. In PHPUnit, the `Mock` object is an interface that extends the `Stub` interface. This means that in the code, a `Mock` object is an implementation of a `Stub` interface. The process of replacing the instances of `ToyValidatorInterface` and `WriterInterface` with a Mock object and setting a return value when a specific method is executed is called stubbing. Let's try it for real:

1. Go back to the ToyCarProcessorTest class and refactor it with the following content:

codebase/symfony/tests/Integration/Processor/ToyCarProcessorTest.php

```php
<?php

namespace App\Tests\Integration\Repository;

use App\DAL\Writer\WriterInterface;
use App\Model\CarManufacturer;
use App\Model\ToyCar;
use App\Model\ToyColor;
use App\Processor\ToyCarProcessor;
use Symfony\Bundle\FrameworkBundle\Test\
    KernelTestCase;

class ToyCarProcessorTest extends KernelTestCase
{
    /**
     * @param ToyCar $toyCarModel
     * @throws \App\Validator
     *     \ToyCarValidationException
     * @dataProvider provideToyCarModel
     */
    public function testCanCreate
        (ToyCar $toyCarModel): void
    {
        // Mock: Data writer
        $toyWriterStub = $this->createMock
            (WriterInterface::class);
        $toyWriterStub
            ->method('write')
            ->willReturn(true);
```

```php
        // Processor Class
        $processor = new ToyCarProcessor();
        $processor->setDataWriter($toyWriterStub);


        // Execute
        $result = $processor->create($toyCarModel);


        $this->assertTrue($result);
    }


    public function provideToyCarModel(): array
    {
        // Toy Car Color
        $toyColor = new ToyColor();
        $toyColor->setName('Black');


        // Car Manufacturer
        $carManufacturer = new CarManufacturer();
        $carManufacturer->setName('Ford');


        // Toy Car
        $toyCarModel = new ToyCar();
        $toyCarModel->setName('Mustang');
        $toyCarModel->setColour($toyColor);
        $toyCarModel->setManufacturer
            ($carManufacturer);
        $toyCarModel->setYear(1968);


        return [
            [$toyCarModel],
        ];
    }
}
```

In the `testCanCreate` function here, we are creating mock objects for the `ValidationModel`, `ToyCarValidator`, and `ToyCarWriter` classes. We then instantiate the main `ToyCarCreator` class while passing the mock `ToyCarValidator` and `ToyCarWriter` classes into its constructor. This is called dependency injection, which will be discussed further later in the chapter. Lastly, we then run the `ToyCarCreator`'s `create` method to simulate a developer trying to create a new toy car record:

2. Let's run the test by entering the following command and see what result we get:

```
/var/www/html/symfony# ./vendor/bin/phpunit --filter
ToyCarProcessorTest
```

You should then see the following result:

```
root@webhost:/var/www/html/symfony# ./vendor/bin/phpunit --filter ToyCarProcessorTest
PHPUnit 9.5.5 by Sebastian Bergmann and contributors.

Testing
.                                                                1 / 1 (100%)

Time: 00:00.082, Memory: 10.00 MB

OK (1 test, 1 assertion)
root@webhost:/var/www/html/symfony#
```

Figure 8.5 – Passed the test using a stub

We passed the test, even though we have not really persisted anything in the database yet. It's very common in bigger and more complex projects that you'll have to rely on test doubles just to isolate and focus on your test even if other dependencies are either not built yet or are too cumbersome to include as a part of your test.

Now going back to the SRP, our `ToyCarProcessor` now has two responsibilities – to validate and create a toy car model. Equally, other developers are using your class's `validate` method. Let's refactor our code to redefine the focus and responsibility of our `ToyCarProcessor` class:

1. Rename the following classes:

    *   `ToyCarProcessor.php` to `ToyCarCreator.php`
    *   `ToyCarProcessorTest.php` to `ToyCarCreatorTest.php`

2. Next, let's refactor the `ToyCarCreatorTest.php` class. Open the following class and replace the content with the following:

codebase/symfony/tests/Integration/Processor/ToyCarCreatorTest.php

```php
<?php

namespace App\Tests\Integration\Repository;

use App\DAL\Writer\WriterInterface;
use App\Model\CarManufacturer;
use App\Model\ToyCar;
use App\Model\ToyColor;
use App\Processor\ToyCarCreator;
use App\Validator\ValidatorInterface;
use Symfony\Bundle\FrameworkBundle\Test\KernelTestCase;

class ToyCarCreatorTest extends KernelTestCase
{
    /**
     * @param ToyCar $toyCarModel
     * @throws \App\Validator
         \ToyCarValidationException
     * @dataProvider provideToyCarModel
     */
    public function testCanCreate
        (ToyCar $toyCarModel): void
    {
        // Mock 1: Validator
        $validatorStub = $this->createMock
            (ValidatorInterface::class);
        $validatorStub
            ->method('validate')
            ->willReturn(true);

        // Mock 2: Data writer
```

```php
        $toyWriterStub = $this->createMock
            (WriterInterface::class);
        $toyWriterStub
            ->method('write')
            ->willReturn(true);

        // Processor Class
        $processor = new ToyCarCreator();
        $processor->setValidator($validatorStub);
        $processor->setDataWriter($toyWriterStub);

        // Execute
        $result = $processor->create($toyCarModel);

        $this->assertTrue($result);
    }

    public function provideToyCarModel(): array
    {
        // Toy Car Color
        $toyColor = new ToyColor();
        $toyColor->setName('Black');

        // Car Manufacturer
        $carManufacturer = new CarManufacturer();
        $carManufacturer->setName('Ford');

        // Toy Car
        $toyCarModel = new ToyCar();
        $toyCarModel->setName('Mustang');
        $toyCarModel->setColour($toyColor);
        $toyCarModel->setManufacturer
            ($carManufacturer);
        $toyCarModel->setYear(1968);

        return [
```

```
                [$toyCarModel],
        ];
    }
}
```

As you can see, we added a new `Mock` object for the validation. I will explain why we must do that after we refactor the content of the `ToyCarCreator.php` class. Let's create a validator interface, and then refactor the `ToyCarCreator` class.

3. Create the following file with the following content:

codebase/symfony/src/Validator/ValidatorInterface.php

```php
<?php

namespace App\Validator;

interface ValidatorInterface
{
    /**
     * @param $input
     * @return bool
     * @throws ToyCarValidationException
     */
    public function validate($input): bool;
}
```

4. Open `codebase/symfony/src/Processor/ToyCarCreator.php` and use the following content:

```php
<?php

namespace App\Processor;

use App\DAL\Writer\WriterInterface;
use App\Model\ToyCar;
use App\Validator\ToyCarValidationException;
use App\Validator\ValidatorInterface;

class ToyCarCreator
```

```php
{
    /**
     * @var ValidatorInterface
     */
    private $validator;

    /**
     * @var WriterInterface
     */
    private $dataWriter;

    /**
     * @param ToyCar $toyCar
     * @return bool
     * @throws ToyCarValidationException
     */
    public function create(ToyCar $toyCar): bool
    {
        // Do some validation here and so on...
        $this->getValidator()->validate($toyCar);

        // Write the data
        $result = $this->getDataWriter()->write
            ($toyCar);

        // Do other stuff.

        return $result;
    }
}
```

Next, add the necessary accessors and mutators for the private properties we have declared in the class.

We renamed the class just to give it a more specific name. Sometimes, just naming the class to something else helps you clean up your code. Also, you will notice that we have removed the publicly visible validate class. This class will no longer contain any validation logic – it only knows that it will run a validation routine before it tries to persist the data. This is the class's main responsibility.

We still have not written any validation and data persistence code, but let's see whether we can still pass the test to test the main responsibility of the class, which is to do the following:

I.   Accept a `ToyCar` model object.

II.   Run a validation routine.

III.   Attempt to persist the data.

IV.   Return the result.

5.   Run the following command:

```
/var/www/html/symfony# ./vendor/bin/phpunit --filter
ToyCarCreatorTest
```

Now, you should see the following result:

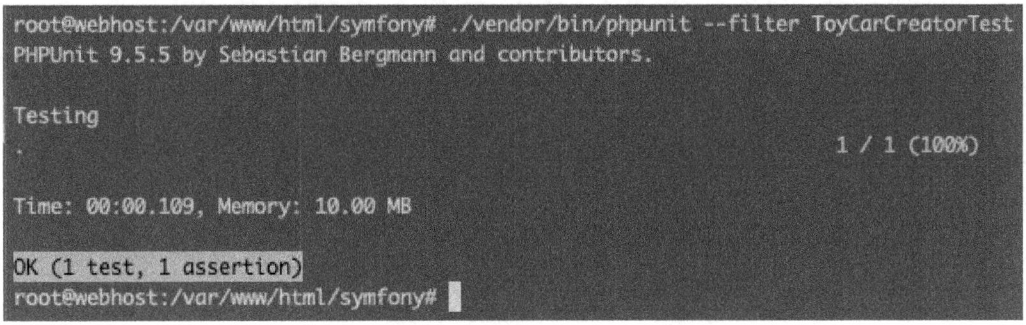

Figure 8.6 – Passing the test using two stubs

In this section, we used BDD and TDD to direct us into writing the solution code. We have created POPOs with a single responsibility. We have also created a `ToyCarCreator` class that does not contain the validation logic, nor the persistence mechanism. It knows it needs to do some validation and some persistence, but it does not have the concrete implementation of those programs. Each class will have its own specialization or a specific job, or a specific single responsibility.

Great – now, we can pass the test again even after refactoring. Next, let's continue writing the solution code by following the O in the SOLID principle, which is the **Open-Closed Principle (OCP)**.

TDD with the Open-Closed Principle

The OCP was first defined by *Bertrand Meyer*, but in this chapter, we will follow the later version defined by *Robert C. Martin*, which is also called the polymorphic OCP.

The OCP states that objects should be open to extension and closed to modification. The aim is that we should be able to modify the behaviour or a feature by extending the original code instead of directly refactoring the original code. That's great because that will help us developers and testers be more confident about the ticket we're working on, as we haven't touched the original code that might be used somewhere else – less risk of regression.

In our `ToyCarCreateTest` class, we are stubbing a validator object because we have not written a concrete validator class yet. There are a lot of different ways of implementing validation, but for this example, we'll try to make it very simple. Let's go back to the code and create a validator:

1. Create a new test class with the following content:

codebase/symfony/tests/Unit/Validator/ToyCarValidatorTest.php

```php
<?php

namespace App\Tests\Unit\Validator;

use App\Model\CarManufacturer;
use App\Model\ToyCar;
use App\Model\ToyColor;
use App\Validator\ToyCarValidator;
use PHPUnit\Framework\TestCase;

class ToyCarValidatorTest extends TestCase
{
    /**
     * @param ToyCar $toyCar
     * @param bool $expected
     * @dataProvider provideToyCarModel
     */
    public function testCanValidate(ToyCar $toyCar,
        bool $expected): void
    {
        $validator  = new ToyCarValidator();
        $result     = $validator->validate($toyCar);

        $this->assertEquals($expected, $result);
    }
}
```

```php
public function provideToyCarModel(): array
{
    // Toy Car Color
    $toyColor = new ToyColor();
    $toyColor->setName('White');

    // Car Manufacturer
    $carManufacturer = new CarManufacturer();
    $carManufacturer->setName('Williams');

    // Toy Car
    $toyCarModel = new ToyCar();
    $toyCarModel->setName(''); // Should fail.
    $toyCarModel->setColour($toyColor);
    $toyCarModel->setManufacturer
        ($carManufacturer);
    $toyCarModel->setYear(2004);

    return [
        [$toyCarModel, false],
    ];
}
}
```

After creating the test class, as usual, we need to run the test to make sure that PHPUnit recognizes your test.

2. Run the following command:

```
/var/www/html/symfony# ./vendor/bin/phpunit
--testsuite=Unit --filter ToyCarValidatorTest
```

Make sure that you get an error, as we have not created the validator class yet. Remember the red phase? You'll notice that in the data provider, we have set an empty string for the name. We will make the validator class return `false` whenever it sees an empty string for the toy car name.

3. Now, that we have the failing test, let's proceed with creating the class to pass it. Create a new PHP class with the following content:

codebase/symfony/src/Validator/ToyCarValidator.php

```php
<?php

namespace App\Validator;

use App\Model\ToyCar;

class ToyCarValidator
{
    public function validate(ToyCar $toyCar): bool
    {
        if (!$toyCar->getName()) {
            return false;
        }

        return true;
    }
}
```

We have created a very simple validation logic where we only check for the toy car's name if it's not an empty string. Now, let's run the test again.

4. Run the following command:

```
/var/www/html/symfony# ./runDebug.sh --testsuite=Unit
--filter ToyCarValidatorTest
```

You should now see a passing test.

Okay, so for now, we can make sure that the toy car model's name should always be a string that is not empty – but here's the thing, what if we want to add more validation logic? We will have to keep on modifying the ToyCarValidator class. That's not wrong. It's just that it's arguably better to follow the OCP so that we don't keep modifying our code – less class modification, less risk of breaking things. Let's refactor our solution code to pass the test again:

1. Let's add some validation logic for the year and retain the toy car name validation as well.

2. Right now, we are in the green phase, moving to the refactor phase. We'll be using polymorphism, which we discussed in *Chapter 4, Using Object-Oriented Programming in PHP*, instead of inheritance in this solution. Create the following interface with the following content:

codebase/symfony/src/Validator/ToyCarValidatorInterface.php

```php
<?php

namespace App\Validator;

use App\Model\ToyCar;
use App\Model\ValidationModel;

interface ToyCarValidatorInterface
{
    public function validate(ToyCar $toyCar):
        ValidationModel;
}
```

3. We created a new `ToyCarValidatorInterface` interface that will replace the `ToyCarValidator` concrete class. You will notice that the validate method returns an object – let's create that object too:

codebase/symfony/src/Model/ValidationModel.php

```php
<?php

namespace App\Model;

class ValidationModel
{
    /**
     * @var bool
     */
    private $valid = false;

    /**
     * @var array
```

```
        */
    private $report = [];
}
```

After creating the class, generate the accessors and mutators for the properties.

Instead of simply returning `true` or `false` on our validation program, we can now return an array containing the field name and validation result for that field name as well. Let's continue coding.

4. Create the following test class with the following content:

codebase/symfony/tests/Unit/Validator/ToyCarValidatorTest.php

```php
<?php

namespace App\Tests\Unit\Validator;

use PHPUnit\Framework\TestCase;
use App\Validator\YearValidator;

class YearValidatorTest extends TestCase
{
    /**
     * @param $data
     * @param $expected
     * @dataProvider provideYear
     */
    public function testCanValidateYear(int $year,
        bool $expected): void
    {
        $validator  = new YearValidator();
        $isValid    = $validator->validate($year);

        $this->assertEquals($expected, $isValid);
    }

    /**
     * @return array
```

```
    */
    public function provideYear(): array
    {
        return [
            [1,     false],
            [2005,  true],
            [1955,  true],
            [312,   false],
        ];
    }
}
```

5. If you run this test, you will see four failures, as we have four sets of values inside the `provideYear` data provider. Run the test by running the following command:

    `/var/www/html/symfony# ./runDebug.sh --testsuite=Unit`
    `--filter YearValidatorTest --debug`

If the test fails, that's good. Let's proceed with the solution code:

1. Create the following solution class with the following content:

codebase/symfony/src/Validator/YearValidator.php

```php
<?php

namespace App\Validator;

class YearValidator implements ValidatorInterface
{
    /**
     * @param $input
     * @return bool
     */
    public function validate($input): bool
    {
        if (preg_match("/^(\d{4})$/", $input,
            $matches)) {
            return true;
```

```
        }

        return false;
    }
}
```

Now, we have a simple validation class for checking whether a year is acceptable for our car. If we want to add more logic here, such as checking for the minimum and maximum acceptable value, we can put all that logic here.

2. Run the following command again and see whether the tests pass:

```
/var/www/html/symfony# ./runDebug.sh --testsuite=Unit
--filter YearValidatorTest --debug
```

You should see the following result:

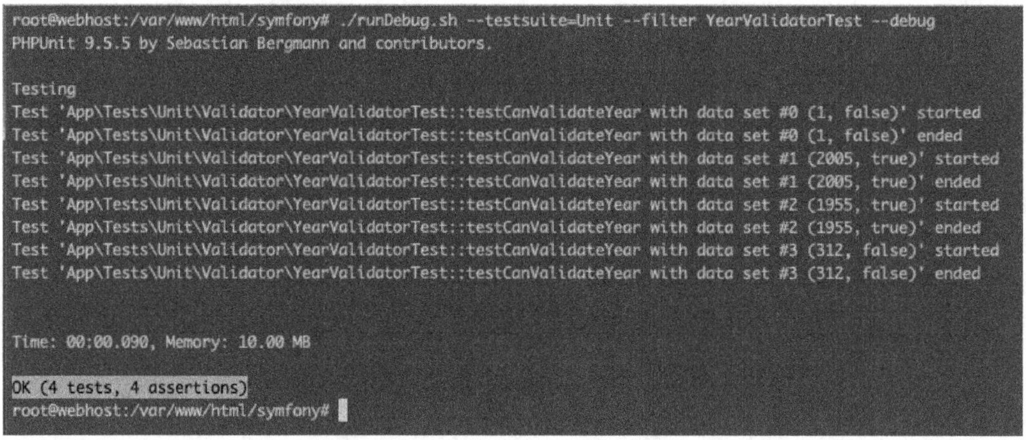

Figure 8.7 – Simple date validation test

Now that we have passed the very simple test for the year validator, next, let's move on to the name validator:

3. Create the following test class with the following content:

codebase/symfony/tests/Unit/Validator/NameValidatorTest.php

```php
<?php

namespace App\Tests\Unit\Validator;

use App\Validator\NameValidator;
```

```php
use PHPUnit\Framework\TestCase;

class NameValidatorTest extends TestCase
{
    /**
     * @param $data
     * @param $expected
     * @dataProvider provideNames
     */
    public function testCanValidateName(string $name,
        bool $expected): void
    {
        $validator  = new NameValidator();
        $isValid     = $validator->validate($name);

        $this->assertEquals($expected, $isValid);
    }


    /**
     * @return array
     */
    public function provideNames(): array
    {
        return [
            ['',            false],
            ['$50',         false],
            ['Mercedes',    true],
            ['RedBull',     true],
            ['Williams',    true],
        ];
    }
}
```

4. As with the year validator, if you run this test now, you will encounter multiple errors, but we have to make sure that it does fail or error out. Run the following command:

```
/var/www/html/symfony# ./runDebug.sh --testsuite=Unit
--filter NameValidatorTest
```

5. After running the command, you should see five errors. That's okay. Let's build the solution code for it now. Create the following class with the following content:

codebase/symfony/src/Validator/NameValidator.php

```php
<?php

namespace App\Validator;

class NameValidator implements ValidatorInterface
{
    public function validate($input): bool
    {
        if (preg_match("/^([a-zA-Z' ]+)$/", $input)) {
            return true;
        }

        return false;
    }
}
```

6. Now, we have a simple logic to validate a name. Let's run the name validator test again, and see whether it passes. Run the following command again:

```
/var/www/html/symfony# ./runDebug.sh --testsuite=Unit
--filter NameValidatorTest
```

You should now see five passing tests.

Let's summarize what we have added so far. We created two new validation classes, and both are working as expected based on our unit tests – but how is this better than the first solution we created? How is this relevant to the OCP? Well, first we need to tie things together and pass the bigger `ToyCarValidatorTest`.

7. Let's refactor the `ToyCarValidator` class with the following content:

codebase/symfony/src/Validator/ToyCarValidator.php

```php
<?php

namespace App\Validator;
```

```php
use App\Model\ToyCar;
use App\Model\ValidationModel as ValidationResult;

class ToyCarValidator implements
    ToyCarValidatorInterface
{
    /**
     * @var array
     */
    private $validators = [];

    public function __construct()
    {
        $this->setValidators([
            'year'  => new YearValidator(),
            'name'  => new NameValidator(),
        ]);
    }

    /**
     * @param ToyCar $toyCar
     * @return ValidationResult
     */
    public function validate(ToyCar $toyCar
        ValidationResult
    {
        $result     = new ValidationResult();
        $allValid   = true;

        foreach ($this->getValidators() as $key =>
            $validator) {
            $accessor   = 'get' . ucfirst(strtolower
                ($key));
            $value      = $toyCar->$accessor();
            $isValid    = false;
```

```
            try {
                $isValid = $validator->validate
                    ($value);
                $results[$key]['message']   = '';
            } catch (ToyCarValidationException $ex) {
                $results[$key]['message']   = $ex->
                    getMessage();
            } finally {
                $results[$key]['is_valid']   =
                    $isValid;
            }


            if (!$isValid) {
                $allValid = false;
            }
        }


        $result->setValid($allValid);
        $result->setReport($results);


        return $result;
    }
}
```

Then, generate the accessors and mutators for the $validators property.

8. You will notice that in the constructor, we are instantiating two validator classes, and within the validate method, we are using those validator classes. Each validator class will then have its own custom logic on how to run the validate method. Now, refactor the following test class with the following content:

codebase/symfony/tests/Unit/Validator/ToyCarValidatorTest.php

```php
<?php


namespace App\Tests\Unit\Validator;


use App\Model\CarManufacturer;
use App\Model\ToyCar;
```

```php
use App\Model\ToyColor;
use App\Validator\ToyCarValidator;
use PHPUnit\Framework\TestCase;

class ToyCarValidatorTest extends TestCase
{
    /**
     * @param ToyCar $toyCar
     * @param array $expected
     * @dataProvider provideToyCarModel
     */
    public function testCanValidate(ToyCar $toyCar,
        array $expected): void
    {
        $validator  = new ToyCarValidator();
        $result     = $validator->validate($toyCar);

        $this->assertEquals($expected['is_valid'],
            $result->isValid());
        $this->assertEquals($expected['name'],
            $result->getReport()['name']['is_valid']);
        $this->assertEquals($expected['year'],
            $result->getReport()['year']['is_valid']);
    }

    public function provideToyCarModel(): array
    {
        // Toy Car Color
        $toyColor = new ToyColor();
        $toyColor->setName('White');

        // Car Manufacturer
        $carManufacturer = new CarManufacturer();
        $carManufacturer->setName('Williams');

        // Toy Car
```

```
$toyCarModel = new ToyCar();
$toyCarModel->setName(''); // Should fail.
$toyCarModel->setColour($toyColor);
$toyCarModel->setManufacturer
    ($carManufacturer);
$toyCarModel->setYear(2004);

return [
    [$toyCarModel, ['is_valid' => false,
        'name' => false, 'year' => true]],
];
    }
}
```

9. Now, in this test, we are checking for the validity of the entire toy car model object, as well as checking which specific field of the toy car model has passed or failed the validation. Let's see whether the test passes. Run the following command:

    /var/www/html/symfony# ./runDebug.sh --testsuite=Unit
    --filter ToyCarValidatorTest

    Now, you should see the following result:

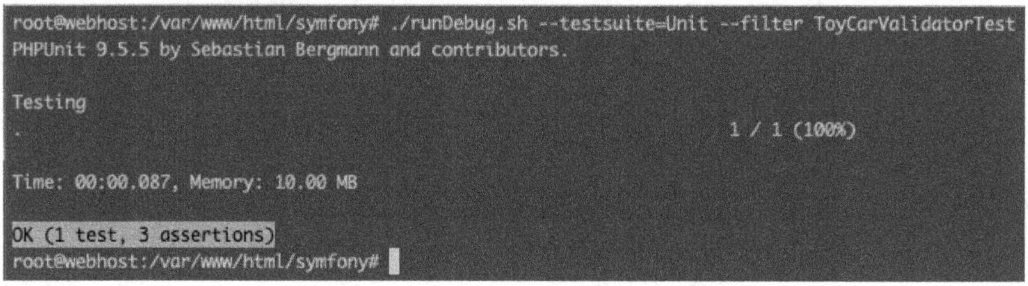

Figure 8.8 – Passing toy car validation test

You will notice that we passed three assertions. It looks like we are starting to get a test with more responsibilities. It's still better to do one assertion per test, just so that we don't end up having a god test class! For now, we'll move on.

Now, what have we achieved by refactoring? Well, first, we no longer have the validation logic for checking the validity of the toy name inside the `ToyCarValidatorTest` class. Second, we can now check for the validity of the year. If we want to improve the date and name validation logic, we won't have to do it in the main `ToyCarValidator` class – but what if we want to add more validator classes? Such as a `ToyColorValidator` class? Well, we can still do that without even touching the main class! We'll refactor `ToyCarValidator` and discuss how to do so later in the chapter in the *TDD with the Dependency Inversion Principle* section.

But what if we want to change the entire behavior of the `ToyCarValidator.php` class we created and change the logic entirely? Well, there's no need to modify it – we can just replace the entire `ToyCarValidator.php` class with a different concrete implementation of the `ToyCarValidatorInterface` interface!

Next, we'll talk about the **Liskov Substitution Principle (LSP)**.

TDD with the Liskov Substitution Principle

The LSP was introduced by Barbara Liskov. The way that I use it is that an implementation of an interface should be replaceable with another implementation of that interface without changing the behavior. If you are extending a superclass, the child class must be able to substitute the superclass without breaking the behavior.

In this example, let's try adding a business rule to reject toy car models that were built on or before 1950.

As usual, let's start with a test:

1. Open the `YearValidatorTest.php` class we created earlier and modify the test class with the following:

codebase/symfony/tests/Unit/Validator/YearValidatorTest.php

```php
<?php

namespace App\Tests\Unit\Validator;

use App\Validator\ToyCarTooOldException;
use PHPUnit\Framework\TestCase;
use App\Validator\YearValidator;

class YearValidatorTest extends TestCase
{
    /**
     * @param $data
     * @param $expected
     * @dataProvider provideYear
     */
```

```php
    public function testCanValidateYear(int $year,
        bool $expected): void
    {

        $validator  = new YearValidator();
        $isValid    = $validator->validate($year);


        $this->assertEquals($expected, $isValid);
    }


    /**
     * @return array
     */
    public function provideYear(): array
    {

        return [
            [1,     false],
            [2005,  true],
            [1955,  true],
            [312,   false],
        ];
    }


    /**
     * @param int $year
     * @dataProvider provideOldYears
     */
    public function testCanRejectVeryOldCar(int
        $year): void
    {

        $this->expectException
            (ToyCarTooOldException::class);
        $validator  = new YearValidator();
        $validator->validate($year);


    }
```

```php
    /**
     * @return array
     */
    public function provideOldYears(): array
    {
        return [
            [1944],
            [1933],
            [1922],
            [1911],
        ];
    }

}
```

2. We added a new test so that we check for `ToyCarTooOldException`. Let's add this exception class as well, but first, let's run the test.

3. Run the following command:

    /var/www/html/symfony# ./runDebug.sh --testsuite=Unit
    --filter testCanRejectVeryOldCar

4. Now you will see four errors. That's okay. Now, let's add the missing exception class:

---

codebase/symfony/src/Validator/ToyCarTooOldException.php

```php
<?php

namespace App\Validator;

class ToyCarTooOldException extends \Exception
{

}
```

As you can see, it's just a simple exception class that extends the main PHP `\Exception` class.

If we run the test again, we should now pass the test, as we have told PHPUnit that we are expecting exceptions for this test by using the `$this->expectException()` method.

5. Run the following command:

```
/var/www/html/symfony# ./runDebug.sh --testsuite=Unit
--filter testCanRejectVeryOldCar
```

Now, we should be able to pass the test – you should see the following result:

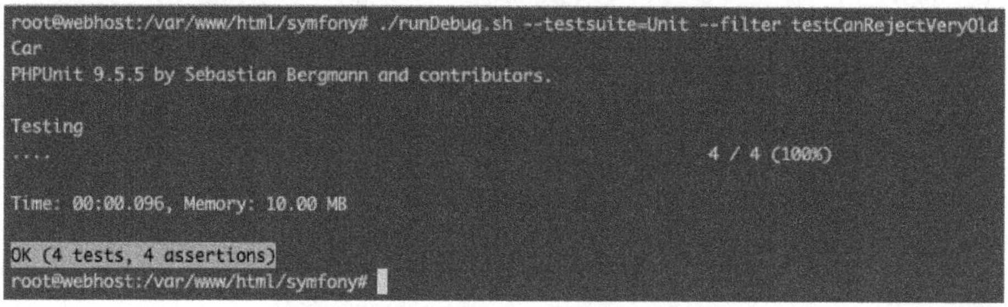

Figure 8.9 – Passing the old car rejection test

This means that we are correctly throwing the `ToyCarTooOldException` object whenever we submit a year that is less than or equal to 1950 – but what will happen to our `ToyCarValidatorTest`?

Let's modify the test data with a year less than 1950 and see what happens:

1. Modify the data provider content with the following:

codebase/symfony/tests/Unit/Validator/ToyCarValidatorTest.php

```php
public function provideToyCarModel(): array
{
    // Toy Car Color
    $toyColor = new ToyColor();
    $toyColor->setName('White');

    // Car Manufacturer
    $carManufacturer = new CarManufacturer();
    $carManufacturer->setName('Williams');

    // Toy Car
    $toyCarModel = new ToyCar();
    $toyCarModel->setName(''); // Should fail.
    $toyCarModel->setColour($toyColor);
    $toyCarModel->setManufacturer($carManufacturer);
```

```
    $toyCarModel->setYear(1935);

    return [
        [$toyCarModel, ['is_valid' => false, 'name' =>
            false, 'year' => false]],
    ];
}
```

2. Now, run the following command and see what happens:

    **/var/www/html/symfony# ./runDebug.sh --filter
    ToyCarValidatorTest**

You will notice that we have failed the test with the following message:

```
root@webhost:/var/www/html/symfony# ./runDebug.sh --filter ToyCarValidatorTest
PHPUnit 9.5.5 by Sebastian Bergmann and contributors.

Testing
E                                                                    1 / 1 (100%)

Time: 00:00.092, Memory: 10.00 MB

There was 1 error:

1) App\Tests\Unit\Validator\ToyCarValidatorTest::testCanValidate with data set #0 (App\Model\Toy
Car Object (...), array(false, false, true))
App\Validator\ToyCarTooOldException: Car is too old.

/var/www/html/symfony/src/Validator/YearValidator.php:22
/var/www/html/symfony/src/Validator/ToyCarValidator.php:37
/var/www/html/symfony/tests/Unit/Validator/ToyCarValidatorTest.php:21

ERRORS!
Tests: 1, Assertions: 0, Errors: 1.
root@webhost:/var/www/html/symfony#
```

Figure 8.10 – Failed toy car validation

Now, we can see that we have an uncaught exception. Our `ToyCarValidator` program is not programmed to handle this exception object. Why is that? Well, the interface in this example is the `codebase/symfony/src/Validator/ValidatorInterface.php` interface. This interface throws a `ToyCarValidationException` object. The problem now is that our implementing class, the `YearValidator.php` class, throws a different exception compared to its contract or interface. Therefore, it breaks the behavior. To fix this problem, we simply need to throw the correct exception as declared in the interface.

3. Let's modify the `ToyCarTooOldException` class:

---

codebase/symfony/src/Validator/ToyCarTooOldException.php

```php
<?php

namespace App\Validator;

class ToyCarTooOldException extends
    ToyCarValidationException
{

}
```

As you can see, we simply replaced the class it extends to `ToyCarValidationException`. The `ToyCarValidator.php` class is designed to catch this exception.

4. Now, let's run the test by running the following command and see whether it really works:

    /var/www/html/symfony# ./runDebug.sh --filter
    ToyCarValidatorTest

    We should now pass the test and see the following result:

    ```
    root@webhost:/var/www/html/symfony# ./runDebug.sh --filter ToyCarValidatorTest
    PHPUnit 9.5.5 by Sebastian Bergmann and contributors.

    Testing
    .                                                                1 / 1 (100%)

    Time: 00:00.102, Memory: 10.00 MB

    OK (1 test, 3 assertions)
    root@webhost:/var/www/html/symfony#
    ```

    Figure 8.11 – Passing the toy car validator test, with old car validation

5. Now that we are passing the test again, let's see what is being returned by our `ToyCarValidator` program. Remember the shell scripts we wrote back in *Chapter 5, Unit Testing*? Let's use one of them. Put a breakpoint in `codebase/symfony/tests/Unit/Validator/ToyCarValidatorTest.php` at line **23**. Then, run the following command:

    /var/www/html/symfony# ./runDebug.sh --filter
    ToyCarValidatorTest

6. Inspect the $result variable, and you should see the following content:

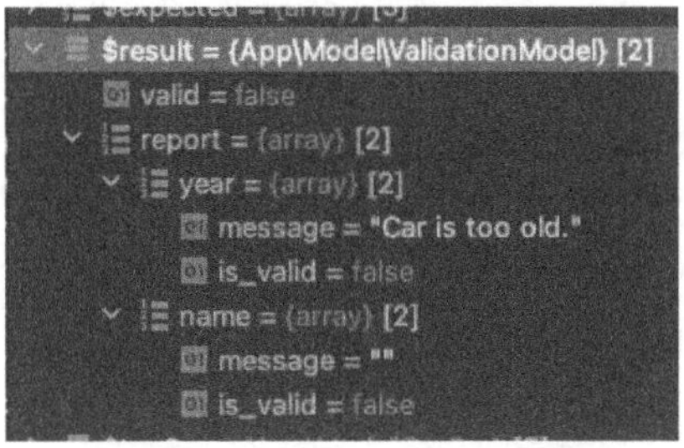

Figure 8.12 – Validation model

You can see that our `ToyCarValidator`'s validate method returns a `ValidationModel` object. It gives a summary of the fields we validated for, as well as the exception message for the `year` field.

We've seen how interfaces can be useful, but sometimes they become too powerful. Next, we'll talk about the **Interface Segregation Principle (ISP)** to help stop this from happening.

TDD with the Interface Segregation Principle

Interfaces are very helpful, but sometimes it can be very easy to pollute them with capabilities that are not really supposed to be a part of the interface. I used to encounter this violation a lot. I was asking myself how I kept on creating empty methods with to-do comments, only to find classes a few months or years later, still with those to-do comments and the methods still empty.

I used to touch my interfaces first and stuff them with all the methods I thought I needed. Then, when I finally wrote the concrete implementations, these concrete classes mostly had empty methods in them.

An interface should only have methods that are specific to that interface. If there's a method in there that is not entirely related to that interface, you need to segregate it into a different interface.

Let's see that in action. Again, let's start with a – you guessed it right – test:

1. Open the `codebase/symfony/tests/Unit/Validator/NameValidatorTest.php` test class and add the following content:

```
/**
 * @param $data
 * @param $expected
 * @dataProvider provideLongNames
 */
public function testCanValidateNameLength(string
```

```
    $name, bool $expected): void
{

    $validator  = new NameValidator();
    $isValid    = $validator->validateLength($name);


    $this->assertEquals($expected, $isValid);
}


/**
 * @return array
 */
public function provideLongNames(): array
{
    return [
        ['TheQuickBrownFoxJumpsOverTheLazyDog',
            false],
    ];
}
```

We introduced a new function in the test called `validateLength`, which is common for strings. We also added a very long name, and we set `false` to be expected to be returned in the data provider.

2. Run the following test:

```
/var/www/html/symfony# ./runDebug.sh --testsuite=Unit
--filter testCanValidateNameLength
```

You should get an error, as we have not created the new method yet.

3. Now, open the `ValidatorInterface.php` interface and add the `validateLength` method we are expecting to have in our test:

codebase/symfony/src/Validator/ValidatorInterface.php

```php
<?php

namespace App\Validator;

interface ValidatorInterface
{
```

```
    /**
     * @param $input
     * @return bool
     * @throws ToyCarValidationException
     */
    public function validate($input): bool;

    /**
     * @param string $input
     * @return bool
     */
    public function validateLength(string $input):
        bool;
}
```

4. Great – now we have the contract for validating a string's length. If we go back to the NameValidator.php class, we'll get the following error from the IDE:

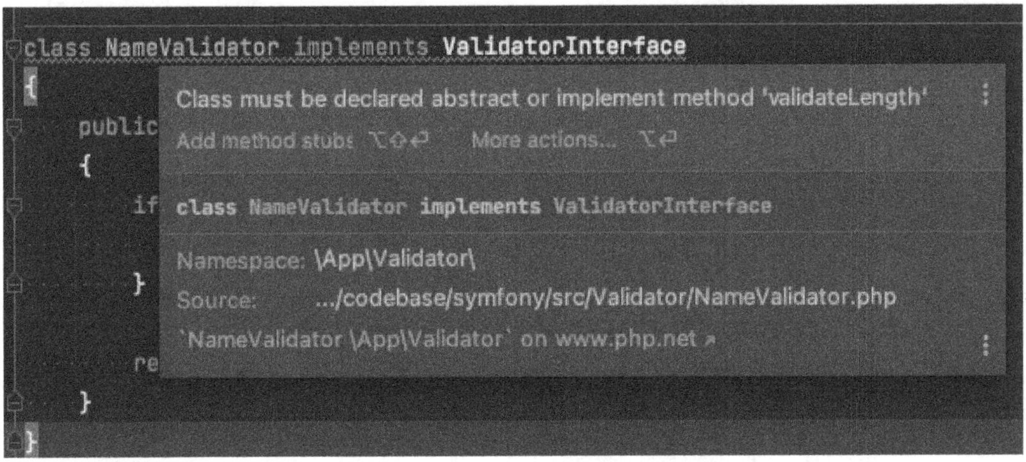

Figure 8.13 – Must implement the method

Obviously, we need to implement the validateLength method for the NameValidator. php class, which is okay, as we want to validate the string length – but what would happen if we also wanted to create a validator for the ToyCar model's color? The ToyCar model's color property expects a ToyColor.php object, not a string! Therefore, the solution is to delete the validateLength method from ValidatorInterface. Certain classes will implement ValidatorInterface without the need to implement this logic. What we can do instead is create a new interface called the `StringValidator` interface that can have the `validateLength` method.

5. Refactor the `codebase/symfony/src/Validator/ValidatorInterface.php` interface and delete the `validateLength` method we just added, and create the following file with the following content:

codebase/symfony/src/Validator/StringValidatorInterface.php

```php
<?php

namespace App\Validator;

interface StringValidatorInterface
{
    /**
     * @param string $input
     * @return bool
     */
    public function validateLength(string $input):
        bool;
}
```

At this stage, we have segregated the `validateLength` method into a separate interface, removing it from the `ValidatorInterface.php` interface.

6. Now, open the `NameValidator.php` class, and refactor it with the following content:

codebase/symfony/src/Validator/NameValidator.php

```php
<?php

namespace App\Validator;

class NameValidator implements ValidatorInterface,
    StringValidatorInterface
{
    const MAX_LENGTH = 10;

    /**
```

```php
 * @param $input
 * @return bool
 */
public function validate($input): bool
{
    $isValid = false;

    if (preg_match("/^([a-zA-Z' ]+)$/", $input)) {
        $isValid = true;
    }

    if ($isValid) {
        $isValid = $this->validateLength($input);
    }

    return $isValid;
}

/**
 * @param string $input
 * @return bool
 */
public function validateLength(string $input):
    bool
{
    if (strlen($input) > self::MAX_LENGTH) {
        return false;
    }

    return true;
}
}
```

7. We have refactored the `NameValidator` class so that it now also checks for the name's length. Let's run the test and see whether it passes:

```
/var/www/html/symfony# ./runDebug.sh --testsuite=Unit
--filter testCanValidateNameLength
```

Now, you should see the following result:

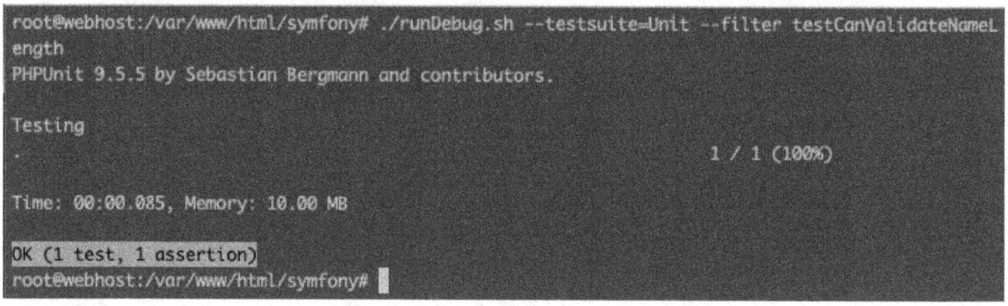

```
root@webhost:/var/www/html/symfony# ./runDebug.sh --testsuite=Unit --filter testCanValidateNameL
ength
PHPUnit 9.5.5 by Sebastian Bergmann and contributors.

Testing
.                                                                   1 / 1 (100%)

Time: 00:00.085, Memory: 10.00 MB

OK (1 test, 1 assertion)
root@webhost:/var/www/html/symfony#
```

Figure 8.14 – Passing the string length validation test

What we did is instead of combining different methods into `ValidatorInterface`, we segregated them into two different interfaces. Then, we only implement the `StringValidator` interface for the validator objects that will need this `validateLength` method. That's basically what the ISP is all about. This is a very basic example, but it is very easy to fall victim to these very powerful interfaces if you don't watch out.

Next, we will go back to the `ToyCarValidator` class and see how we can improve what we had earlier in the *TDD with the Open-Closed Principle* example, using the **Dependency Inversion Principle** (**DIP**).

TDD with the Dependency Inversion Principle

In terms of making a class more testable, the DIP is probably the most important principle on the list for me. The DIP suggests that details should depend on abstractions. To me, this means that the specifics of a program that does not really belong to a class should be abstracted. The DIP allows us as developers to remove a concrete implementation of a routine or program and put it in a different object altogether. We can then use the DIP to inject the object that we need, whenever we need it. We can inject the object that we need in the constructor, passed as an argument upon class instantiation, or simply expose a mutator function.

Let's revisit the `ToyCarValidator` class that we created earlier in this chapter to see how we can implement the DIP.

How will this look in our code?

Going back to the `ToyCarValidator.php` class, you will notice that in the `__constructor` method, we have instantiated two classes:

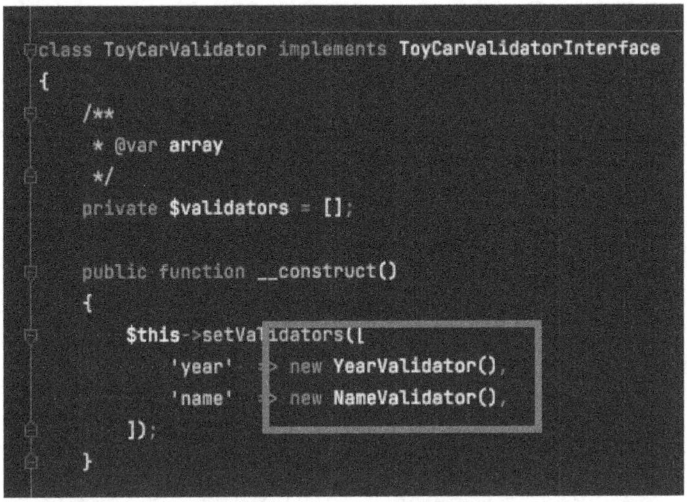

Figure 8.15 – Hardcoded dependencies

How can we improve this? Well, this program works – as you have seen, we are passing
`ToyCarValidatorTest`. The only problem is that our `ToyCarValidator` class is now
hardcoded to its dependencies – the `YearValidator` and `NameValidator` classes. What if we
want to replace these classes – or what if we want to add more validators? Well, what we can do is
remove the dependency from inside of the class. Follow these steps:

1. Refactor the following test class, and replace the `testCanValidate` method with the
    following content:

codebase/symfony/tests/Unit/Validator/ToyCarValidatorTest.php

```php
/**
 * @param ToyCar $toyCar
 * @param array $expected
 * @dataProvider provideToyCarModel
 */
public function testCanValidate(ToyCar $toyCar, array
    $expected): void
{
    $validators = [
        'year'  => new YearValidator(),
        'name'  => new NameValidator(),
    ];
```

```php
    // Inject the validators
    $validator = new ToyCarValidator();
    $validator->setValidators($validators);

    $result = $validator->validate($toyCar);

    $this->assertEquals($expected['is_valid'],
        $result->isValid());
    $this->assertEquals($expected['name'],
        $result->getReport()['name']['is_valid']);
    $this->assertEquals($expected['year'],
        $result->getReport()['year']['is_valid']);
}
```

You will notice that the objects that `ToyCarValidator` depends on are now being instantiated outside the `ToyCarValidator` class – and we then set the validators using the `setValidators` mutator.

2. Now, remove the hardcoded validator instantiations from the `ToyCarValidator`'s constructor:

codebase/symfony/src/Validator/ToyCarValidator.php

```php
<?php

namespace App\Validator;

use App\Model\ToyCar;
use App\Model\ValidationModel as ValidationResult;

class ToyCarValidator implements
    ToyCarValidatorInterface
{
    /**
     * @var array
     */
    private $validators = [];
```

```php
/**
 * @param ToyCar $toyCar
 * @return ValidationResult
 */
public function validate(ToyCar $toyCar):
    ValidationResult
{
    $result     = new ValidationResult();
    $allValid   = true;
    $results    = [];

    foreach ($this->getValidators() as $key =>
        $validator) {
        $accessor   = 'get' . ucfirst(strtolower
            ($key));
        $value      = $toyCar->$accessor();
        $isValid    = false;

        try {
            $isValid = $validator->validate
                ($value);
            $results[$key]['message']   = '';
        } catch (ToyCarValidationException $ex) {
            $results[$key]['message']   =
                $ex->getMessage();
        } finally {
            $results[$key]['is_valid']  =
                $isValid;
        }

        if (!$isValid) {
            $allValid = false;
        }
    }

    $result->setValid($allValid);
```

```
        $result->setReport($results);

        return $result;
    }

    /**
     * @return array
     */
    public function getValidators(): array
    {
        return $this->validators;
    }

    /**
     * @param array $validators
     */
    public function setValidators(array $validators):
        void
    {
        $this->validators = $validators;
    }
}
```

3. We no longer have the hardcoded validator instantiations – now, let's run the test and see whether the tests still pass:

```
/var/www/html/symfony# ./runDebug.sh --testsuite=Unit
--filter testCanValidateNameLength
```

After running the command, you should see that the tests still pass. At this point, we can keep creating new validators and just add them to the array of validators we want to inject into the ToyCarValidator.php class.

4. Now, open the ToyCarCreator.php class we created earlier in this chapter, and you'll see that it's already prepared to accept dependencies from the outside. We can also refactor the class so that we can automatically inject the dependencies it needs during instantiation.

5.   Open the following test class and refactor it with the following content:

codebase/symfony/tests/Integration/Processor/ToyCarCreatorTest.php

```php
<?php

namespace App\Tests\Integration\Repository;

use App\DAL\Writer\WriterInterface;
use App\Model\CarManufacturer;
use App\Model\ToyCar;
use App\Model\ToyColor;
use App\Model\ValidationModel;
use App\Processor\ToyCarCreator;
use App\Validator\ToyCarValidatorInterface;
use Symfony\Bundle\FrameworkBundle\Test\KernelTestCase;

class ToyCarCreatorTest extends KernelTestCase
{
    /**
     * @param ToyCar $toyCarModel
     * @throws \App\Validator
            \ToyCarValidationException
     * @dataProvider provideToyCarModel
     */
    public function testCanCreate(ToyCar
        $toyCarModel): void
    {
        $validationResultStub = $this->createMock
            (ValidationModel::class);
        $validationResultStub
            ->method('isValid')
            ->willReturn(true);

        // Mock 1: Validator
        $validatorStub = $this->createMock
```

```php
                    (ToyCarValidatorInterface::class);
        $validatorStub
            ->method('validate')
            ->willReturn($validationResultStub);

        // Mock 2: Data writer
        $toyWriterStub = $this->createMock
            (WriterInterface::class);
        $toyWriterStub
            ->method('write')
            ->willReturn(true);

        // Processor Class
        $processor = new ToyCarCreator($validatorStub,
            $toyWriterStub);

        // Execute
        $result = $processor->create($toyCarModel);

        $this->assertTrue($result);
    }

public function provideToyCarModel(): array
{
    // Toy Car Color
    $toyColor = new ToyColor();
    $toyColor->setName('Black');

    // Car Manufacturer
    $carManufacturer = new CarManufacturer();
    $carManufacturer->setName('Ford');

    // Toy Car
    $toyCarModel = new ToyCar();
    $toyCarModel->setName('Mustang');
    $toyCarModel->setColour($toyColor);
```

```
        $toyCarModel->setManufacturer
            ($carManufacturer);
        $toyCarModel->setYear(1968);


        return [
            [$toyCarModel],
        ];
    }
}
```

As you can see, we have instantiated the dependencies of the `ToyCarCreator`. php class and then injected them as a parameter when we instantiated the class in `ToyCarCreator($validatorStub, $toyWriterStub);`.

6. Then, open the `ToyCarCreator.php` solution class and refactor it with the following content:

codebase/symfony/src/Processor/ToyCarCreator.php

```php
<?php

namespace App\Processor;

use App\DAL\Writer\WriterInterface;
use App\Model\ToyCar;
use App\Validator\ToyCarValidationException;
use App\Validator\ToyCarValidatorInterface;

class ToyCarCreator
{
    /**
     * @var ToyCarValidatorInterface
     */
    private $validator;

    /**
     * @var WriterInterface
     */
    private $dataWriter;
```

```php
public function __construct
    (ToyCarValidatorInterface $validator,
        WriterInterface $dataWriter)
{

    $this->setValidator($validator);
    $this->setDataWriter($dataWriter);
}


/**
 * @param ToyCar $toyCar
 * @return bool
 * @throws ToyCarValidationException
 */
public function create(ToyCar $toyCar): bool
{
    // Do some validation here and so on...
    $this->getValidator()->validate($toyCar);

    // Write the data
    $result = $this->getDataWriter()->write
        ($toyCar);

    // Do other stuff.

    return $result;
}


/**
 * @return WriterInterface
 */
public function getDataWriter(): WriterInterface
{
    return $this->dataWriter;
}
```

```
/**
 * @param WriterInterface $dataWriter
 */
public function setDataWriter(WriterInterface
    $dataWriter): void
{
    $this->dataWriter = $dataWriter;
}

/**
 * @return ToyCarValidatorInterface
 */
public function getValidator():
    ToyCarValidatorInterface
{
    return $this->validator;
}

/**
 * @param ToyCarValidatorInterface $validator
 */
public function setValidator
    (ToyCarValidatorInterface $validator): void
{
    $this->validator = $validator;
}
}
```

Upon instantiation, both the validator and writer dependencies are set through the constructor.

If we run the test, it should still pass:

```
/var/www/html/symfony# ./runDebug.sh --testsuite=Integration
--filter ToyCarCreatorTest
```

After running the command, you should still see a passing test.

The most obvious thing that you will notice with this approach is that you will have to manage all the dependencies yourself and then inject them into the object that needs them. Luckily, we are not the first people to encounter this headache. There are a lot of service containers out there that help manage the dependencies that your application needs, but the most important thing when selecting a service container for PHP is that it should follow the PSR-11 standards. You can read more about PSR-11 at `https://www.php-fig.org/psr/psr-11/`.

Summary

In this chapter, we've gone through the SOLID principles one by one. We used our tests to kickstart the development of our solution code so that we can use them as examples for implementing the SOLID principles in real life.

We have covered the SRP, which helped us make a PHP class's responsibility or capability more focused. The OCP helped us avoid the need for touching or modifying a class in some instances when we want to change its behavior. The LSP helped us be stricter about the behavior of an interface, making it easier for us to switch concrete objects implementing that interface without breaking the parent class's behavior. The ISP helped us make the responsibility of an interface more focused – classes that implement this interface will no longer have empty methods just because they were declared by the interface. The DIP helped us quickly test our `ToyCarCreator` class even without creating a concrete implementation of its dependencies, such as the `ToyCarValidator` class.

When working on real-life projects, some principles are hard to strictly follow, and sometimes the boundaries are vague. Add the pressure of real-life deadlines and it gets even more interesting. One thing is for sure, using BDD and TDD will help you be more confident about the features you are developing, especially when you are already a few months deep into a project. Adding SOLID principles on top of that makes your solution even better!

In the next chapter, we will try to utilize automated tests to help us make sure that any code changes that any developer in your team pushes into your code repository will not break the expected behavior of your software. We will try to automate this process by using Continuous Integration.

Part 3 – Deployment Automation and Monitoring

In this part of the book, you will learn how to utilize automated tests to improve and automate the code integration process, as well as automate the deployment process of an application. You will also learn how to monitor a PHP application after it's been deployed.

This section comprises the following chapters:

- *Chapter 9, Continuous Integration*
- *Chapter 10, Continuous Delivery*
- *Chapter 11, Monitoring*

Continuous Integration

In the previous chapters, we went through the software development process of a toy car model inventory solution. We followed the test-driven development process, and at this stage, we should now be familiar with it. However, there are still a lot of missing features in the software that we are building. In this chapter, we will start with an almost complete solution that you can get from the GitHub repository for this chapter. We will then make sure our solution works.

In this chapter, we'll start with an almost complete software solution except for the missing last feature, which is to filter the table containing the toy car models. We have built a lot of tests; wouldn't it be great if we could automatically trigger the execution of these tests whenever we created a pull request to the develop or main branch? Automatically triggering the test suites that we have spent so much time developing will help us catch bugs or defects before they even get merged into the main branch. This is where continuous integration will be able to help us.

In this chapter, we will go through the following topics:

- Running and passing all the Symfony application tests
- Using Bitbucket Pipelines for continuous integration

Technical requirements

In this chapter, you are expected to have basic knowledge of using Git version control for web applications. You should also use the development environment and solution code from this book's GitHub repository: `https://github.com/PacktPublishing/Test-Driven-Development-with-PHP-8/tree/main/Chapter%209`.

Preparing the development environment for this chapter

First, download the code found at `https://github.com/PacktPublishing/Test-Driven-Development-with-PHP-8/tree/main/Chapter%209`.

To run the containers and execute the commands in this chapter, you should be inside the `docker-server-web-1` container.

Run the following command to confirm the container name for our web server:

```
docker ps
```

To run the containers, run the following command from the `/docker` directory from the repository in your host machine:

```
docker-compose build && docker-compose up -d
docker exec -it docker-server-web-1 /bin/bash
```

Once inside the container, run the following commands to install the libraries required through Composer:

```
/var/www/html/symfony# ./setup.sh
/var/www/html/behat# ./setup.sh
```

Running and passing all the Symfony application tests

In the previous chapter, we started writing solution code by trying to follow the SOLID principles. To develop the other parts of the application, we can just continue following the same process. In this chapter, I have taken the liberty to complete all other tests and the solution code needed to pass those tests. We will go through the tests and make sure they pass.

Setting up the local environment

Check out the source code provided in the *Technical requirements* section into your local development machine and run the following commands from the host machine to configure your development environment:

```
$ cd docker
$ docker-compose build && docker-compose up -d
```

After running these commands, make sure that the containers we built earlier in this book are up and running by running the following command:

```
$ docker ps
```

You should see the following Docker container names:

```
docker_server-web_1
docker_app-phpmyadmin_1
docker_server-mysql_1
```

Now that the containers are running, we need to prepare the Symfony and Behat applications running inside the `docker_server-web_1` container by installing the packages they depend on, as well as creating the database and tables that our example PHP application needs.

Preparing the Symfony application and tests

Now, let's set up the required database tables and libraries needed by our Symfony application. While still inside the `docker` directory, run the following command from your host machine:

```
$ docker exec -i docker_server-web_1 /var/www/html/symfony/
setup.sh
```

Alternatively, run the following command inside the `docker_server-web_1` container:

```
/var/www/html/symfony# ./setup.sh
```

The `setup.sh` file is just a shell script I have added to easily configure our Symfony application and prepare the database and tables we need to run the tests.

If you open the following shell file, you will see that we are simply running some Doctrine commands and using Composer to install all the Symfony dependencies needed:

codebase/symfony/setup.sh

```bash
#!/bin/bash
composer install -d /var/www/html/symfony/


# Test DB
php /var/www/html/symfony/bin/console doctrine:database:create
-n --env=test
php /var/www/html/symfony/bin/console
doctrine:migrations:migrate -n --env=test
```

```
php /var/www/html/symfony/bin/console doctrine:fixtures:load -n
--env=test

# Main DB
php /var/www/html/symfony/bin/console doctrine:database:create
-n
php /var/www/html/symfony/bin/console
doctrine:migrations:migrate -n
php /var/www/html/symfony/bin/console doctrine:fixtures:load -n
```

This shell script will come in handy once we are running the application in the **continuous integration** **(CI)** machine.

After running the `setup.sh` command, your development environment should be ready to run all the unit and integration tests from inside our Symfony application.

In *Chapter 5, Unit Testing*, we created a shell script called `codebase/symfony/runCoverage.sh`. This shell script will help us run all the tests and check how much test coverage we have against our solution code. Realistically speaking though, we don't have to cover all the code inside our application since some of them are third-party libraries with no tests, or some of them might be just **Plain Old PHP Object (POPO)** classes. But for the code that we develop, we should add automated tests for them.

If you think you need to exclude some classes from the code coverage report, you can open the `codebase/symfony/phpunit.xml` configuration file and add the directories you want to exclude from the coverage report.

From within the `docker_server-web_1` container, if you open the `codebase/symfony/tests` directory inside our Symfony application, you will see the following tests:

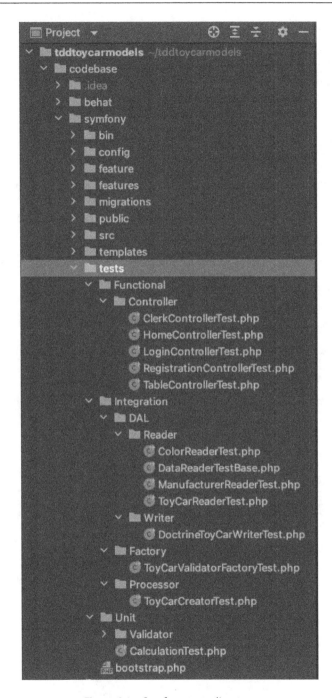

Figure 9.1 – Symfony tests directory

We have three main directories for the tests: **Functional**, **Integration**, and **Unit**. The **Functional** tests in this example are the controller tests, which are the tests that use HTTP requests; you can think of them as Integration tests as well but they cover more integrated code. The **Integration** tests are the tests that run through the different custom classes and how they interact with each other, making sure that they all work as expected. Finally, the **Unit** tests are simple tests that focus on single units or functions inside a specific class.

You can browse through the directories and classes inside `codebase/symfony/src` to check the actual classes our tests are testing against.

Let's see whether the tests pass; from the host machine, run the following command:

```
$ docker exec -i docker_server-web_1 /var/www/html/symfony/
runTests.sh
```

Alternatively, run the following command inside the `docker_server-web_1` container:

```
/var/www/html/symfony# ./runTests.sh
```

Since we have configured the database and tables needed for the tests, you should see the following result:

```
rainsarabia@Rains-MacBook-Pro docker % docker exec -i docker_server-web_1 /var/www/html/
symfony/runTests.sh
PHPUnit 9.5.5 by Sebastian Bergmann and contributors.

Testing
.........................................                    43 / 43 (100%)

Time: 00:01.225, Memory: 34.00 MB

OK (43 tests, 143 assertions)
rainsarabia@Rains-MacBook-Pro docker %
```

Figure 9.2 – Passing Symfony tests

It looks like we have a lot of passing tests, but let's open one of the test classes and see exactly what we are testing for.

Open `codebase/symfony/tests/Integration/DAL/Reader/ColorReaderTest.php`; you will see the following content:

```php
<?php

namespace App\Tests\Integration\DAL\Reader;
```

```
use App\DAL\Reader\Doctrine\ColorReader;
use App\Entity\Color;
use App\Model\ToyColor;

class ColorReaderTest extends DataReaderTestBase
{
    public function testCanReadColors()
    {
        $reader = $this->getServiceContainer()-
>get(ColorReader::class);
        $colorsFromDb = $reader->getAll();

        /** @var Color $color */
        foreach ($colorsFromDb as $color) {
            $this->assertInstanceOf(ToyColor::class, $color);
            $this->assertIsInt($color->getId());
            $this->assertNotNull($color->getName());
        }
    }
}
```

You will notice that in this test class, we are reading data from the database and running some assertions against the results from the database. In *Chapter 7, Building Solution Code with BDD and TDD*, we created the databases we needed for both testing and the main database for the actual solution code.

We have the following databases inside the `docker_server-mysql_1` container:

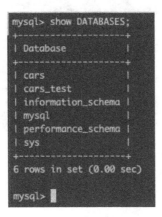

Figure 9.3 – MySQL databases

We are using the `cars` database for the actual solution code, and `cars_test` for the automated tests. This way, our automated tests won't contaminate our main application database.

Now, finally, before we deploy to the CI solution, let's run the `runCoverage.sh` shell script we built earlier.

Run the following command from the host machine:

```
$ docker exec -i docker_server-web_1 /var/www/html/symfony/
runCoverage.sh
```

Alternatively, run the following command inside the `docker_server-web_1` container:

```
/var/www/html/symfony# ./runCoverage.sh
```

Now, you should see the following test result:

```
rainsarabia@Rains-MacBook-Pro docker % docker exec -i docker_server-web_1 /var/www/html/
symfony/runCoverage.sh
PHPUnit 9.5.5 by Sebastian Bergmann and contributors.

Testing
.............................................               43 / 43 (100%)

Time: 00:02.216, Memory: 48.00 MB

OK (43 tests, 163 assertions)


Code Coverage Report:
  2022-10-10 09:45:22

 Summary:
  Classes: 100.00% (12/12)
  Methods: 100.00% (33/33)
  Lines:   100.00% (131/131)

App\DAL\Reader\Doctrine\ColorReader
  Methods: 100.00% ( 1/ 1)   Lines: 100.00% ( 8/ 8)
App\DAL\Reader\Doctrine\ManufacturerReader
  Methods: 100.00% ( 1/ 1)   Lines: 100.00% ( 8/ 8)
App\DAL\Reader\Doctrine\ReaderBase
  Methods: 100.00% ( 5/ 5)   Lines: 100.00% ( 6/ 6)
```

Figure 9.4 – Test coverage report

Great! At this stage, we are sure that the tests are running properly and that they can also connect to the test database:

```
mysql> SELECT * FROM toy_car;
+----+-----------------+----------+--------+------+
| id | manufacturer_id | color_id | name   | year |
+----+-----------------+----------+--------+------+
|  1 |               1 |        1 | ABC123 | 1998 |
+----+-----------------+----------+--------+------+
1 row in set (0.01 sec)
```

Figure 9.5 – Test data

If you check the `toy_cars` table inside the `cars_test` MySQL database, you should see some sample data created by the automated tests.

Next, let's move on to our more elaborate functional tests defined inside the Behat application.

Preparing the Behat application and tests

In the previous section, we were able to run and pass all the Symfony application tests. Now, we'll need to make sure that we have also passed our behavior-driven tests living inside the Behat application.

Run the following command from your host machine to set up the Behat application:

```
$ docker exec -i docker_server-web_1 /var/www/html/
behat/setup.sh
```

Alternatively, run the following command inside the `docker_server-web_1` container:

```
/var/www/html/behat# ./setup.sh
```

Just like what we did earlier in the Symfony application, we first need to set up the Behat application and install its dependencies.

In *Chapter 6*, *Applying Behavior-Driven Development*, we created test features and scenarios using the Gherkin language. We also created some Context PHP classes that contain steps we have defined in the feature files we've created. These Context classes will be executed by Behat to serve as functional PHP tests.

The difference between the Symfony tests and the tests from our Behat application is that the Behat tests do not care about how we achieve the results or how specific PHP classes interact with other PHP classes. They only care about testing very high-level functional and behavioral scenarios.

That's it – now, we are ready to run our behavior-driven tests.

Run the following command from the host machine and see whether you can pass our Behat tests:

```
docker exec -i docker_server-web_1 /var/www/html/behat/
runBehatTests.sh
```

Alternatively, run the following command inside the `docker_server-web_1` container:

```
/var/www/html/behat# ./runBehatTests.sh
```

You should see the following results:

```
    Then I should be able to register a new account              # InventoryClerkRegistrat
ionContext::iShouldBeAbleToRegisterANewAccount()

Feature: Inventory Clerk Login
  In order to access the inventory system
  As a registered user
  I need to be able to login

  Scenario: Login                                                # features/suite_b/invent
ory_clerk_login.feature:6
    Given I am in the login "/login" path                        # InventoryClerkLoginCont
ext::iAmInTheLoginPath()
    When I fill in Email "Email" with "clerk_email@phptdd.bdd"   # InventoryClerkLoginCont
ext::iFillInEmailWith()
    And I fill in Password "Password" with "password"            # InventoryClerkLoginCont
ext::iFillInPasswordWith()
    And I click on the "login" button                            # InventoryClerkLoginCont
ext::iClickOnTheButton()
    Then I should be able to access the clerk page               # InventoryClerkLoginCont
ext::iShouldBeAbleToAccessTheClerkPage()

Feature: Clerk creates new toy car record
  In order to have a collection of toy car model records
  As an Inventory Clerk
  I need to be able to create a single record

  Scenario: Create new record                        # features/suite_c/create_toy_car_record
.feature:6
    Given I am in the inventory system page          # CreateToyCarRecordContext::iAmInTheInv
entorySystemPage()
    When I submit the form with correct details      # CreateToyCarRecordContext::iSubmitTheF
ormWithCorrectDetails()
    Then I should see the created record             # CreateToyCarRecordContext::iShouldSeeT
heCreatedRecord()

5 scenarios (5 passed)
20 steps (20 passed)
0m13.93s (12.52Mb)
```

Figure 9.6 – Behat tests passing

Great! We have passed all the test scenarios that we have defined. If you want to check all the feature files and scenarios, you can open the files in `codebase/behat/features`.

Now that we are sure that our automated tests are working properly from our development machine, we are ready to use them in Bitbucket Pipelines for our CI solution.

Using Bitbucket Pipelines for CI

We've spent a lot of effort building our automated tests and solution code, and all these efforts are aimed to help us develop maintainable and more reliable software. CI is the practice of being able to integrate code changes from different sources. With the addition of automated tests, this is where our hard work will start to pay off on a bigger scale with all the tests we've been writing. This will help in preventing us from introducing regressions into the main code base. For example, the CI process can reject a git pull request if there are broken automated tests.

There are a lot of CI tools out there, but in this example, since I am using Bitbucket for the version control in the project, I'll just use Bitbucket Pipelines as it's already integrated well with Bitbucket Cloud. It is extremely easy to use, as you will see. Let's get started:

1. In the Bitbucket Cloud dashboard, select the repository you are using for your project, and click on the **Pipelines** link on the left menu:

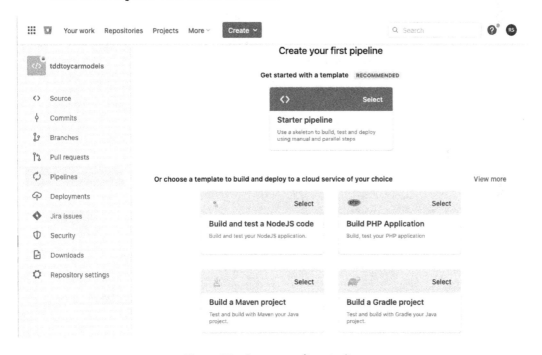

Figure 9.7 – Create your first pipeline

2. Then, select the **Build PHP Application** box. You will see the example template for creating your first pipeline:

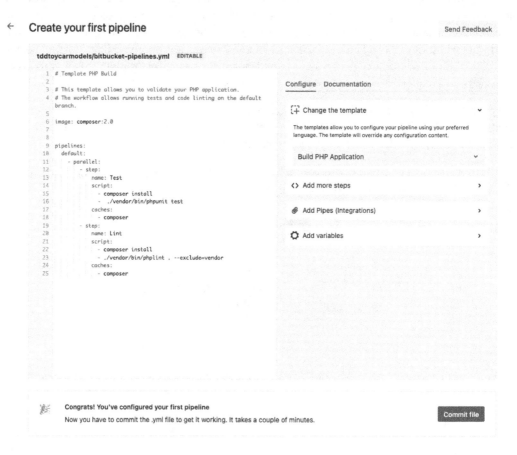

Figure 9.8 – Create your first pipeline

3. Here, you will see a simple .yml file; you can edit it to run your script. For our example project, you can use the following content:

bitbucket-pipelines.yml

```
image: docker:stable

options:
  docker: true
```

```
pipelines:
  default:
    - parallel:
      - step:
          name: Prepare environment
          script:
            - set -eu
            - apk add --no-cache py-pip bash
            - apk add --no-cache gcc
            - apk add --update --no-cache --virtual
.tmp-build-deps gcc libc-dev linux-headers postgresql-dev
&& apk add libffi-dev
            - apk update && apk add python3-dev gcc
libc-dev
            - pip install --upgrade pip setuptools
wheel
            - pip install --no-cache-dir docker-compose
            - docker-compose -v
            - ls -lap
            - pwd
            - cd docker
            - docker-compose build && docker-compose up
-d
            - docker exec -i docker_server-web_1 /var/
www/html/symfony/setup.sh
            - docker exec -i docker_server-web_1
/var/www/html/symfony/runCoverage.sh
            - docker exec -i docker_server-web_1
/var/www/html/behat/setup.sh
            - docker exec -i docker_server-web_1
/var/www/html/behat/runBehatTests.sh
          caches:
            - composer
```

As you can see, these are just some commands we want to run while setting up the Docker containers we need to use in the CI cloud. You will notice that we are using the codebase/ symfony/setup.sh and codebase/behat/setup.sh files to install all the dependencies and libraries that our Symfony and Behat applications need. This includes creating the `cars` and `cars_test` databases we are using inside our Symfony application!

4. Paste the script into the text area and click on the **Commit File** button. You'll be redirected to the **Pipelines** page, where you will see your build running:

Figure 9.9 – Pipeline running

You will notice from the preceding screenshot that we were able to build the same containers we were working with from our local machine.

The build will take a few minutes to run. Here, we want the following to happen in the CI cloud:

1. Create a host machine.

2. Install the necessary libraries we need to run `docker-compose`.

3. Build the Docker containers we are using for our solution.

4. Install Composer packages for Symfony.

5. Run the Doctrine Database migrations for Symfony.

6. Execute the `runCoverage.sh` test script for Symfony.

7. Make sure we pass all the Symfony tests.

8. Install Composer packages for Behat.

9. Execute the `runBehatTests.sh` test script for Behat.

10. Make sure we pass all the Behat tests.

That's a lot of steps! But we need to do all of these things to make sure we can run our automated tests as if we are just running them from our local machine. After a few minutes, check back on your **Build** and see whether we have passed the Symfony tests:

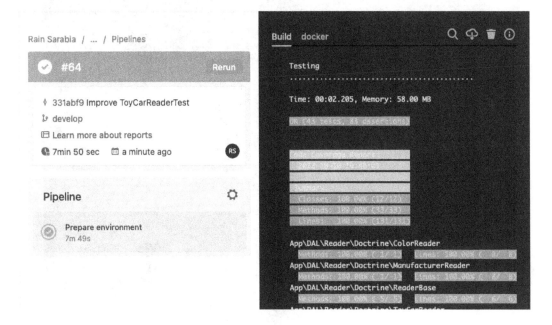

Figue 9.10 – CI pass Symfony tests

Great! By running the `runCoverage.sh` shell script from inside the CI, we can make sure that all the tests and code are still running as expected! Now, let's see whether our Behat tests also pass. Keep scrolling down the build screen until you find the Behat test results:

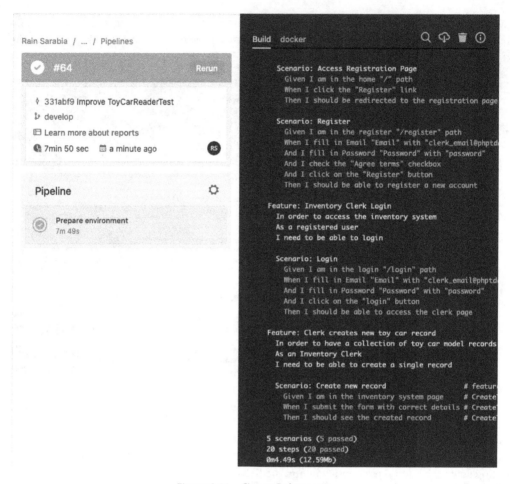

Figure 9.11 – CI pass Behat tests

As you can see from the log, we passed the same five scenarios that we passed earlier from our local development machine!

At this stage, **Pipelines** will show a green bar with a check indicating that we have passed the entire build.

In *Chapter 2, Understanding and Organizing the Business Requirements of Our Project*, we created some Jira tickets and integrated our Bitbucket repository into the Jira project. Now, this is going to be very handy for Bitbucket Pipelines as it is also seamlessly integrated with Jira.

In the root directory of the solution code, as cloned from `https://github.com/ PacktPublishing/Test-Driven-Development-with-PHP-8/tree/main/ Chapter%209`, you will find a `bitbucket-pipelines.yml` file containing the scripts we have used to run our first pipeline. Now, each time you push an update into the Bitbucket branch that is connected to the Jira ticket that you're working on, Jira will be automatically able to detect the Pipelines build that is running for your Jira ticket as well:

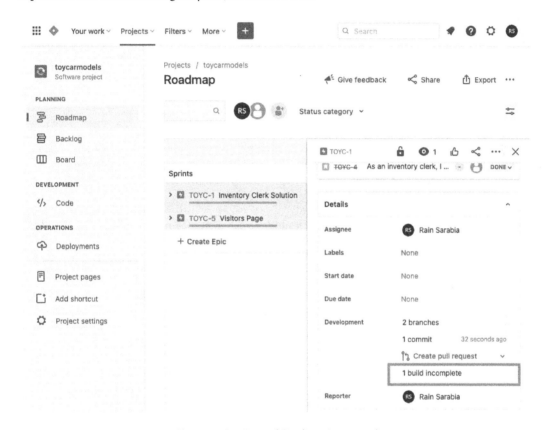

Figure 9.12 – Jira and Pipelines integrated

Click on the **1 build incomplete** link below the **Create pull request** link area highlighted in the preceding screenshot; you will see a popup containing the list of builds that have been executed for that branch and ticket:

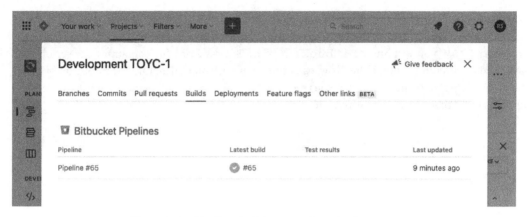

Figure 9.13 – Pipelines builds popup from the Jira page

This is a set of very powerful tools. Your team can monitor tasks using Jira, and you can make sure that the source code being pushed by you, or any other developer, is not detrimental to the existing software before you decide whether you want to deploy the solution.

If a developer pushes code that changes the behavior of your application negatively, and there are enough automated tests to cover it, then you'll be able to catch the problem as it will fail the CI build.

Summary

In this chapter, we went through the process of setting up our updated development environment complete with all the test and solution code we need to build our example project. We created and used shell scripts to help us install dependencies, set up databases, and seed data, making sure that we have everything we need to easily run our tests from a local machine or in the cloud.

We also created our first Bitbucket Pipeline to help us implement continuous integration. By using CI, we can run all our automated tests in the cloud to make sure that we do not break anything in the code base each time we commit and push changes to a branch.

In the next chapter, we will deploy our solution into an external web server, where we will also be able to test the application using a web browser.

10
Continuous Delivery

We've built a software solution complete with automated tests and have set up a continuous integration pipeline to run those automated tests. Now, if a developer in your team pushes some code that changes the expected behavior of the solution, our automated tests and continuous integration solution will catch those issues and will help you and your team stop releasing detrimental code. But what if all the tests have passed after pushing all the new code to the repository? Wouldn't it be great if we had a solution to help us prepare and deploy the application into a development, staging, or production server?

In this chapter, we will add the last missing piece to our development process. We will prepare a remote server in AWS, and we will automatically deploy our application into that server using **continuous delivery (CD)**.

Figure 10.1 shows the steps we are going to take to deploy our solution code to a public-facing web server. We will go through the process of pushing new code to the repository, which, in turn, will trigger the CI pipeline we configured in the previous chapter. The CI pipeline will run the automated tests we've built and, when successful, the CD process will upload our solution code into AWS S3. Then, we will use AWS CodeDeploy to deploy our application into an AWS EC2 instance that will serve as our example production server:

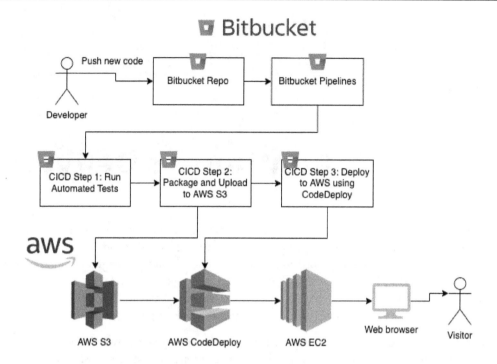

Figure 10.1 – Entire flow

From a developer pushing new code and running all automated tests in the cloud to automatically deploying the solution code into a Linux server, we will be covering all of that!

In this chapter, we will go through the following topics:

- Setting up an AWS EC2 instance
- Creating an AWS CodeDeploy application
- Installing Docker and other dependencies inside the AWS EC2 instance
- Continuous delivery with Bitbucket Pipelines and AWS CodeDeploy

Technical requirements

In this chapter, you should follow the instructions provided in the previous chapter and configure a Bitbucket Pipelines pipeline. You are also expected to have basic knowledge of AWS and should use the code in this book's code base at `https://github.com/PacktPublishing/Test-Driven-Development-with-PHP-8/tree/main/Chapter%2010`.

To see all the tests running properly, you can run the following command to download the complete code of this chapter, and run the Docker containers:

```
curl -Lo phptdd.zip "https://github.com/PacktPublishing/Test-
Driven-Development-with-PHP-8/raw/main/Chapter%2010/complete.
zip" && unzip -o phptdd.zip && cd complete && ./demoSetup.sh
```

To run the containers and execute the commands in this chapter, you should be inside the `docker-server-web-1` container.

Run the following command to confirm the container name for our web server:

```
docker ps
```

To run the containers, run the following command from the `/phptdd/docker` directory from the repository in your host machine:

```
docker-compose build && docker-compose up -d
docker exec -it docker_server-web_1 /bin/bash
```

Once inside the container, run the following command to install the libraries required through Composer:

```
/var/www/html/symfony# ./setup.sh
```

Within the `/var/www/html/symfony` directory, run the following command to see all the tests passing:

```
/var/www/html/symfony# ./runCoverage.sh
```

After running the `runCoverage.sh` command, it should execute all our Symfony tests, and you can make sure that they all pass.

Setting up an AWS EC2 instance

If you don't already have an AWS account, you can follow the instructions at `https://aws.amazon.com/premiumsupport/knowledge-center/create-and-activate-aws-account/` to create one. You will also have to create an AWS IAM User group. The instructions can be found on https://docs.aws.amazon.com/IAM/latest/UserGuide/id_groups_create.html. You will need an AWS IAM User, and follow the official documentation from AWS to create an IAM user in your AWS account at `https://docs.aws.amazon.com/IAM/latest/UserGuide/id_users_create.html`.

We will also need the following AWS resources to complete the EC2 setup:

- AWS EC2 key pair

- IAM instance profile

Why do we need an EC2 instance? Well, this will serve as our remote server. You can think of it as your host computer running in the cloud. We will use this server to host our Docker containers to run and serve our application:

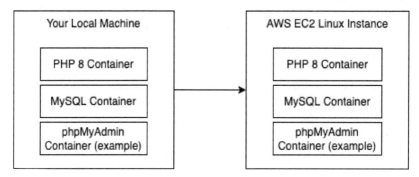

Figure 10.1 – EC2 instance

As you can see from the diagram, it's going to serve as almost a replica of your local development environment. That's the big benefit of using containers, as we discussed in *Chapter 3, Setting Up Our Development Environment Using Docker Containers*.

Follow these steps to create an EC2 instance:

1. Sign in to the AWS console and search for EC2 in the **Services** search bar to go to the EC2 dashboard.

2. In the EC2 dashboard, click on the **Launch instance** button:

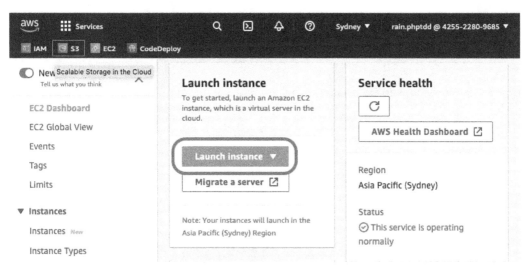

Figure 10.2 – The Launch instance button

You will be shown the **Launch an instance** wizard.

3.   In the **Name** field, enter tddphp-instance1. This name tag is going to be very important. We will use this tag for our CodeDeploy application later in this chapter:

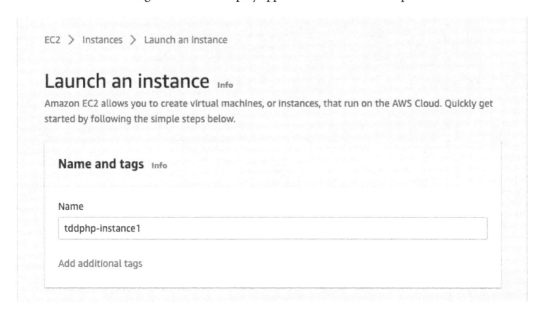

Figure 10.3 – Instance name tag

4. Next, in the **Application and OS Images (Amazon Machine Image)** area, select **Amazon Linux 2 AMI**:

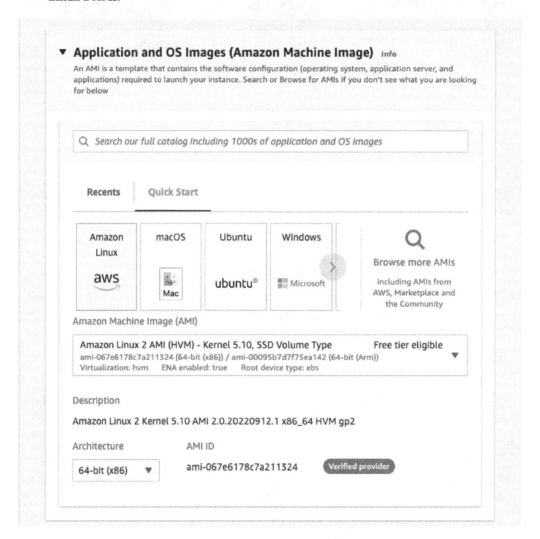

Figure 10.4 – Amazon Linux 2 AMI

5. Next, you can select the EC2 instance type. For this example, you can stick to the **t2.micro** instance as this type is free tier eligible. You can also select a more powerful instance configuration – that's entirely up to you:

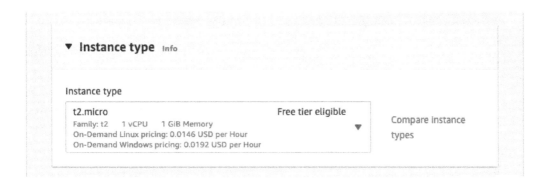

Figure 10.5 – t2.micro instance type

6. You will need a key pair to be able to SSH into this machine instance. If you don't already have one set up, just click on the **Create new key pair** link; a popup will appear for you to create a new key pair:

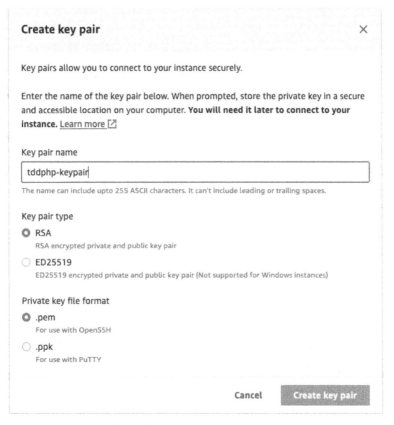

Figure 10.6 – Creating a new key pair

7.   After creating the key pair, you can assign it to the key pair field in the EC2 instance wizard.

8.   Next, in the **Network settings** section, allow all HTTP and HTTPs traffic. This is so that we can easily access the web application from a browser:

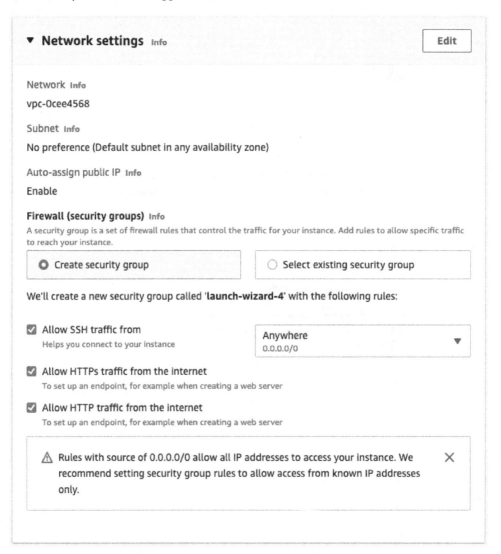

Figure 10.7 – Network settings; allow HTTP and HTTPS

9. Next, in the **Advanced details** section, if you don't already have an IAM instance profile, you can easily create one by clicking on the **Create new IAM profile** link:

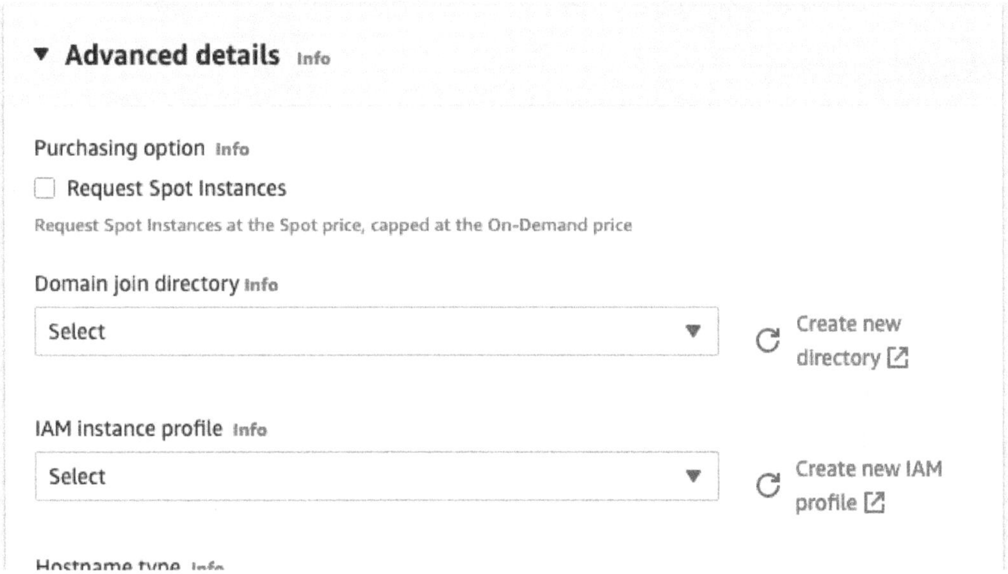

Figure 10.8 – Creating a new IAM profile link

10. You will be redirected to the IAM wizard. Enter any IAM role name you want to use; then, select the **Custom trust policy** option in the **Trusted entity type** section:

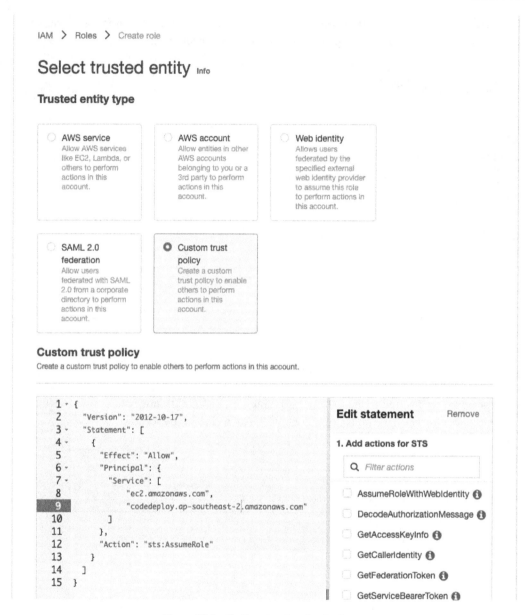

Figure 10.9 – Custom trust policy text area

11. In the text area, use the following policy:

```
{
    "Version": "2012-10-17",
    "Statement": [
```

```
        {
            "Effect": "Allow",
            "Principal": {
                "Service": [
                    "ec2.amazonaws.com",
                    "codedeploy.ap-southeast-2.
                        amazonaws.com"
                ]
            },
            "Action": "sts:AssumeRole"
        }
    ]
}
```

Since I am in Australia, I usually use the Sydney ap-southeast-2 region. You can replace this with any region you prefer.

12. Click the **Next** button to proceed.

13. In the **Add permissions** section, search for the following policies, and tick the checkbox before the policy name:

- **AmazonEC2FullAccess**
- **AmazonS3FullAccess**
- **AWSCodeDeployFullAccess**

14. After selecting these policies, click **Next**.

Make sure these policies are displayed in the IAM wizard review screen before creating the role:

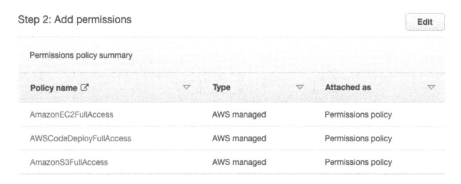

Figure 10.10 – Access policies

15. Next, click on the **Create role** button, then go back to the **EC2 instance** wizard. You can now select the IAM role you just created from the **Advanced details** section:

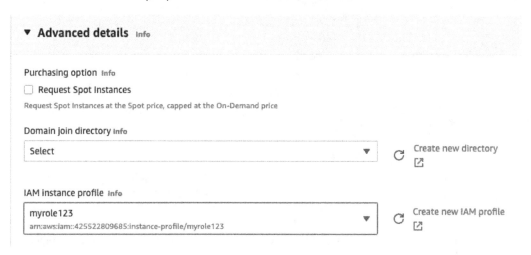

Figure 10.11 – Newly created IAM instance profile

16. And that's it – scroll to the very bottom of the page and click on the **Launch instance** button. It will take a few minutes for AWS to launch your new EC2 instance. After a few minutes, go back to the dashboard; you should now see your EC2 instance running:

Figure 10.12 – Amazon Linux 2 instance running

We now have a running Amazon Linux 2 instance; we will use this instance to run our containers.

Before proceeding with the CodeDeploy setup, we need to create an S3 bucket. This bucket will be used both by our Bitbucket Pipelines and the CodeDeploy application:

1. While in the AWS console, search for S3 and click the **S3** service item:

Figure 10.13 – S3 service

You will be redirected to the Amazon S3 dashboard.

2. Click on the **Create bucket** button:

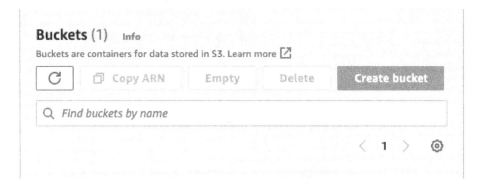

Figure 10.14 – The Create bucket button

3. Use any unique name you want for the bucket and select the same region you used for your EC2 instance. For me, it's **ap-southeast-2**:

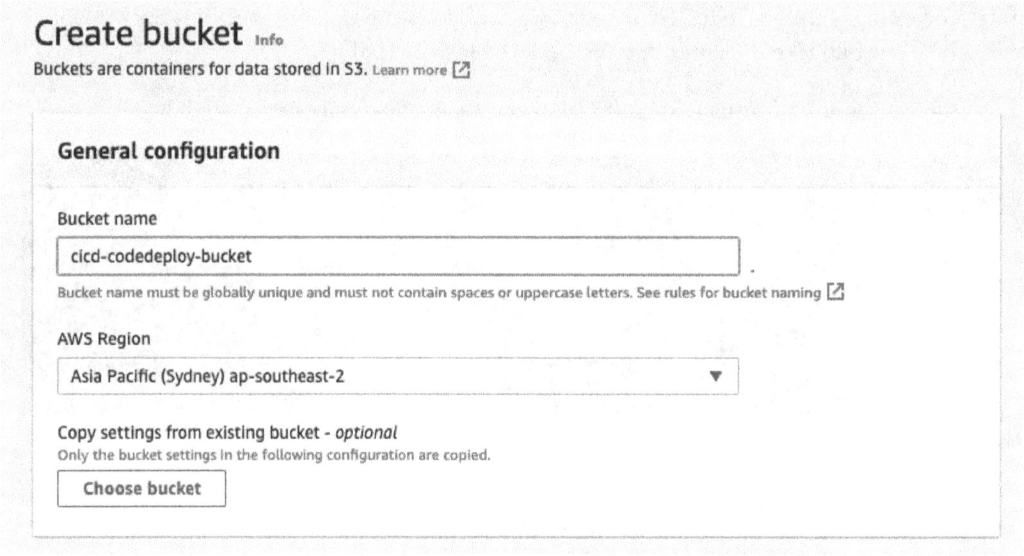

Create bucket Info

Buckets are containers for data stored in S3. Learn more ⧉

General configuration

Bucket name

cicd-codedeploy-bucket

Bucket name must be globally unique and must not contain spaces or uppercase letters. See rules for bucket naming ⧉

AWS Region

Asia Pacific (Sydney) ap-southeast-2   ▼

Copy settings from existing bucket - *optional*
Only the bucket settings in the following configuration are copied.

Choose bucket

Figure 10.15 – Creating an S3 bucket

4.   You can leave all the default settings as-is and click on the **Create bucket** button.

And that's it. We can now proceed with creating the CodeDeploy application. The CodeDeploy application will use the EC2 instance and S3 bucket we just created.

Creating an AWS CodeDeploy application

We will be using AWS CodeDeploy to automate the deployment of our PHP application into an EC2 server. But where will CodeDeploy get the files to deploy? It will get them from an S3 bucket. But how will our solution code end up in S3 in the first place? Well, we will tell Bitbucket Pipelines to upload it there! We will cover that later in this chapter:

Figure 10.16 – CodeDeploy flow

Follow these steps to set up AWS CodeDeploy, which will be triggered by our Bitbucket CI pipeline once all of our automated tests have passed:

1.   In the AWS console, search for the CodeDeploy service and click on the **Create application** button:

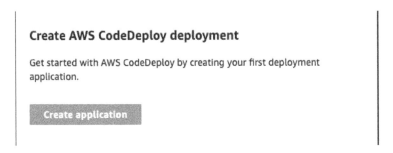

Figure 10.17 – Creating the CodeDeploy application

2. In the CodeDeploy wizard, use any name you want in the **Application configuration** section. Then, in the **Compute platform** field, select the **EC2/On-premises** option and click on the **Create application** button:

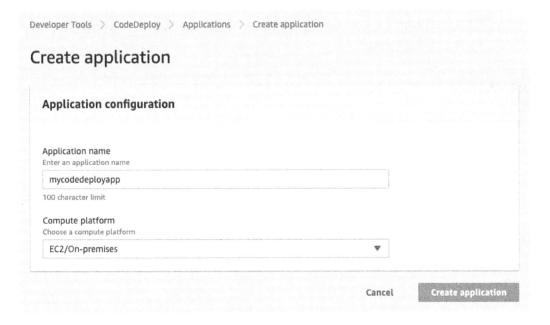

Figure 10.18 – Application configuration section

You will be redirected to the CodeDeploy **Applications** page.

3. Next, click on the **Create deployment group** button:

Figure 10.19 – The Create deployment group button

- In the **Deployment group name** section, use any name you want. In this example, I will use `codedeploy_group1`:

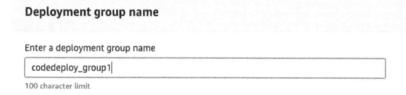

Figure 10.20 – Deployment group wizard – group name

4. Next, in the **Service role** section, select the IAM role we created earlier in this chapter:

Figure 10.21 – Deployment group wizard – IAM role

5. Next, in the **Environment configuration** section, check the **Amazon EC2 instances** checkbox. Then, in the **Tag group** section, add the EC2 instance name we created earlier, which is `tddphp-instance1`. This is very important. This is how we tell CodeDeploy that we want

to deploy the application in this specific instance. You can add more tags here if you want to deploy to other instances as well:

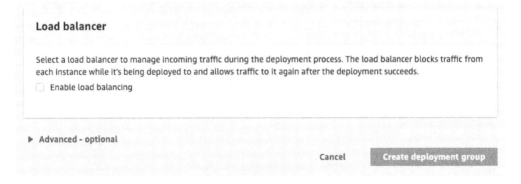

Environment configuration

Select any combination of Amazon EC2 Auto Scaling groups, Amazon EC2 instances, and on-premises instances to add to this deployment

☐ Amazon EC2 Auto Scaling groups

☑ Amazon EC2 instances
  1 unique matched instance. Click here for details ↗

You can add up to three groups of tags for EC2 instances to this deployment group.
One tag group: Any instance identified by the tag group will be deployed to.
Multiple tag groups: Only instances identified by all the tag groups will be deployed to.

Tag group 1
Key

🔍 Name   ✕

Value - *optional*

🔍 tddphp-instance1   ✕

Remove tag

Figure 10.22 – Deployment group wizard – EC2 instance details

6. Next, in the **Load balancer** section, uncheck the **Enable load balancing** checkbox, then click on the **Create deployment group** button:

Load balancer

Select a load balancer to manage incoming traffic during the deployment process. The load balancer blocks traffic from each instance while it's being deployed to and allows traffic to it again after the deployment succeeds.
☐ Enable load balancing

▶ Advanced - optional

                                                    Cancel   Create deployment group

Figure 10.23 – Deployment group wizard – Load balancer

Great! That's it for the CodeDeploy configuration from the AWS console.

Next, we will need to get inside the EC2 instance we just created and install some applications we need for it to be able to connect to CodeDeploy, and for us to be able to run Docker containers.

Installing Docker and other dependencies inside the AWS EC2 instance

We will need three very important applications inside the EC2 instance. First, we will need the AWS CodeDeploy agent, after which we'll need to install Docker and docker-compose so that we can build and run the Docker containers we need for our application.

Connecting to the EC2 instance

We need to get inside the instance before we can install anything. Thankfully, we can do this by using the AWS console from a browser:

1. In the EC2 dashboard, select the running instance we created earlier and click on the **Connect** button at the top of the table:

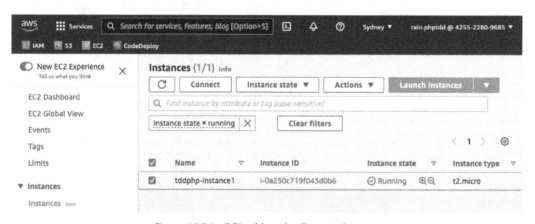

Figure 10.24 – EC2 table – the Connect button

You will be redirected to the **Connect to instance** page.

2. Click on the **Connect** button on that page. Finally, you will be redirected to the browser's terminal window:

Figure 10.25 – EC2 terminal window

Great! Now, we can install the applications we need for CD and our PHP solution.

Installing CodeDeploy Agent

The CodeDeploy application we created earlier in the chapter will need additional software installed inside our EC2 instance so that it can communicate with it. This is why we need CodeDeploy Agent. You can read more about it on the official AWS documentation page for CodeDeploy Agent: https://docs.aws.amazon.com/codedeploy/latest/userguide/codedeploy-agent.html.

Follow these steps to install CodeDeploy Agent:

1. In the terminal, enter the following commands to install the agent:

    ```
    sudo yum update -y
    sudo yum install -y ruby
    sudo yum install -y wget
    wget https://aws-codedeploy-ap-southeast-2.s3.ap-
        southeast-2.amazonaws.com/latest/install
    chmod +x ./install
    sudo ./install auto
    ```

2. After running those commands, verify that the agent is running by running the following command:

    ```
    sudo service codedeploy-agent status
    ```

    You should now get the following result:

```
Complete!
I, [2022-10-15T02:26:00.700668 #3569]  INFO -- : Update check complete.
I, [2022-10-15T02:26:00.700782 #3569]  INFO -- : Stopping updater.
[ec2-user@ip-172-31-3-12 ~]$ sudo service codedeploy-agent status
The AWS CodeDeploy agent is running as PID 3650
[ec2-user@ip-172-31-3-12 ~]$
```

i-0a250c719f043d0b6 (tddphp-instance1)

PublicIPs: 13.211.240.163   PrivateIPs: 172.31.3.12

Figure 10.26 – CodeDeploy Agent is running

Awesome! Our EC2 instance can now be used by our CodeDeploy application. Next, we can proceed with installing Docker.

Installing Docker

We've been using Docker containers to run our PHP solution. Now, CodeDeploy will try to deploy our code in the EC2 instance we just created, but our solution code depends on Docker and docker-compose being installed.

Follow these steps to install Docker:

1. Run the following commands in the AWS terminal window:

    ```
    sudo amazon-linux-extras install -y docker
    sudo service docker start
    sudo usermod -aG docker ec2-user
    sudo chkconfig docker on
    ```

2. After running the installation commands, check whether Docker is installed correctly by running the following command:

    ```
    docker --version
    ```

    You should see the following result:

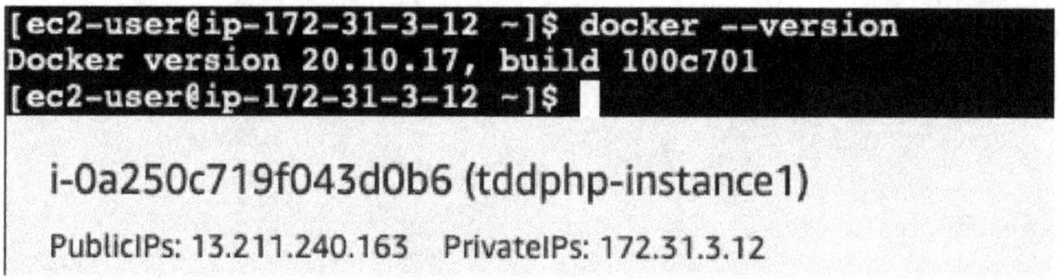

```
[ec2-user@ip-172-31-3-12 ~]$ docker --version
Docker version 20.10.17, build 100c701
[ec2-user@ip-172-31-3-12 ~]$
```

i-0a250c719f043d0b6 (tddphp-instance1)

PublicIPs: 13.211.240.163   PrivateIPs: 172.31.3.12

Figure 10.27 – Docker installed

3. Next, we will need to reboot the instance to make sure that we can execute Docker with the correct permissions. Run the following command:

```
sudo reboot
```

4. After running the command, the terminal window will hang up. Give it a few minutes, then connect to the EC2 portal again, as we did earlier:

Figure 10.28 – Terminal error while rebooting

If you see the preceding error message, don't fret. Just wait a few minutes and then try connecting again.

Lastly, we'll need to install docker-compose.

Installing docker-compose

We've been using the docker-compose tool to run and configure our multi-container setup in our local development environment. We will also need to install it in the EC2 instance. Follow these steps:

1. Back in the AWS terminal window, run the following commands:

```
sudo curl -L "https://github.com/docker/compose/releases/
download/v2.11.2/docker-compose-$(uname -s)-$(uname -m)"
-o /usr/local/bin/docker-compose
sudo chmod +x /usr/local/bin/docker-compose
```

2. After running those two commands, to make sure that docker-compose has been installed properly, run the following command:

```
docker-compose --version
```

You should see the version that is installed. Great! At this stage, we have installed everything we need for CodeDeploy to be able to deploy our PHP application in this EC2 instance.

Next, we will add an Elastic IP to our EC2 instance.

Attaching Elastic IP to the EC2 instance

To make our EC2 instance easily accessible through a web browser, we will add an AWS Elastic IP to the EC2 instance. We can also easily attach this Elastic IP to a different EC2 instance when we need to.

To create an Elastic IP, follow these steps:

1. Go back to the EC2 dashboard in the AWS console, then click on the **Elastic IPs** button:

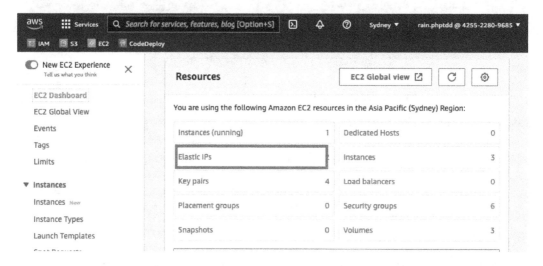

Figure 10.29 – The Elastic IPs button

2. On the next screen, select the **Amazon's pool of Ipv4 addresses** radio button in the **Public Ipv4 address pool** section. Then, click on the **Allocate** button:

Figure 10.30 – Allocate Elastic IP address

3.   Next, click on the newly created Elastic IP address, then click on the **Associate Elastic IP address** button:

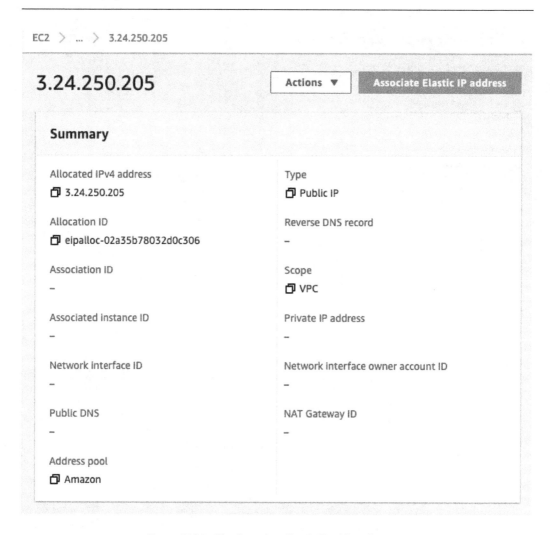

Figure 10.31 – The Associate Elastic IP address button

4. On the next screen, in the **Instance** field, select the EC2 instance we created earlier. Then, click on the **Associate** button:

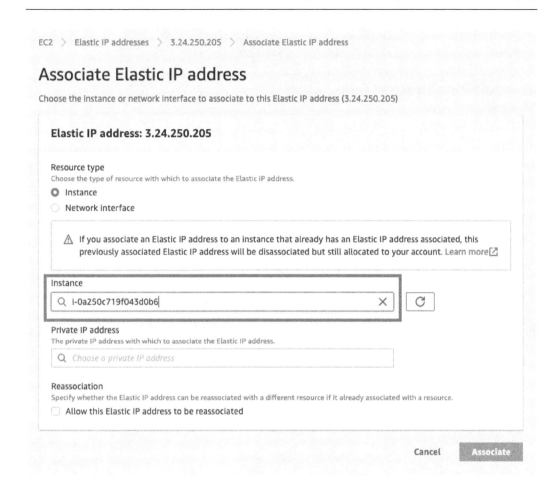

Figure 10.32 – Associating the Elastic IP address with the EC2 instance

At this stage, we will have a permanent IP address pointed to our EC2 instance. Once we deploy the PHP application into the EC2 instance, we will use this IP to access the web application.

Next, we will need to configure Bitbucket Pipelines to tell it that we want to automatically deploy our code using AWS CodeDeploy.

Continuous delivery with Bitbucket Pipelines and AWS CodeDeploy

In the previous section, we prepared an AWS EC2 instance for our PHP application. Now, we will need a way to get our solution code from Bitbucket into the EC2 instance itself. For this, we will need to configure Bitbucket Pipelines to use AWS CodeDeploy. You can read more about Bitbucket Pipelines to AWS CodeDeploy deployments at `https://support.atlassian.com/bitbucket-cloud/docs/deploy-to-aws-with-codedeploy/`.

Bitbucket Pipelines settings

We will need to add some AWS-specific information into Bitbucket as we will be using this information to connect to our AWS CodeDeploy application. To add this information, follow these steps:

1. In the Bitbucket repository dashboard, click on the **Repository settings** option:

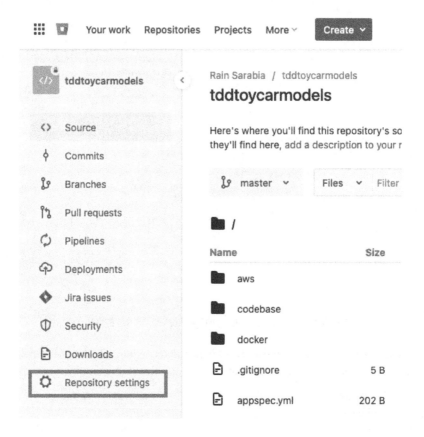

Figure 10.32 – Repository settings

2. Then, select the **Repository variables** link from the left menu. You should be redirected to the **Repository variables** page. In the **Name** and **Value** fields, add the following names and values:

    *   **AWS_ACCESS_KEY_ID**: Use the value from the key pair file

    *   **AWS_SECRET_ACCESS_KEY**: Use the value from the key pair file

- **AWS_DEFAULT_REGION: ap-southeast-2**
- **S3_BUCKET**: \<your unique S3 bucket name>
- **DEPLOYMENT_GROUP: codedeploy_group1**
- **APPLICATION_NAME: mycodedeployapp:**

Rain Sarabia / tddtoycarmodels / tddtoycarmodels / Repository settings

Repository variables

Environment variables added on the repository level can be accessed by any users with push permissions in the repository. To access a variable, put the $ symbol in front of its name. For example, access AWS_SECRET by using $AWS_SECRET. Learn more about repository variables.

Repository variables override variables added on the workspace level. View workspace variables

If you want the variable to be stored unencrypted and shown in plain text in the logs, unsecure it by unchecking the checkbox.

Name	Value	☑ Secured	Add
AWS_ACCESS_KEY_ID	••••••	🔒	🗑
AWS_SECRET_ACCESS_KEY	••••••	🔒	🗑
AWS_DEFAULT_REGION	ap-southeast-2	🔓	🗑
S3_BUCKET	cicd-codedeploy-bucket	🔓	🗑
DEPLOYMENT_GROUP	codedeploy_group1	🔓	🗑
APPLICATION_NAME	mycodedeployapp	🔓	🗑

Figure 10.33 – Repository variables; AWS values

Next, we will need to tell Bitbucket Pipelines that we want to zip and upload our application to AWS S3. Then, we will deploy it to our EC2 instance using AWS CodeDeploy.

3. Back to our code base, in the root directory, you will find the `bitbucket-pipelines.`
    `yml` file we created in the previous chapter. Add the following lines to the file:

/bitbucket-pipelines.yml

```
- step:
    name: Package and Upload
    script:
      - apk add zip
      - zip -r phptddapp.zip .
      - pipe: atlassian/aws-code-deploy:0.2.10
        variables:
            AWS_DEFAULT_REGION: $AWS_DEFAULT_REGION
            AWS_ACCESS_KEY_ID: $AWS_ACCESS_KEY_ID
            AWS_SECRET_ACCESS_KEY:
                $AWS_SECRET_ACCESS_KEY
            COMMAND: 'upload'
            APPLICATION_NAME: 'mycodedeployapp'
            ZIP_FILE: 'phptddapp.zip'
            S3_BUCKET: $S3_BUCKET
            VERSION_LABEL: 'phptdd-app-1.0.0'
- step:
    name: Deploy to AWS
    script:
      - pipe: atlassian/aws-code-deploy:0.2.5
        variables:
            AWS_DEFAULT_REGION: $AWS_DEFAULT_REGION
            AWS_ACCESS_KEY_ID: $AWS_ACCESS_KEY_ID
            AWS_SECRET_ACCESS_KEY:
                $AWS_SECRET_ACCESS_KEY
            APPLICATION_NAME: $APPLICATION_NAME
            DEPLOYMENT_GROUP: $DEPLOYMENT_GROUP
            S3_BUCKET: $S3_BUCKET
            COMMAND: 'deploy'
            VERSION_LABEL: 'phptdd-app-1.0.0'
            IGNORE_APPLICATION_STOP_FAILURES: 'true'
```

```
        FILE_EXISTS_BEHAVIOR: 'OVERWRITE'
        WAIT: 'true'
```

Here, we will be using the AWS values we entered in the repository variables page in the previous section.

Next, we need to tell CodeDeploy what scripts to run when deploying our application.

Creating a CodeDeploy configuration file

CodeDeploy will need a base configuration file called `appspec.yml`. Here, we can tell CodeDeploy to run scripts for us, such as running docker-compose and running our Symfony application's `setup.sh` script.

Create the `/appspec.yml` file and add the following content to it:

```
version: 0.0
os: linux
files:
  - source: /
    destination: /home/ec2-user/phptdd
hooks:
  AfterInstall:
    - location: aws/codedeploy/containers_setup_php.sh
      timeout: 3600
      runas: ec2-user
```

In this file, we are telling CodeDeploy that we want our code to be copied into `/home/ec2-user/phptdd directory`. Then, after the installation process, we want to run the `containers_setup_php.sh` file, which we will create next. Create this file with the following content:

aws/codedeploy/containers_setup_php.sh

```bash
#!/bin/bash


# Build and run containers (PHP, MySQL)
docker-compose -f ~/phptdd/docker/docker-compose-production.yml
down
docker-compose -f ~/phptdd/docker/docker-compose-production.yml
build
docker-compose -f ~/phptdd/docker/docker-compose-production.yml
```

```
up -d

# Setup the PHP Applications inside the containers (install
composer packages, setup db, etc).
docker-compose -f ~/phptdd/docker/docker-compose-production.yml
exec server-web php --version
docker-compose -f ~/phptdd/docker/docker-compose-production.yml
exec server-web /var/www/html/symfony/setup.sh
docker-compose -f ~/phptdd/docker/docker-compose-production.yml
exec server-web /var/www/html/behat/setup.sh
```

You will notice that we are running docker-compose. After that, we are running the custom `setup.sh` files we created for the Symfony and Behat applications.

Next, we need to run the entire CI/CD process using Bitbucket Pipelines.

Running Bitbucket Pipelines

Now that we have everything we need, just commit and push the files to your repository to trigger a Bitbucket pipeline to run, or just manually run a pipeline.

Our pipeline is now divided into three steps:

- **Run automated tests**: These will run our Symfony and Behat tests
- **Package and upload**: This will zip and upload our code to AWS S3
- **Deploy to AWS**: This will use CodeDeploy to deploy our solution inside the EC2 instance we configured

It will take a few minutes to run everything, but imagine replacing the manual process of testing tens, hundreds, or thousands of features and server deployment manually:

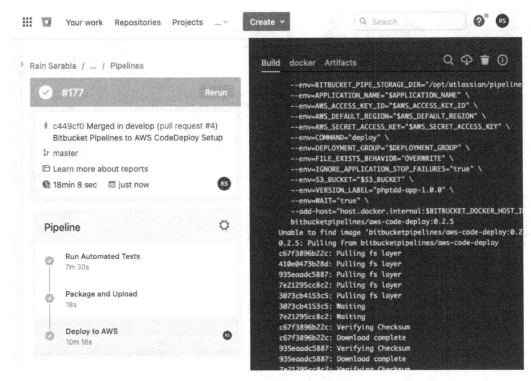

Figure 10.34 – CI/CD result

Great – after 18 minutes, we have completed the entire process! This setup and process can still be tweaked and optimized, but in just a few minutes, we were able to automatically run all our test scenarios, and automatically deploy them into a remote server!

But did the deployment work? Let's find out.

Go back to the AWS console and connect to the EC2 instance again:

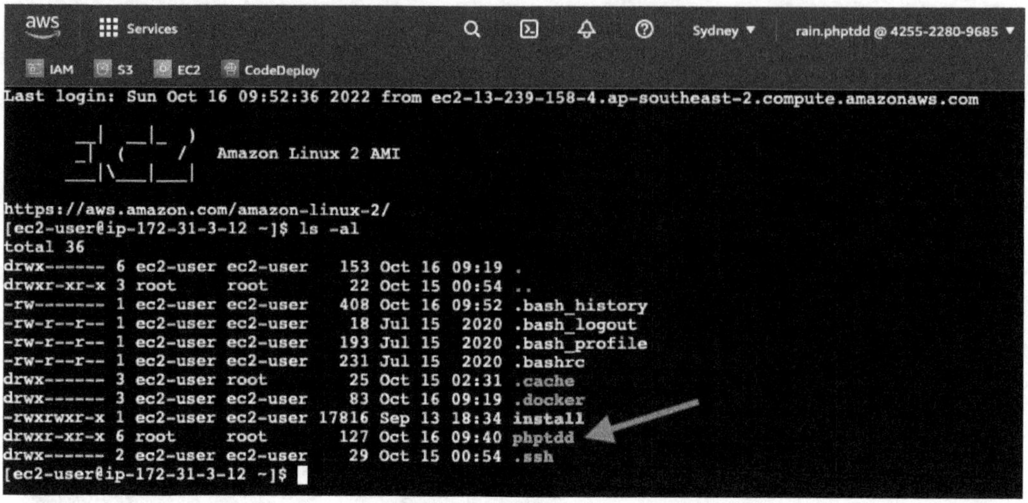

Figure 10.35 – New phptdd directory

The first thing you'll notice if the code deployment worked is that there should be a new /phptdd directory. Let's see whether it's got something in it:

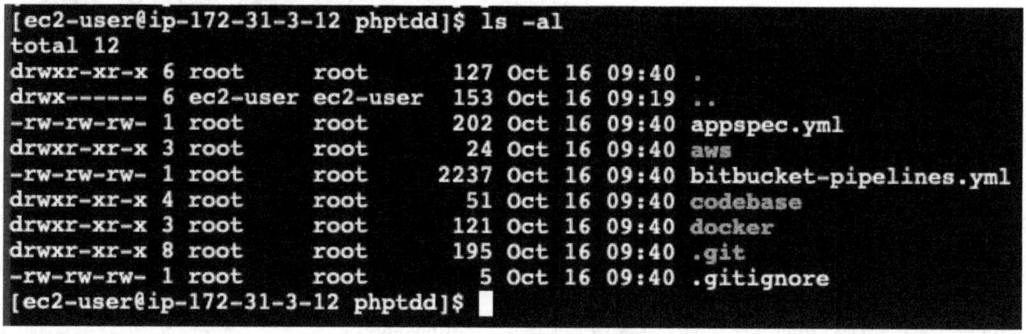

Figure 10.36 – /phptdd content

As you can see, we have all the files we pushed into our Bitbucket repository! But what about our Docker containers? Let's see whether they are running.

Run the following command:

```
docker ps
```

If everything got installed properly by CodeDeploy, we should see our containers running:

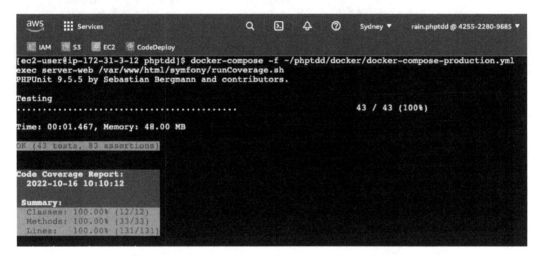

```
[ec2-user@ip-172-31-3-12 phptdd]$ docker ps
CONTAINER ID    IMAGE                      COMMAND                 CREATED          STATUS
     PORTS                                             NAMES
cacd4ba10ccd    mysql:8.0.19               "docker-entrypoint.s…"  16 minutes ago   Up 16 minut
es   33060/tcp, 0.0.0.0:3336->3306/tcp, :::3336->3306/tcp    docker-server-mysql-1
b9ff27b2cff3    phpmyadmin/phpmyadmin:5.0.1 "/docker-entrypoint…"  16 minutes ago   Up 16 minut
es   0.0.0.0:3333->80/tcp, :::3333->80/tcp             docker-app-phpmyadmin-1
c76a101e50cl    docker-server-web          "docker-php-entrypoi…"  16 minutes ago   Up 16 minut
es   0.0.0.0:80->80/tcp, :::80->80/tcp                 docker-server-web-1
[ec2-user@ip-172-31-3-12 phptdd]$
```

Figure 10.37 – Docker containers running

That's good – all our containers are running! Now, what if we run our automated tests? Let's see how it goes. Run the following command:

```
docker-compose -f -/phptdd/docker/docker-compose-production.yml
```

You should see the following:

Figure 10.38 – Running a Symfony coverage test in EC2

Great! All our Symfony PHP tests are passing! But what about the actual web application? The automated tests won't make sense to our visitors.

Go back to the EC2 dashboard and click on the EC2 instance we created. Then, click on the **Elastic IP addresses** link:

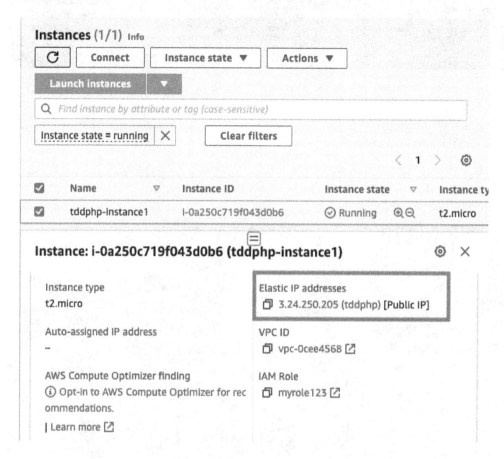

Figure 10.39 – Elastic IP addresses link

The Elastic IP address details will be loaded. Then, copy the **Public DNS** value:

Figure 10.40 – Elastic IP – Public DNS

After copying the public DNS, just simply paste it into your web browser and see whether it loads:

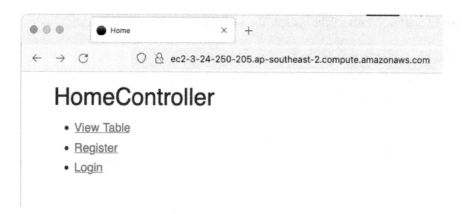

Figure 10.41 – HomeController

As you can see, we can now access our web application from a web browser. You can try to register an account, log in, and add new toy car entries.

Let's try the registration feature first:

1. Click on the **Register** link and enter an email address and a password:

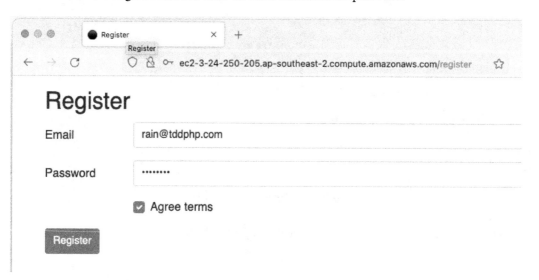

Figure 10.42 – Register

2. Click **Register**. Next, click on the **login** button:

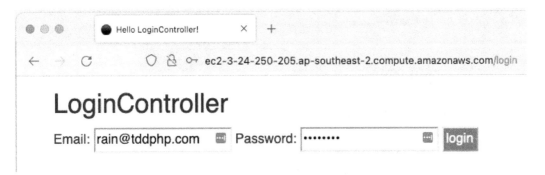

Figure 10.40 – Login

If it works properly, it will redirect you to the **Add Toy Car** page.

3. On the **Add Toy Car** page, add some values in the fields:

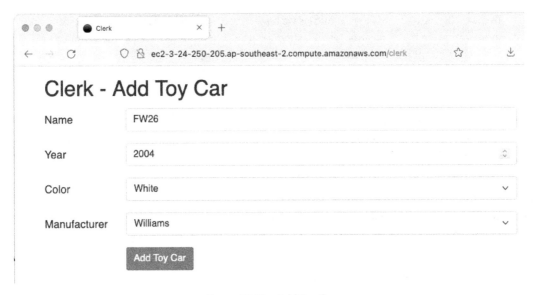

Figure 10.41 – Add Toy Car

4.   Click on the **Add Toy Car** button. If it works, it should redirect you to the table controller:

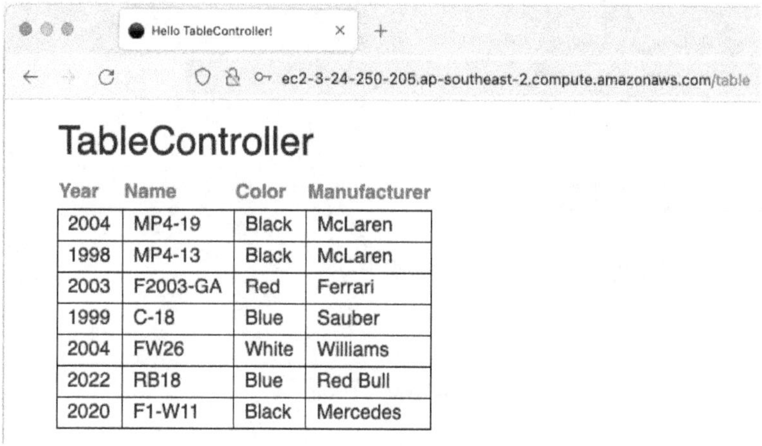

Figure 10.42 – Table controller

In the table controller, the toy car entries we have created will all be displayed. If we want to add more features to the application, we can simply start with a Jira ticket, create a new branch, write some code, commit it, and push the code – that's it. The CI/CD process will take care of the rest!

Summary

In this chapter, we covered the process of setting up an AWS EC2 instance, AWS CodeDeploy, and all the other AWS resources we need to host our PHP application. We integrated Bitbucket Pipelines with our AWS CodeDeploy application, and we used custom scripts to automatically configure our Docker containers inside the AWS EC2 instance whenever CodeDeploy runs.

We covered this process from a developer pushing new code changes to the application, running all the automated tests, and deploying the entire solution to a Linux server through AWS. We are also able to manually test our web application using a web browser to make sure consumers can use the application.

In the next chapter, we will investigate some tools to help us monitor our application. This will be very helpful when working on large applications as this will help us, as developers, analyze our application's performance and health.

11

Monitoring

Out in the real world, in a production environment, is where your application gets really tested to its limits. Despite all the effort in developing test scenarios, and going through different stages of quality assurance, there will come a time when there are edge case scenarios that the development team or the quality assurance team might have not considered and, therefore, these missed edge case scenarios might cause bugs to occur. There are times when hardware-related issues will be encountered, or sometimes there will be some code-related performance bottlenecks causing timeouts and unhappy clients. It happens, but it's not the end of the world. It would be great if the development team had access to a production environment's usage statistics, the CPU or memory usage of the containers, the most accessed controllers, the stack trace of an exception, and so on.

Having this information will help you and your team resolve issues more quickly when they happen. It will give you and your team a better understanding of how heavily your application is being used. In this chapter, we'll use an **application performance monitoring** (APM) tool to give us the ability to collect and go through this valuable application performance and usage data.

In this chapter, we will go through the following topics:

- Setting up New Relic APM for PHP
- Going through the application performance data

Technical requirements

For this chapter, you are expected to have gone through the processes and steps in *Chapter 10*, *Continuous Delivery*, and need to have access to the AWS EC2 instance that is used to host the PHP application; the code base for the PHP application can be found at `https://github.com/PacktPublishing/Test-Driven-Development-with-PHP-8/tree/main/Chapter%2010`.

Setting up New Relic APM for PHP

There are a lot of different APM tools available out there, but in this book, we will just focus on using New Relic.

New Relic offers a lot of performance monitoring tools, but in this book, we will focus on monitoring our PHP application, and the infrastructure it runs on top of.

In this section, we will install and configure the New Relic PHP agent in our EC2 instance so that we can start collecting PHP and server data.

Creating a New Relic account and license key

The first thing you will need before installing the New Relic agent into the EC2 instance is a free New Relic account. You can sign up at `https://newrelic.com/signup` to create a free account. You will need your license key later in the setup process.

The license key can be found on the New Relic **API keys** page under the **Administration** dashboard:

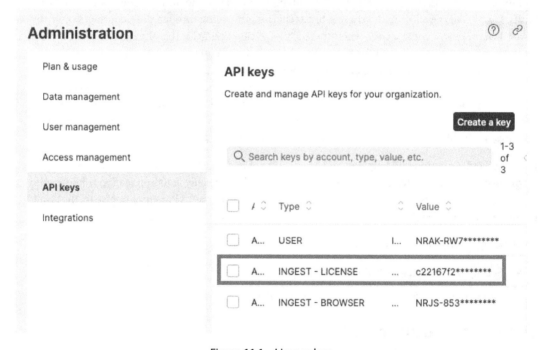

Figure 11.1 – License key

You can copy the license key from this page, and use it to set up the agent in the next steps.

Installing a New Relic agent in the PHP 8 container

To install the PHP agent, we'll need to connect to the AWS EC2 instance we are using to serve the application.

Connect to the EC2 instance using SSH or the AWS EC2 Instance Connect web application.

Once inside the instance, we'll install the agent inside the container. This can be a part of your deployment automation, but in this book, we will install it manually. You can run the following command to connect to your PHP container:

```
docker exec -it docker-server-web-1 /bin/bash
```

Once inside the container, run the following commands to install the PHP agent:

```
curl -L "https://download.newrelic.com/php_agent/release/
newrelic-php5-10.2.0.314-linux.tar.gz" | tar -C /tmp -zx
export NR_INSTALL_USE_CP_NOT_LN=1
/tmp/newrelic-php5-*/newrelic-install install
```

After running these commands, you will be prompted to enter your New Relic license key. Paste the license key from the New Relic **API keys** page, and finish the installation process:

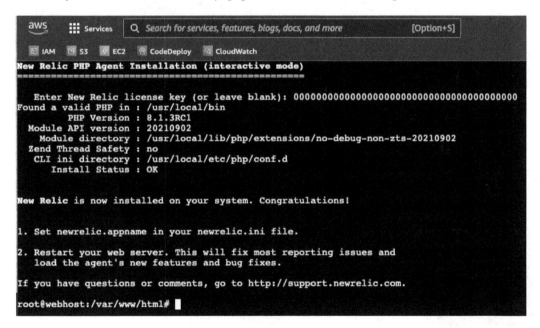

Figure 11.2 – PHP Agent Installation result

After the installation process, you will notice that there is a new ini file created in /usr/local/etc/php/conf.d/newrelic.ini. You can modify this manually to set the PHP application name of your choice, or just run the following command:

```
sed -i \
      -e 's/newrelic.appname = "PHP Application"/newrelic.
```

```
appname = "NEWRELIC_TDDPHP"/' \
        -e 's/;newrelic.daemon.app_connect_timeout =.*/newrelic.
daemon.app_connect_timeout=15s/' \
        -e 's/;newrelic.daemon.start_timeout =.*/newrelic.daemon.
start_timeout=5s/' \
        /usr/local/etc/php/conf.d/newrelic.ini
```

After updating the `newrelic.ini` file, restart `apache2` by running the following command:

```
service apache2 restart
```

The New Relic PHP agent is now installed in the PHP container serving the Symfony and Behat applications.

Next, we'll see whether the agent is able to send data to New Relic, and we'll go through the New Relic dashboard to see what performance data will be available to us.

Going through the application performance data

In the previous section, we installed a tool to collect performance and usage data from our PHP application. This data will be useless unless we are able to view and make sense of the data.

To view the data being gathered by the PHP agent we just installed, follow these steps:

1. Go back to the **new relic** dashboard at `https://one.newrelic.com` and then click on the **APM & services** menu item:

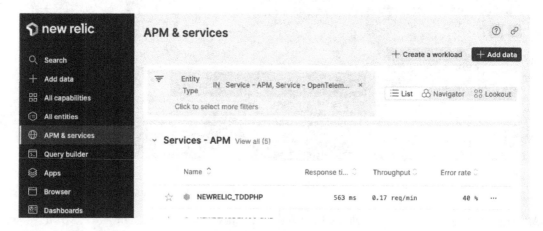

Figure 11.3 – New Relic services – APM

2. Next, click on the `NEWRELIC_TDDPHP` item on the dashboard. You'll notice that this is the same PHP name we used in the `/usr/local/etc/php/conf.d/newrelic.ini` file.

```
; Setting: newrelic.appname
; Type    : string
; Scope   : per-directory
; Default: "PHP Application"
; Info    : Sets the name of the application that metrics will be reported into.
;           This can in fact be a list of up to 3 application names, each of
;           which must be separated by a semi-colon. The first name in any such
;           list is considered the 'primary' application name and must be unique
;           for each account / license key.
;
newrelic.appname = "NEWRELIC_TDDPHP"
```

Figure 11.4 – newrelic.ini – newrelic.appname

Once you are monitoring a lot of applications, these app names will come in very handy so it would be great if you could standardize your app names. You can read more about New Relic's APM best practices in the official documentation found at https://docs.newrelic.com/docs/new-relic-solutions/best-practices-guides/full-stack-observability/apm-best-practices-guide/.

After clicking on the NEWRELIC_TDDPHP item, you will be redirected to the APM dashboard:

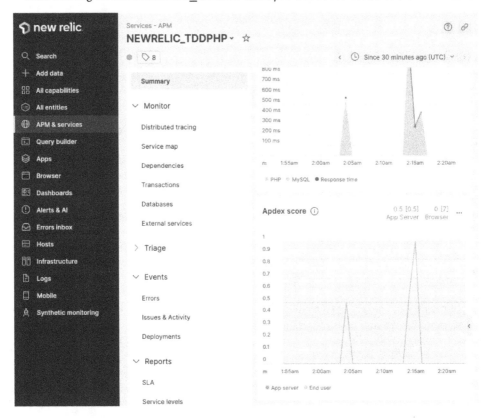

Figure 11.5 – PHP APM dashboard

On the dashboard, you will be able to view different metrics regarding the PHP application we are monitoring. For example, we can check which DB operations take the longest to execute:

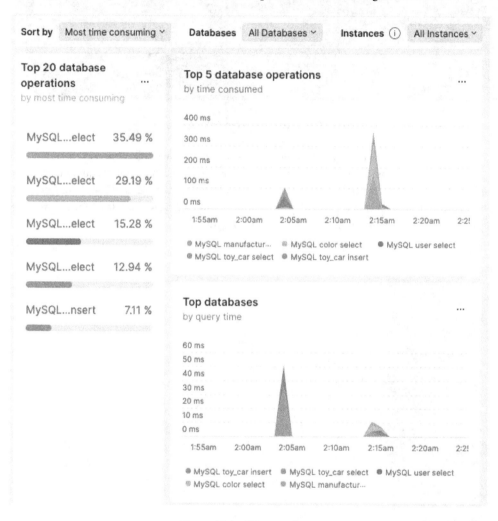

Figure 11.6 – DB operations

You and your team can learn a lot from the data being reported on these dashboards. You can spot performance bottlenecks, and go through the error exceptions that the users are encountering.

On the **Errors** dashboard, you will be able to view metrics about the errors being reported by the application:

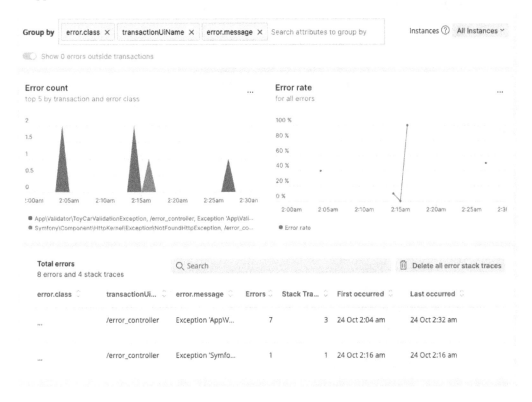

Figure 11.7 – Errors dashboard

You can also click on the error item itself to get a deeper understanding of what's going on:

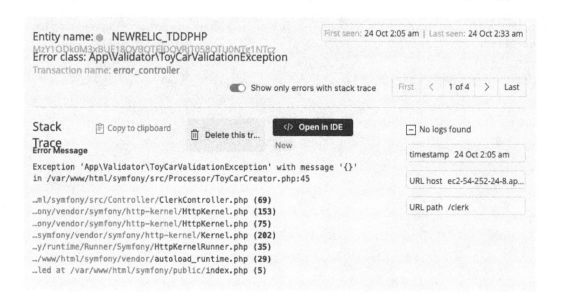

Figure 11.8 – Exception trace

Here, you can see which specific object threw an exception, and what exception was thrown, along with the stack trace. This is all valuable information that can help you and your team spot and fix issues.

Monitoring other containers in your setup

In our example application, we are using more than one container. We can also monitor these containers, such as the MySQL server, and that example phpMyAdmin container we were using.

In the EC2 Console, run the following command to install the New Relic agent into our AWS EC2 Linux instance:

```
curl -Ls https://download.newrelic.com/install/newrelic-cli/
scripts/install.sh | bash && sudo NEW_RELIC_API_KEY=<your
licence key> NEW_RELIC_ACCOUNT_ID=<your account id> /usr/
local/bin/newrelic install -n logs-integration
```

Make sure to include your New Relic license key and account ID, which can be found on the **API keys** page, as shown earlier in the chapter.

After the installation process, go back to the **New Relic** dashboard, and in the left-hand menu, click on the **All entities** menu item, then select **Containers**. You'll then see all of the Docker containers we have in that EC2 instance:

Entities

See all the entities reporting in the past 30 minutes. You can select up to 25 to compare.

Since less than a minute ago   Update

View selected   Reset table

	Name	Containe...	CPU u...	CPU u...	Stora...	Memo...	Netw...	
☐	docker-app-phpmyad...	running	37 µ	0.056 %	36.2 MB	6.35 MB	4.67 B/s	...
☐	docker-server-mysql-1	running	0	7.23 %	127 MB	412 MB	532 B/s	...
☐	docker-server-web-1	running	0.06	87.99 %	95.7 MB	108 MB	11.6 kB/s	...
☐	newrelic-infra	exited	-	-	-	-	-	...
☐	newrelic-php-daemon	exited	-	-	-	-	-	...

Figure 11.9 – Docker containers performance monitoring

If you click on one of those containers in the list, you'll be able to get more metrics about that container such as memory usage, CPU utilization, and so on:

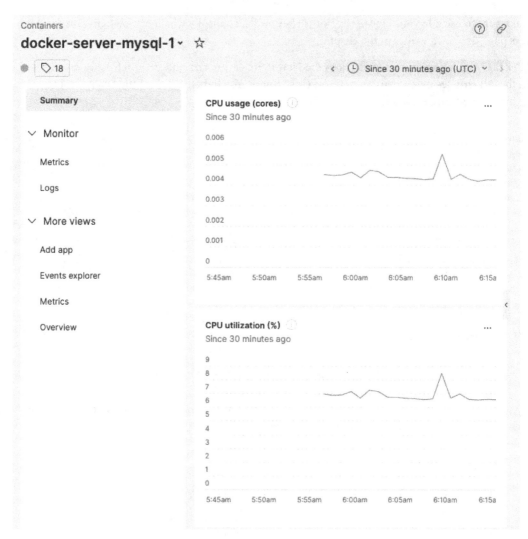

Figure 11.10 – MySQL container metrics

All of these data visualization tools will help you get a better understanding of how heavily your containers and applications are being used and will be able to help you diagnose performance issues when they occur.

Summary

In this chapter, we have gone through the importance of having an APM tool as a part of your setup. We have installed the New Relic APM agent into our AWS EC2 instance and Docker container to start recording performance and usage data. Using an APM tool is entirely optional, but having one will help you and your team address issues more quickly by giving you and your team real production performance data. By having an APM tool, you will be able to understand your application much better, and it will help you to optimize and improve your application.

Index

Packt.com

Subscribe to our online digital library for full access to over 7,000 books and videos, as well as industry leading tools to help you plan your personal development and advance your career. For more information, please visit our website.

Why subscribe?

- Spend less time learning and more time coding with practical eBooks and Videos from over 4,000 industry professionals

- Improve your learning with Skill Plans built especially for you

- Get a free eBook or video every month

- Fully searchable for easy access to vital information

- Copy and paste, print, and bookmark content

Did you know that Packt offers eBook versions of every book published, with PDF and ePub files available? You can upgrade to the eBook version at packt.com and as a print book customer, you are entitled to a discount on the eBook copy. Get in touch with us at customercare@packtpub.com for more details.

At www.packt.com, you can also read a collection of free technical articles, sign up for a range of free newsletters, and receive exclusive discounts and offers on Packt books and eBooks.

Other Books You May Enjoy

If you enjoyed this book, you may be interested in these other books by Packt:

Clean Code in PHP

Carsten Windler | Alexandre Daubois

ISBN: 978-1-80461-387-0

Build a solid foundation in clean coding to craft human-readable code

Understand metrics to determine the quality of your code

Get to grips with the basics of automated tests

Implement continuous integration for your PHP applications.

High Performance with Laravel Octane

Roberto Butti

ISBN: 9781801819404

- Understand the dynamics of the request life cycle in a classic Laravel application
- Explore possibilities with OpenSwoole and Roadrunner and choose the best solution for your application
- Analyze the potential bottlenecks of a classic web application
- Configure Laravel Octane with Roadrunner and OpenSwoole)

Packt is searching for authors like you

If you're interested in becoming an author for Packt, please visit `authors.packtpub.com` and apply today. We have worked with thousands of developers and tech professionals, just like you, to help them share their insight with the global tech community. You can make a general application, apply for a specific hot topic that we are recruiting an author for, or submit your own idea.

Hi!

I am Rainier Sarabia, author of *Test-Driven Development with PHP 8*. I really hope you enjoyed reading this book and found it useful for increasing your productivity and efficiency in PHP.

It would really help me (and other potential readers!) if you could leave a review on Amazon sharing your thoughts on *Test-Driven Development with PHP 8*.

Go to the link below or scan the QR code to leave your review:

https://packt.link/r/1803230754

Your review will help us to understand what's worked well in this book, and what could be improved upon for future editions, so it really is appreciated.

Best Wishes,

Download a free PDF copy of this book

Thanks for purchasing this book!

Do you like to read on the go but are unable to carry your print books everywhere?

Is your eBook purchase not compatible with the device of your choice?

Don't worry, now with every Packt book you get a DRM-free PDF version of that book at no cost.

Read anywhere, any place, on any device. Search, copy, and paste code from your favorite technical books directly into your application.

The perks don't stop there, you can get exclusive access to discounts, newsletters, and great free content in your inbox daily

Follow these simple steps to get the benefits:

1. Scan the QR code or visit the link below

https://packt.link/free-ebook/978-1-80323-075-7

2. Submit your proof of purchase
3. That's it! We'll send your free PDF and other benefits to your email directly

CPSIA information can be obtained
at www.ICGtesting.com
Printed in the USA
LVHW051110200123
737523LV00006B/403

9 781803 230757